Why Christians Can't Trust Psychology

Ed Bulkley, Ph.D.

HARVEST HOUSE PUBLISHERS
Eugene, Oregon 97402

WHY CHRISTIANS CAN'T TRUST PSYCHOLOGY

Copyright © 1993 Harvest House Publishers
Eugene, Oregon 97402

Library of Congress Cataloging-in-Publication Data

Bulkley, Ed, 1947–
    Why Christians can't trust psychology / Ed Bulkley.
        p.   cm.
    Includes bibliographical references and index.
    ISBN 1-56507-026-7
        1. Pastoral counseling.   2. Christianity—Psychology.
    3. Bible—Psychology.   4. Psychology and religion.   I. Title.
    BV4012.2.B85   1994
    261.5'15—dc20   93-31617
                                                            CIP

Printed in the United States of America.

94 95 96 97 98 99 00 01 — 10 9 8 7 6 4 4 3

Acknowledgments

A book is rarely the work of one individual. In my case it involved family, friends, professional peers, my secretary, our elders, and our congregation.

Primary thanks goes to my family, who have patiently endured my long preoccupation with this volume. Their patience and understanding of the amount of time I had to spend away from them made the work much easier.

I thank my wife, Marlowe, for her steadfast encouragement and unselfish love. A great deal of additional responsibility fell on her, but she maintained her composure as a wife, mother, and gifted leader within our church. I share the opinion that a former member expressed to me one day: "Pastor Ed, we've found a lot of good preachers in other churches, but we've never met another pastor's wife that even comes close to Marlowe." I admire her for her sweet spirit under pressure as she divides her time between the ministries she leads. She is my best friend and I praise God for her.

I thank our "4-H Club"—Heidi, Holly, Heather, and Hans—for adding credibility to our ministry by their lives. All of our children have been a joy during every phase of their lives and I treasure their love and trust. As they move into their adult years I am enjoying their friendship as well. Through the practical application of biblical principles, we have seen God's Word make our home a small preview of heaven, and we are so thankful for it.

I also want to express my deepest gratitude to the Lord for having blessed me with loving parents, Bob and Pat Bulkley, who engraved my young heart and mind with the solid conviction that the Bible is the infallible, inerrant Word of God and that it provides practical solutions for daily living in a desperately wicked world. Their quiet example of consistent godly living convinced me that the secrcts to happiness and success are found in simple obedience to the Scriptures. They raised their four children to love and serve the Lord, all without the aid of psychological training!

I appreciate my secretary, Janet Davis, who has patiently helped with printing, binding, and mailing of multiple manuscript drafts. I am also indebted to a variety of readers who made helpful observations and suggestions.

I want to give a special word of thanks to the dear people at Harvest House, who have worked so patiently with me to bring the message of this book to the public. All new authors should be so blessed as to work with folks like Bob, Eileen, and Steve.

Lastly, I want to express my deepest appreciation to the elders and congregation of LIFE Fellowship for the encouragement and support I have received during this project. Few pastors experience greater freedom and joy in the ministry than I do at LIFE. How I praise the Lord for the longtime friendships, mutual respect, firm commitment, and genuine love we share.

*I dedicate this book
to the local biblical churches
and thousands of pastors who faithfully
minister the Word of God publicly and
privately from their pulpits and counseling
offices. May this book reinforce their
confidence in God's Word and the power of
the Holy Spirit to change lives. I pray that
their churches will reclaim the spiritual
authority found in the Scriptures to
administer healing to the damaged souls
of suffering people.*

My Challenge

Thank you for opening this book. Perhaps you are standing in the counseling section of a Christian bookstore at this very moment, leafing through the book to sneak a preview of *Why Christians Can't Trust Psychology*. Maybe the chapter titles will be enough to draw you into one of the most important debates of modern Christianity.

Are you a pastor? A counselor? A Christian layperson? Whoever you are, psychology has touched your life in one way or another. Newspapers, television broadcasts, talk shows, and magazines regularly publicize the latest psychological "findings" and "studies" about why people act the way they do and how dysfunctional people can be helped.

Your obvious interest in counseling, or at least in psychology, may stem from a personal need. Maybe you are currently seeing a psychologist or a professional counselor. Or perhaps you are having trouble with one of your children, or your marriage is shaky. Possibly you have been told that you have a psychological disorder or that you need a psychoactive drug. And now you see a book that boldly proclaims that Christians cannot trust psychology.

I am not trying to add to your confusion and pain. I believe in the need for counsel; where I differ with my psychological brethren is the *source* of the counsel Christians are to receive. If you have the courage to read on, I will share my reasons with you. You may be surprised to find that much of the documentation I offer comes from secular sources.

When speaking of psychology and psychiatry in this book, I am referring to them in the counseling or therapeutic sense, which involves efforts to diagnose and change human behavior, thinking, attitudes, values, and beliefs through "psychotherapies." This is not an indictment against all forms of psychological research, such as those dealing with physical causes of psychopathologies, the physiological workings of the brain, or other non-value-oriented studies.

The terms "integration" and "integrationists" refer to the counseling system and its adherents who seek to combine the Bible with secular psychological theories and practices. I do not use the terms in a derogatory way, but to accurately contrast its hybrid system from genuine biblical counseling.

I will try to avoid name-calling and judging the motives of those who favor integrating psychological concepts and theories with Christian counseling. I have no intention of attacking any individual, though I question many of the assumptions, conclusions, theories, and practices that prevail in Christian counseling centers.

I have read the bitter attacks made by some critics of psychology and I have listened to and spoken with some of the authors who have written books labeling Christian psychologists and psychiatrists as heretics. In all honesty, I must admit that I agree with them on many points, but I don't like their tone of voice. I don't appreciate their barbed sarcasm and judgmental attitudes. But I understand their frustration that they cannot get a fair hearing in the evangelical community.

One of the drawbacks of the written word is that it cannot communicate the author's tone of voice or facial expression. If you could sit across the table from me right now, perhaps you would sense the sincere urgency in my heart and the genuine love I have for you. You might detect a twinkle in my eye when I quote some of the statements that reveal how foolish we humans become when we seek solutions from psychological "experts" rather than the unadulterated Word of God. I am writing this book in a spirit of meekness, good humor, and genuine humility, realizing my own shortcomings and fallibility.

I challenge you to read this book from cover to cover! Read it thoughtfully and slowly, if necessary, to understand why I believe that Bible-believing Christians are being shortchanged by the empty promises of psychology.

Realize that I write this book hesitantly, for I recognize my own inadequacies, intellectual limitations, and inconsistencies. I do not believe that I alone am right and everyone else is wrong, though when taking a stand that opposes the prevailing view it may look that way. I confess that for years I also sent my parishioners to Christian psychologists for major problems needing counsel. It was not until I began to research the issues that I became aware of the dangers of integrating biblical counseling with psychological precepts.

God bless you as you read. My prayer is that you will be drawn back to the pure waters of God's refreshing Word.

—Ed Bulkley

Contents

PART FOUR:
A Biblical Alternative
to Psychology

PART FIVE:
Appendices

A Pastor's Dilemma

Pastor Clifford Chase walked to the pulpit and looked out over his Sunday morning congregation, unaware that the attractive woman sitting in the third row to his left would change his life forever. Cliff, age 34, had just begun his sixth year of ministry at the Evangelical Bible Church. A graduate of Moody Bible Institute and Dallas Theological Seminary, no one could question his orthodox evangelical credentials.

Cliff's wife, Miriam, looked up at him with loving confidence. She had listened to him preach hundreds of sermons, but she never got tired of hearing his clear explanation of the Scriptures. *He gets better every year,* she thought proudly. Then, *Oh, I wish I had pressed his slacks this morning.* The Chase children sat next to Miriam hoping that Daddy would keep it short this morning.

Cliff bowed his head and began to pray. "Father, You know that there are hurting people here this morning. They are waiting to hear from Your Word, hoping to find answers for their deepest needs. How thankful I am, O God, that Your Word is truth—that You have revealed in it everything we need to become the happy, productive, and fulfilled people You designed us to be. Holy Spirit, instruct our hearts as we listen to Your still, small voice. I pray this in Jesus' blessed name. Amen."

The congregation stirred in their places, coughed, sniffed, and cleared their throats.

"Turn with me to 2 Timothy 3:16,17," Cliff said as he smiled at his congregation. *How I love these people, O God,* he prayed silently as the congregation flipped the pages of their Bibles to 2 Timothy. An attractive, professional-looking woman sat in the third row on his left. *I wonder who that woman is. I've never seen her before.*

He began to read the passage in his powerful baritone voice. "'All Scripture is God-breathed and is useful for

13

teaching, rebuking, correcting and training in righteousness, so that the man of God may be thoroughly equipped
for every good work.' Keep your finger in this passage, and
turn to 2 Peter 1:3 and 4.''

Cliff's youngest child, Eric, nudged his sister Becky with
his elbow as he whispered, "The sermon isn't gonna be
short." He looked for a piece of paper to draw on. He heard
his dad read, "His divine power has given us everything we
need for life and godliness through our knowledge of him
who called us." Eric's mind tuned out his father's voice as he
began to draw Luke Skywalker's spaceship.

"I want to show you today that no matter what problem
you have, God has a solution. Note that Peter says that God
has provided 'everything we need for life and godliness.'
And He provides everything we need 'through our knowledge of him who called us'—Jesus Christ. How do we get
that knowledge of Christ? Through the Word of God.''

Cliff couldn't help but notice tears in the eyes of the
woman in the third row. As the sermon progressed, her
sorrowful expression began to change to a look of tentative
hope. Others in the congregation were also being visibly
moved as Cliff exhorted them to seek wisdom from God's
holy Word.

He moved from behind the pulpit and walked from one
end of the platform to the other as his voice increased
in volume. "Television doesn't have the answers! Science
doesn't have the answers! Philosophy doesn't have the
answers! No, my friends, the answers for your deepest needs
are found in the Word of God!"

Wallace Kramer, one of the elders, shouted "Amen!"
and Peter Bryant, a scruffy new believer, spiked an imagin-
ary football as he yelled "Right on!" Others around him
chuckled good-naturedly at his irreverent enthusiasm.

After the service, as Cliff shook hands at the door, parishioners congratulated him on his powerful message.
"Good preaching!" Thelma Trent said as she pumped his
hand. She was the church's oldest saint and her praise
encouraged Cliff's heart.

"Powerful, Preacher! Powerful!" Wally Phillips affirmed loudly as he pumped Cliff's hand and nodded his head in admiration.

When the crowd was gone, Cliff, Miriam, and the kids walked to the car and got in. Miriam looked over at him with a proud smile and said, "Honey, that was one of your best!"

"Yeah, Dad, that was cool!" Becky chimed in. "You made me want to read my Bible more." Cliff looked in the rearview mirror at Eric. "What did you think, Son?" Eric shrugged his shoulders.

"Aw, he didn't even hear you, Dad." Becky tattled. "He was drawing."

"I did too hear him!" Eric said loudly.

"Oh, yeah? What did he preach about?"

"The Bible!" Eric answered and made a face at Becky.

"Lucky guess," Becky said under her breath as she adjusted her skirt.

That afternoon, as Cliff sat in the family room reading the Sunday paper, the phone rang. He sighed as he finished the paragraph he was reading. The phone rang again. He laid down the paper and picked up the receiver.

"Hello?"

A hesitant voice came over the line. "Pastor Chase?"

"Yes."

"Pastor, my name is Annette Pearson. I visited your church this morning." *It's the pretty lady from the third row,* Cliff thought.

"What can I do for you, Ms. Pearson?"

"I'm sorry to be calling you on Sunday, but I've got to talk to someone. You answered some questions this morning that I've been asking for years. I've . . . I've been in psychotherapy since I was 17, but nothing has made as much sense as what you shared in your sermon. For the first time in years, I began to have hope."

"I'm glad to hear that," Cliff said with a smile.

Miriam looked over at Cliff and whispered, "Who is it?" Cliff shook his head and mouthed back, "I'll tell you in a minute."

"I was wondering," the lady said softly, "if I could set up an appointment for counseling."

Cliff cleared his throat and shifted uneasily in his chair. "Well, ordinarily I don't counsel, Ms. Pearson. I find that administration and preparing my messages consume most of my time. I can refer you to several competent Christian psychologists, however."

"Oh, I see. No, that won't be necessary. Like I told you, I've already been to psychologists and psychiatrists. They haven't helped me at all. I just thought after what you said this morning that perhaps you had some real answers." Cliff's heart dropped. He suddenly felt ashamed of himself.

"Well, listen, Ms. Pearson, I'm certainly willing to talk with you. I can fit an appointment in on Tuesday morning, about 10:00."

"Oh, thank you, Pastor. I really appreciate it. I'll be there Tuesday."

On Tuesday morning, promptly at 10:00, Cliff's secretary buzzed his phone and said, "Pastor, there's a Mrs. Annette Pearson here to see you." *Good, she's married,* Cliff thought.

"Show her in, Jenny," Cliff said as he sighed quietly. He pretended to be studying as Jenny ushered Mrs. Pearson into his office. After a moment he looked up, smiled, and said, "Hello, Mrs. Pearson. Have a seat."

He couldn't help but notice how attractive the woman was as she sat down and crossed her legs. She appeared to be about 30 years of age. She was neatly dressed, her long dark hair was fashionably arranged, and her makeup was tastefully applied. Behind her beauty, however, Cliff detected uneasiness and pain.

"What did you want to ask me?" he said, trying to appear confident and professional.

"I want to know how God can help me. I'm a nervous wreck. Sometimes I think I hear voices, and I have a hard time accepting myself." Her hands were visibly shaking as she twisted her tissue. "My marriage is getting worse and worse and Harold said if something doesn't happen soon he's going to leave me. I need help, Pastor."

Cliff looked down at his hands, which were folded together on his desk. *God help me!* he prayed silently. *What do I tell this woman?*

He coughed nervously. "Uh...what seems to be the cause of your marriage problems?"

"Can I talk frankly?" she asked as she leaned forward.

"Of course." *Oh, God, give me wisdom!*

"Our physical relationship is almost nonexistent."

Cliff swallowed involuntarily and hoped she didn't notice. "Is that by your choice or his?"

"Harold would say it's my choice." She looked at her lap. "He doesn't understand that what happened to me as a child is still affecting me."

Cliff looked at his desk clock. Less than five minutes had passed. He wondered if she could see the microscopic beads of sweat forming on his brow. "Do you want to tell me what happened when you were a child?" *Please say no.*

"I was sexually abused by my father from the time I was eight until I was fourteen. I finally got up the courage to tell my mom," she said matter-of-factly.

"Did she make him stop?"

"No! She said she didn't believe me! She called me a stinking liar and slapped me so hard my face was bruised. A teacher at school noticed the bruise and asked me what happened. I began crying and finally told her about the incest. She reported my folks to Social Services, and I was placed in a foster home. I was shifted from foster home to foster home—15 of them—over the next four years. I was raped six times by the men and their sons. I finally ran away."

Pastor Clifford Chase was stunned. He had read of such cases and had heard similar stories on talk shows, but he had never personally dealt with anyone who had suffered so severely. He leaned back in his chair. "I'm so very sorry, Mrs. Pearson, for all you've gone through. It's no wonder you have difficulty trusting men. I would like to help you; but, in all honesty, I think this is out of my league."

"What do you mean?" The look of despair began to creep over her face again.

"I've learned to face my limitations. I think you need to seek professional counsel."

"But I thought, as a pastor, you would give me spiritual advice. I thought you would show me from the Bible how to find peace in my heart." Her eyes begged for help.

He shook his head slowly and rubbed a trickle of sweat from behind his ear. "In seminary, I learned that theological training prepares a pastor to deal with spiritual problems. Your problem is much deeper. For serious disorders such as yours, a therapist needs psychological training as well as theological. It would be unprofessional of me to attempt to counsel you." He turned to his Rolodex. "I can recommend several Christian psychologists who specialize in...uh...your problem."

"I don't understand," Mrs. Pearson said. She raised her hands, palms up, and dropped them into her lap helplessly.

"What don't you understand?"

"I thought you said that God has the answers for our deepest problems. That we can find His answers in the Bible."

Cliff hesitated and then replied, "Well, we *can* find the answers to most problems, but we also need the insights of scientific research. Psychologists have specialized training that enables them to uncover subconscious causes for inner problems. They are then able to use individualized therapies to treat specific dysfunctions."

"Have you ever undergone psychotherapy, Pastor Chase?" Mrs. Pearson asked.

"Well, no, I haven't," he admitted.

"I have, and I'm telling you psychologists don't have the answers. They talk and pry and try to explain why you do what you do. Then they experiment with different therapies. When those don't work, they pump you full of drugs so you don't feel the pain. But it always comes back. They try to change the head, but the problems are in the heart." She stood to leave.

"I'm talking about *Christian* psychologists," Cliff protested. "Surely you see that they are different." He stood, knowing that he had failed miserably.

"I've been to Christian psychologists and psychiatrists. Not one prayed with me. Not one opened the Bible to tell me what God would have me do. I thought surely you could help." She walked to the door of his office.

"Well, I hope you'll visit our church again next Sunday," Cliff said because he could think of nothing else to say.

She turned and looked at him. With tight lips she said, "Thank you" and walked out.

PART ONE

A Look
at the Issues

The Psychological Counselor

The Bible's primary purpose is to tell us how to be right with God, not what to do when someone has a nervous breakdown.

The Biblical Counselor

Is the Bible lacking the information needed to understand why man acts as he does and how he can be changed? ... How miserable believers must have been from the first century until the latter part of the nineteenth century when psychology was finally discovered.

The Word of God

We have the word of the prophets made more certain, and you will do well to pay attention to it, as to a light shining in a dark place, until the day dawns and the morning star rises in your hearts.
—2 Peter 1:19

1

Christian Counseling Today

There is growing confusion in today's Christian community about the best way to help people overcome their personal problems of living. Some believe that Christians should submit only to biblical counseling, while others passionately support psychological counseling so long as it is integrated with the Scriptures.

Integrating Psychology into Christian Counseling

Fully persuaded that psychological training is necessary to counsel effectively, most pastors today refer their parishioners to psychologists and psychiatrists for treatment of serious emotional and behavioral disorders. Christian publishing houses pour out an endless stream of books written by psychologists to help believers solve their problems of living. These experts appear on Christian radio and television and produce film series to communicate their belief that pastors and churches can help parishioners with minor problems, but serious disorders must be entrusted to "professional counselors."

23

Denver Seminary, Talbot Seminary, Trinity Evangelical Divinity School, Liberty University, Moody Bible Institute, Fuller Theological Seminary, and a host of other Christian schools are convinced that psychology and the Bible must be integrated in counseling if the church is to remain relevant to our contemporary culture. Dallas Seminary employs one of the nation's best-known Christian psychiatrists on its teaching faculty. Colorado Christian University offers a counseling degree built on the theories of a prominent Christian psychologist.

The president of one Bible college believes that "there are many helpful insights to be gleaned from this field [of secular counseling]."[1] He states the common integrationist position:

> We live in a season when life is increasingly complex and the fragility of precious souls is demonstrated by growing brokenness and complicated conflicts. We dare not waste their sorrows on the battlefield of careless counsel that violates biblical parameters or with simplistic, unqualified solutions that plunge them ultimately into deeper despair.[2]

As much as I respect this man of God and believe that he is fully committed to the Lord and to the Scriptures, I am convinced that he has not adequately researched the issue. In trying to strike a balance between psychology and biblical counseling, he insists that secular counseling has much to offer the church and he implies that biblical counseling produces "simplistic, unqualified solutions."[3] It appears that he is in agreement with the prevailing view that is sweeping the evangelical church—that without the insights of secular psychology, pastors and churches are simply inadequate to deal with the deepest hurts of modern man.

Is Psychology Needed Today?

How did the apostle Paul counsel people in his day? Paul himself answers that in Colossians 1:28: "We proclaim him, admonishing [*noutheteo*] and teaching everyone with all wisdom, so that we may present everyone perfect in Christ." He then warns us in Colossians 2:8, "See to it that no one takes you captive through hollow and deceptive philosophy, which depends on human tradition and the basic principles of this world rather than on Christ."

Am I misreading Paul? Is he in error to suggest that we can find *all* wisdom in Christ? Do we in fact need the insights of psychology to provide for the deepest needs of Christians? Is modern life truly more complex than it was in the days of Paul? Those who believe we desperately need the insights of psychology seem to think so.

A professor of counseling psychology at Trinity Evangelical Divinity School is committed to the concept of integrating secular psychology with biblical counseling. He argues that psychological truths fall under the category of general revelation and that new insights can be accepted if they are true and do not contradict the Bible. He offers this example:

> I think all Christians would agree that when you bury negative feelings, you bury them alive, and that can cause ulcers, even heart attacks. This process is undeniably true, but you can't find it specifically in the Bible. If it's true, then we embrace it and use it; if it isn't true, then we don't.[4]

One could argue with the professor whether "this process is undeniably true" and what it means to "bury negative feelings." But a greater problem is *how* one determines whether a psychological discovery is true. He implies that the Bible is as silent about the human condition as it is about modern technologies:

> It isn't a textbook on how to tune up our automobiles, or on physics, chemistry, or psychology. It does contain statements that relate to geology, anthropology, and psychology that must be integrated into those disciplines, but

the Bible's primary purpose is to tell us how to
be right with God, not what to do when someone has a nervous breakdown.[5]

Are we to assume that there is no connection between
one's standing with God and a nervous breakdown? Is the
Bible really silent on the issues of psychological health? Are
mental/emotional problems the same as tuning one's car or
mixing chemicals? Integrationists see a categorical difference between psychological and spiritual problems and
how to solve those problems. They say that the medical
doctor should treat the body, the psychologist or psychiatrist should treat the mind, and the pastor should deal with
the spirit.

Those who insist that we must use psychology along
with biblical counseling argue that "even though the Bible
is all true, it does not follow that all truth is in the Bible."[6]
They give examples: "In mathematics, medicine, physics,
geography, marine biology and a host of other areas, there
is much truth that is not mentioned in the Bible. God in his
wisdom has allowed human beings to discover truths about
the universe that are not discussed in Scripture."[7]

While it is true that the Bible does not list mathematical
formulae, modern medical procedure, every physical law,
every geographic location, or every species of marine life,
one must remember that none of those areas deal with
essential spiritual truths.

In reply, integrationists say:

Some critics of psychology seem to argue
... that God has not allowed human beings to
discover any truths about interpersonal relations, mental health, counseling techniques,
mental disorders, personal decision making or
any other issues related to stress management
and daily living. Such a view maintains that
God has allowed human beings to discover
truth in almost every field of human study
except psychology.[8]

The problem is that many integrationists seem unable to discern the significant difference between the physical sciences and the so-called "social sciences." We will deal with that subject at length later on.

The question remains: Is psychology necessary today? Integrationists seem to think so because "some human problems are not mentioned in the Scriptures."[9] They believe that "the Bible was not written as a self-help, question-and-answer book covering every possible human problem. It does not claim to be a textbook of counseling techniques or personal problem solving."[10]

No, the Bible claims to be far more—the very Word of God that "is useful for teaching, rebuking, correcting and training in righteousness, so that the man of God may be thoroughly equipped for every good work" (2 Timothy 3:16,17).

Of course, the Bible does not tell a student which specific college to choose, nor does it name the precise person a Christian is to marry. God does not remove from the individual the privilege and responsibility to use his mind, experience, and common sense, as well as the advice of godly counselors, to make important decisions. But those kinds of decisions involve specific *applications* of biblical truths, not universal *principles*. Contrary to integrationist reasoning, the Bible *does* present the principles which, if followed, will provide the answers for *every* human problem.

The Bible provides the principles necessary to deal with eating disorders, nonbiogenic depressions, scholastic failure, child abuse, bitter memories, anxiety, and a host of other modern problems. Thus integrationists are grossly mistaken when they say that "many, perhaps most, of the problems people bring to modern counselors are never discussed in the Bible."[11]

Though they admit that "often principles of behavior can be inferred from the Bible and applied to modern problems,"[12] integrationists believe that psychological training is necessary to help Christians with deep problems:

Surely there are times, many times, when a sensitive, psychologically trained, committed Christian counselor can help people through psychological techniques and with psychological insights that God has allowed us to discover, but that he has not chosen to reveal in the Bible.... The Word of God never claims to have all the answers to all of life's problems.[13]

Twentieth-Century Complexities

Why do integrationists insist that the problems we face today are so different from those which humans have suffered in centuries past? Depression is not a recent discovery of psychology. People have had to cope with disease, disappointments, frustrations, unhappy marriages, confusion, lethargy, and bizarre behavior since the fall of man into sin.

Psychological studies have not shown that mankind is mentally healthier since the introduction of psychological theories and therapies. To the contrary, there is evidence that society has become *more* psychotic rather than better-adjusted. The increase of "mental illness" may someday be found to be in direct proportion to the number of psychologists and psychiatrists who set up practice.

Has psychology really added to our essential knowledge about human behavior, needs, and solutions? Is the Bible lacking the information needed to understand why man acts as he does and how he can be changed? If so, we must pity all the saints of God who struggled with problems of living from the times of Adam, Abraham, Moses, David, Isaiah, Daniel, Jesus, and Paul. How fortunate we are to not be living in the days of the early church, when the only therapeutic resources were the writings of the prophets and apostles, along with the ministry of fellow saints and the Holy Spirit. How miserable believers must have been from the first century until the latter part of the nineteenth century, when psychology was finally "discovered."

I do not dispute the fact that biblical counselors can glean from psychology some helpful ideas, observations, illustrations, and generic methods with which to communicate God's solutions for man's problems. But these are not the same as accepting psychological "findings" as essential truths about man's nature, problems, needs, and solutions.

Integrationists often refer to the "psychological truths about human behavior" not mentioned in the Scriptures. However, we will see in the chapters ahead that the Bible addresses every "dysfunction" and presents the essential truths required to bring humans to full maturity.

Secular Criticisms of Psychology

Generally speaking, Christians have great confidence in psychology. With so many respected Christian leaders expressing the view that the church needs the insights of secular counseling systems, it is no wonder that Christian laity hold psychology in such high esteem. Most Christians, however, are unaware that while the church's confidence in psychological counseling is growing, secular critics of psychology are increasing in number, and research is raising additional doubts about psychological claims, therapies, scientific status, and success rates.

Gary Collins begins his first chapter of *Can You Trust Psychology?* with this statement:

> Bernie Zilbergeld doesn't trust psychology. Despite his Ph.D. from Berkeley, his twelve years' experience as a practicing therapist, and his acclaim as a psychological researcher and author, Dr. Zilbergeld has written a whole book to criticize his own profession. Many psychological conclusions are really myths, he writes. Professional therapy is "overpromoted, overused, and overvalued." These criticisms could be dismissed had they come from a journalist or theologian writing as an outsider. But they come instead from a member of the psychological guild who has gone through all the prescribed training in clinical psychology, has been in therapy himself, has taken the time to

interview 140 former patients, and has met for lengthy discussions with a cross-range of fourteen professional colleagues.[14]

What About Bible-Based Psychology?

One might justify trusting a psychologist if his theory and practice were based on biblical principles rather than theories of human behavior originated by men. And to the casual observer, there seem to be many Christian psychologists who meet that test. But as one prominent Christian therapist confesses:

> When I received my Ph.D. in clinical psychology, I assumed that I knew how to counsel people with problems. ... As I restudied what I had learned in graduate school, it became clearly and frighteningly apparent that most of what I was believing and doing as a professional psychologist was built upon the swaying foundation of humanism, a fervent belief in the self-sufficiency of man. As a Christian committed to a biblical view of man, I could not make the psychological thinking in which I had been trained dovetail with basic biblical beliefs. ... The truths of Christianity seemed to have little bearing on the activities in my counseling office and were at many points flatly contradicted by my professionally orthodox behavior.[15]

I applaud him for further stating that "every concept of biblical counseling must build upon the fundamental premise that there really is an infinite and personal God who has revealed Himself propositionally in the written word, the Bible, and in the living word, Jesus Christ."[16]

Why then do I believe that a Christian should seriously question the counseling systems of such men? I do not question their sincerity or personal integrity. I do, however, disagree with many of their counseling theories, which, I believe, are still deeply influenced by unproven psychological precepts of man. By their own admission, they are intent upon integrating psychology and Christianity in order to form a better counseling system. One Christian psychologist calls this approach "spoiling the Egyptians."[17] He compares this adaptation of secular concepts to the Israelites' taking of Egyptian goods as they made their exodus.

The problem with this comparison is that the Israelites were taking gold, silver, and other material objects, while integration is appropriating concepts, philosophies, and worldviews that are hostile to God's plan for man. It is more akin to the *adoption of Canaanite practices* than spoiling the Egyptians. I appreciate this psychologist for admitting:

> The job of careful screening is no easy matter. In spite of the best intentions to remain biblical, it is frighteningly easy to admit concepts into our thinking which compromise biblical content. Because psychologists have spent up to nine years studying psychology in school and are pressed to spend much of their reading time in their field in order to stay current, it is inevitable that we develop a certain "mind-set." The all-too-common but disastrous result is that we tend to look at Scripture through the eyeglasses of psychology when the critical need is to look at psychology through the glasses of Scripture.[18]

Psychological Thinking

It is inevitable that psychologists will think psychologically, he says. Christians might well suspect that Christian psychologists have admitted concepts into their thinking which compromise biblical content. Anyone familiar with psychological theories should recognize that secular concepts underlie much of their systems, especially in the area of unconscious drives and the need to return to the past to achieve healing in the present.

William Glasser writes that "conventional psychiatry holds that an essential part of treatment is probing into the patient's past life—searching for the psychological roots of his problem."[19] Psychiatry holds that a patient must understand his unconscious drives if he is going to change his way of thinking and acting.

This emphasis on the unconscious is an essential premise of psychological counseling. The prevailing psychological doctrine is that "to really understand your daughter's anorexia or your own lack of self-confidence, you must go outside the Church, or at least to a pastor with psychological training."[20]

I readily admit that some of what integrationists write is helpful and biblically solid. The danger is found in the integrationist *foundation*, which rests upon the psychological concepts of man rather than on the scriptural precepts of God. Prevailing psychological theory says that if you want to be changed from the inside out, you must "explore the imperfections of key relationships until you experience deep disappointment."[21] Counselors who follow this doctrine believe that "keenly felt disappointment in the present supplies the energy for passionate hope for the future."[22]

Most Christians will agree that for genuine change to occur, the Holy Spirit must act on a person's heart as He makes him a "new creation" (2 Corinthians 5:17). But many integrationists believe that all human relationships lead inevitably to disappointment and pain, and that most problems stem from "hidden internal causes." Sin itself is defined in terms of disappointment: "Most habits that we seem powerless to control grow out of our attempts to relieve the unbearable tension that results from our failure to deal with the disappointment of our deepest longings for relationship,"[23] a Christian psychologist writes.

Integrationists theorize that the most devastating sin is the "sin of self-protection,"[24] and that we need to embrace our hurts.[25] "The more deeply we enter our disappointment, the more thoroughly we can face our sin,"[26] one psychologist states authoritatively as though it is a biblical truth.

But one should ask, *Why* must we embrace our hurts and enter our disappointment all over again? *Where* in the Bible do integrationists find this concept of reliving the painful past in order to be healed in the present?

My purpose here is not to critique integrationist counseling systems point by point. It is important, however, to understand that as committed to Christ as many integrationists are, their theories of counseling appear to be strongly influenced by unproven psychological concepts.

The Purpose of This Book

In this book I intend to show that psychologically trained counselors have difficulty in discerning between sacred and secular systems, and that in general, psychology does not merit the trust that Christians have placed in it. I attempt to show from secular sources, as well as Christian writings, that the integrationist position is scientifically invalid, theologically confused, and biblically inconsistent.

My purpose is not to attack the Christian integrity of any individual, but to show in specific detail that much of what is called Christian counseling has conformed to secular psychology, and as a result has lost its spiritual perspective and authority. I believe that integrationists themselves are uncertain whether Christian counseling and secular psychology can be blended without doing great harm to Christian doctrines and standards.

While I genuinely commend Christian psychologists for their desire to serve the Lord and His people, the issue is not their sincere and genuine faith in Christ. The debate is not about their motives for defending psychological counseling. The question is, Can a Christian *trust* psychology?

■ ■ ■

After Annette Pearson walked out, Cliff closed the door of his office and sat at his desk. He pressed the intercom button. "Jenny, hold my calls, please." He sighed deeply and looked at the Bible on his desk. He lovingly touched its worn leather cover and then pulled it in front of him, still closed.

His ego was stinging as he remembered the look Annette had given him as she left. She might as well have shouted, "You're a hypocrite, Pastor Chase! You preach one thing on Sunday from the pulpit, but you teach the very opposite during the week in your office!"

His Rolodex was still open to the listing of Christian psychologists. He leaned forward, picked up the phone, and punched in a number. The phone rang twice at the other end, with no answer. "Come on, come on," he muttered impatiently as he tapped his desk with a pencil.

"Christian Counseling Services. Joan speaking. May I help you?"

"Yes. May I speak to Dr. West, please?"

"May I tell him who is calling?"

"This is Pastor Chase."

"I'll put you right through, Reverend Chase," the secretary replied.

Cliff pulled out his appointment book as he waited for Bryan West to answer the page. Cliff and Bryan had been classmates at Dallas Seminary. Cliff had gone on to pastor, while Bryan had continued his studies at the Minirth-Meier Clinic, eventually becoming a licensed psychologist.

"Dr. West here."

"Bryan! Cliff Chase. How are you doing?"

"Cliff, you old heretic! Good to hear your voice!" Ordinarily, Bryan's use of the endearing term "heretic" wouldn't have bothered Cliff, but today it stung. "What can I do for you?" Bryan asked jovially.

"I wonder if you could squeeze me into your schedule, Bryan. Something just happened that's really got me upset." Though he tried to control his voice, it sounded tense and higher-pitched than normal.

"Sure, Cliff. What's up?"

"I just had a real challenge dropped in my lap, and to tell you the truth, I don't know quite how to deal with it. How soon can you fit me in?"

"How about lunch?"

"Deal! But I'm buying."

"Of course you are. Psychologists don't work for free, you know!" They both laughed. "Where do you want to meet?"

"How about Bennett's, say at 1:00?" Cliff suggested.

"Perfect. I don't have an appointment until 3:00. See you there."

Cliff left his office a few minutes later. "Jenny, I've got a meeting at 1:00 and I don't know how long I'll be. I may not be back today."

"Okay, Pastor. Where can I reach you in case of an emergency?"

"I'll be at Bennett's Barbeque, then possibly at Bryan West's office. You have the number."

Cliff had plenty of time, so he took the scenic route along the river. As he drove, Annette Pearson's accusing face kept appearing in his mind. *I need real help, Pastor. I've already been to psychologists. You said the Bible has all the answers for every human need. I need help . . . I need help . . . I need help . . .*

At 1:00, Cliff drove into the parking lot at Bennett's. He saw Bryan standing on the roomy porch of the old Victorian house that had been converted into a quaint restaurant. Bryan waved as Cliff walked up. "Hi, old buddy! Prompt as always, I see." They went inside and were ushered to a private table near the window overlooking the river.

The waitress came to take their order. Bryan ordered the rib special. Cliff looked at the menu and saw the listing for pulled pork. "What is pulled pork?" he asked as he pointed to the menu.

Bryan interjected, "That's a pig they dragged behind a pickup. Makes for an interesting texture." The waitress tipped her head with an irritated look that said, *How clever. I've never heard that one before.* "Pulled pork is meat the cook pulls away from the piece, rather than slicing it. It's supposed to keep the juices in better," she explained. Cliff ordered the pulled pork and sat back in his chair. He didn't know where to begin.

Bryan leaned forward with his elbows on the table and rested his chin on his hand. "So? Ask away."

Cliff cleared his throat and adjusted the silverware. "Bryan, I had a woman come to my office this morning who thinks I'm a hypocrite for referring people to professional counselors like you."

"Why does she feel that way?"

"Well, I guess I gave her the impression in my sermon on Sunday that all Christians need to solve their personal problems is the Bible. I explained to her that we still need professional counselors to help unravel deeper psychological dysfunctions, but she said that she's been to psychologists and psychiatrists for years and they haven't helped her. She acted like I was her last hope."

"Okay, so what's your question?" The waitress came with their Cokes and Cliff waited until she left.

"What should I have told her? It's hard to explain that God's Word is sufficient to meet the deepest needs of human existence, but that we still need psychology to complete the job."

"Well, that's simple enough, Cliff. When I hold seminars at churches I explain that just as we need medical doctors to treat our bodies, we need psychologists to treat the mind. Just as the Bible does not tell us how to repair automobiles or program computers, neither does it tell us how to heal the wounded heart or come back from a nervous breakdown. Just as the Bible does not deal systematically with chemicals or mathematics, neither does it scientifically handle problems of the brain."

"So just where do I come in, Bryan? Medical doctors for the body and psychologists for the mind. What's left for the pastor?" Cliff asked as Bryan calmly sipped his Coke.

"Pastors teach the Word," Bryan said gently as he patted Cliff's hand condescendingly. "You're dealing at the spiritual level, Cliff. I deal at the cognitive level."

"You make it sound like the human can be neatly subdivided into three distinct parts. In my preaching, I also try to deal on the cognitive level. I mean, I want people to use their minds and think through the claims of Christ. Where does the mind leave off and the spirit begin?"

Bryan shifted in his chair uneasily. Just then the waitress brought their order and they began to eat. Cliff took a

bite and then continued. "I can see a clear distinction between the body, or material part of man, and the immaterial
part. But help me to understand the difference between the
mind, soul, and spirit."

"Well...no one can empirically demonstrate a sharp
division between the mind and soul and spirit. I tend to view
the mind as the cognitive or thinking part. I see the soul as
the feeling part, where the emotions and will reside, and
the spirit as that part of man that interacts with God on an
entirely different level."

"Are you saying, then, that the soul is not involved in the
thinking process or that the mind is not involved in spiritual decisions? Is the will, the making of choices, untouched
by the mind or the spirit?"

"No, Cliff, I'm not saying there is no interaction between
the various aspects of human existence. But the Bible, while
useful in helping us consider spiritual matters, is not a
science book. We need the insights of scientific research
and discoveries to help us understand why man does what
he does and how to help him change. Take alcoholism, for
instance. For years, the standard view was that alcoholics
were just weak-willed, undisciplined losers. Now we realize
that alcoholism is a disease and not a moral weakness."

Cliff ate silently as Bryan continued confidently. "Schizophrenia is another example of how science is helping to
remove the mystery from abnormal behavior. Now we
understand that schizophrenia may be caused by chemical
imbalance and by genetic predisposition. Homosexuality
may also be caused by a genetic dysfunction rather than by
home environment or sinful choice, as we have believed in
the past.

"By failing to differentiate between the mind, soul, and
spirit, we Christians have often added the burden of guilt to
the already troubled and suffering masses. In the past,
Christians condemned those who suffered clinical depression as being unspiritual. But scientific research in psychological areas has shown that some depression is an illness
that can be successfully treated by skillful therapy and
medication.

"Too often, Cliff, preachers make the mistake of prescribing Bible verses as simplistic answers to subconsciously motivated harmful behavior. 'Read two of these, and call me in the morning,'" Bryan chuckled and took a bite of his sandwich.

Cliff's forehead creased with concern. "So you're saying that psychology is a science like medicine and that only psychologically trained experts can really delve into the mysteries of the mind. Is that it?" Cliff's jaw seemed a bit tight to Bryan.

"That's pretty close. Why does that bother you?"

"Because I don't see where God fits into this at all. It seems to me that psychologists are making pastors an unnecessary vestige of the past. It seems as though we could actually do more harm than good by confusing people with biblical theories that may contradict scientific truths. To tell you the truth, Bryan, I feel kind of old and useless."

Cliff drove toward home even more dejected after his lunch with psychologist Bryan West. Rather than feeling justified for having turned Annette Pearson away, he now sensed an uncomfortable bruise of guilt in his heart. Miriam, Cliff's wife, could see he was troubled the moment he walked into the house.

"Hi, Honey!" she greeted him cheerily. "How was your day?"

"Lousy," he answered truthfully.

"What happened, Cliff?" She seldom saw him in such a dark mood.

"It was that counseling appointment I told you about," he said as he flopped down on the couch. "When Mrs. Pearson came in, she told me of an incestuous childhood, her history of psychotherapy, and her disintegrating marriage. I admitted that her problems were too deep for me and suggested that she consult a professional counselor, a Christian psychologist.

"She nearly accused me of malpractice for wanting to refer her to someone else, saying that she had already endured psychologists and psychiatrists for years but hadn't received any help. She insinuated that I'm a real hypocrite because I preached Sunday on the Bible providing all the answers we need." He sat up on the couch. "What's worse is that I'm beginning to agree with her."

Miriam sat quietly, letting him vent his frustration.

"I called Bryan West and had lunch with him," he continued. "Before he was through I began to feel totally irrelevant. I mean, if the real answers to man's deepest problems are found in psychology rather than the Bible, what use are pastors anyway? It would seem that my main ministry should be to refer our people to the experts."

"But are they really experts on the human heart, Cliff?" Miriam asked. "I mean, there are more psychologists and psychiatrists than ever before, but society isn't getting any healthier. Why is crime getting worse? Why are marriages still breaking down? Why is the educational system failing so miserably? I'm not convinced that complex professional answers are as helpful as the simple truths of God's Word."

"I don't know what to think, Miriam. I don't even know who to ask. The seminaries have taken a fairly unified position that psychological training is a must if pastors are to help modern Christians."

"Why don't you call John Kryer? I've seen the brochure on their counseling ministry over at Faith Evangelical. He seems to believe that the Bible alone is sufficient for counseling."

Cliff didn't answer for several moments. "Maybe you have a good idea, Hon," he finally responded, sitting up. "I heard him lecture a couple of years ago on his counseling philosophy. He calls it genuinely biblical counseling. He said that psychologists ridicule his 'simplistic answers to complex problems,' and that they call true biblical counselors 'nothing-butterists.'"

"Nothing *what?*" Miriam asked.

"Nothing-butterists. You know, nothing but the Word, nothing but the Bible. Supposedly, biblical counselors just confront people by calling their failures sin, grabbing their psychic collars, slapping them with a Bible verse, and telling them to shape up. No compassion, no understanding, no practical counsel. Nothing but the Word."

"I can't picture Pastor Kryer that way, Cliff."

"Well, neither can I. I think I'll call him." Cliff phoned John Kryer that evening and set up an appointment for the next morning.

The next day, as Cliff got dressed, he felt a little foolish. *How could I have gotten so worked up over this?* he thought. But even as he looked into the mirror, the suffering eyes of Annette Pearson seemed to stare back at him. He blinked and shook his head slightly. In the back of his mind he heard the accusing words, *I thought surely you could help me. I thought you would open the Bible and tell me what God wants me to do.*

At 10:00 he drove into the parking lot of Faith Evangelical Church for his appointment with John Kryer. He turned off the engine and sat for a moment, staring at the steering wheel. He closed his eyes and his lips moved silently. Then he picked up his Bible off the passenger seat, got out, and walked into the church.

Faith Evangelical was a medium-sized church with about 500 members. The large brick building was well cared for and tastefully decorated. Christian music played softly from ceiling speakers as Cliff walked through the large foyer to the office wing.

The secretary guided him to Pastor Kryer's office. "Come in, Cliff," John welcomed in a hearty voice. "What a pleasure to see you again!" He walked around his desk to shake Cliff's hand enthusiastically. "How is your family?"

"Oh, they're super, John. We've had a wonderful year." Cliff sat down and looked around John's office. Overflowing bookshelves lined three walls. Behind John hung an assortment of diplomas. Cliff was pleased to notice that John's desk was covered with mail, notes, and computer disks. *I'm not the only preacher with a messy office,* he thought. The clutter showed that John was busy, but his relaxed attitude put Cliff at ease.

Pastor Kryer was in his mid-forties, and though he still maintained an athletic build, his hair was starting to thin. His face was creased with smile lines and his eyes seemed to radiate joy mingled with mischief. The Kryer family pic-ture was hung proudly on the wall to the right of the diplomas.

They chatted for a few minutes longer, then John asked, "What did you come to see me about, Cliff?"

"I don't know quite where to begin," Cliff said. He cleared his throat and tugged at his collar, which seemed a bit too tight today. John leaned back in his comfortable desk chair and smiled gently as though to encourage Cliff to continue. "I had a counseling case yesterday that really troubled me, John, and I'd like to get your input. I know you do a lot of counseling, and I remembered from your seminar that you don't follow the standard approach."

"How do you mean?"

"Well, I heard you say that the Bible alone is sufficient for counseling Christians. Is that right?"

"If you're talking about my source of authority and philosophy, you're absolutely right," Pastor Kryer agreed readily. "That doesn't mean that I don't use general coun-seling techniques such as taking notes, giving assignments, and recommending certain authors who have a biblical viewpoint."

"Do you classify yourself as a nouthetic counselor?"

John seemed surprised that Cliff had used the term. "It depends on how you're using the term."

"What do you mean?" Cliff asked.

"I mean, if you're talking about my doctrinal position and whether I believe the Bible provides the essential an-swers for every mental, emotional, and spiritual problem, then I will accept the nouthetic label. But if you're talk-ing about the inaccurate stereotype of an angry, finger-pointing judge who lacks all compassion, I reject the title."

Cliff chuckled and replied, "I guess I'm asking why you believe that a pastor doesn't need psychological training to be an effective counselor. Where did you get your train-ing? . . . if you don't mind my asking, that is," Cliff added, feeling uncomfortable, as though he were interviewing someone for a job.

"I don't mind at all," John laughed. "I got my under-graduate degree in education at the state university in Iowa and my Master of Divinity at Trinity Evangelical Divinity School in Illinois. I got my doctorate from Westminster, in counseling."

"Did you study counseling at Trinity?"

"No, I was a theology major, but my wife, Mary, got her masters in counseling there."

"That's interesting. Trinity doesn't follow a nouthetic philosophy in counseling, does it?" Cliff asked.

John laughed and shook his head. "I'd say not! It was Mary's experience at Trinity that led us into nouthetic counseling, though."

"What happened?"

"Well, Mary felt there was an overemphasis on psychological diagnosis and methodology and far too little training in counseling from the Bible. The students were discouraged from praying with their counselees and were told to avoid pushing their faith on troubled people. The school places a high emphasis on psychology as a necessity in the counsel of God's people."

Cliff leaned forward. "That's why I'm here, John." Cliff told Pastor Kryer about his convicting encounter with Mrs. Pearson the day before and of his subsequent conversation with psychologist Bryan West. "I told my wife last night that I feel as though the pastorate has become a marketing tool used to funnel paying customers to psychologists."

"That is how a lot of psychology clinics view the church, Cliff. Have you noticed how many brochures and letters you receive from psychiatric hospitals offering you one-day seminars and assistance in handling difficult counseling cases?"

Cliff smiled and replied, "I sure have. I probably get four or five of those a month. I even got one from a griefologist who holds seminars to teach pastors how to help people cope with sorrow."

"Isn't that amazing? And the sad fact is that many pastors honestly believe that the psychologist has better information to deal with death and grief than what is provided in the Scriptures," John said, shaking his head. Cliff looked down in conviction. "Those recruiting letters are sent out in the hope that you will refer your parishioners to their clinic or hospital. I'm sure that most psychologists have a sincere desire to help hurting people, but at the same time they are in a position of having to assure themselves of a continual source of revenue."

Cliff scratched his chin in deep thought. He looked up and asked, "Are you sorry you didn't go into secular counseling, John?" revealing a part of his own struggle. "Sometimes when I drive my old sedan and think about the condition of my bank account, I find myself envying Bryan's income."

John smiled sympathetically. "Few pastors get into this work for the money. But honestly, Cliff, I wouldn't trade places with anyone. There is no greater joy than watching lives change in front of your very eyes as people learn to obey the simple truths of God's Word." John picked up his Bible reverently. "This book contains *everything* pertaining to life and godliness. Who knows better than God how to comfort the bereaved? Who has a better solution for chronic depression than the Lord, who changes the very heart rather than dulling the pain with drugs? Isn't it ironic that we who hold forth the Bread of Life refer our people to secular counseling systems that actually enslave people instead of setting them free? And our people are forced to pay for that sort of treatment because we pastors have lost confidence in our calling and the power of God's Word."

PART TWO

The Myths
of Psychology

Scientific Admission

The fact of the matter is that the education of professional scientists is just as narrowly focused as the education of any other group of professionals, and scientists are just as likely to be ignorant of scientific matters as anyone else.

The Biblical Counselor

"Is psychology really a science?" No it isn't. But few pastors are willing to take the time to examine the evidences, consider the implications, confront the deceptions, and inform their people.

The Word of God

For since the creation of the world God's invisible qualities—his eternal power and divine nature—have been clearly seen, being understood from what has been made, so that men are without excuse. For although they knew God, they neither glorified him as God nor gave thanks to him, but their thinking became futile and their foolish hearts were darkened. Although they claimed to be wise, they became fools and exchanged the glory of the immortal God for images made to look like mortal man and birds and animals and reptiles.
—Romans 1:20-23

CHAPTER

2

The Myth That Psychology Is Scientific

An exciting new science explaining the human mind and behavior was introduced by a doctor in Vienna, Austria. His theories influenced prominent writers like Edgar Allan Poe, Walt Whitman, and Ralph Waldo Emerson. Educator Horace Mann declared that he was more indebted to this fresh science than to all the metaphysical books he had ever read. The world-renowned preacher Henry Ward Beecher praised this innovative explanation of human behavior as revealing the principles which underpinned his entire ministry. Horace Greeley thought this new method of evaluating people should be used as the basis for hiring applicants for dangerous jobs. This new understanding of the mind was received enthusiastically at Yale, Harvard, and the Boston Medical Society.

This trailblazing discovery explained intriguing concepts such as amativeness, philoprogenitiveness, alimentiveness, approbativeness, and self-esteem. When this revolutionary hypothesis was first introduced to America, 37 separate organs of the brain had been identified; the number eventually increased to 83.[1] Practitioners of this fascinating new science revealed to a receptive world that one's character could be identified by the shape of the skull!

Coming from the same city that birthed Freudian psychoanalysis, the pseudoscience of *phrenology* influenced American thought for some 30 years. People accepted this scientific pretender because it seemed to explain why man acts the way he does without making him morally responsible.

Though phrenology has long since been discredited, it was the forerunner of another group of practices: psychoanalysis, psychiatry, and psychology. Using more sophisticated techniques to convince the public that they are scientific, these new theories have pulled off a massive deception in our own day.

Psychology As a Science

Is psychology truly a science, as many integrationist counselors claim? Many people have accepted the claim that psychology is scientifically accurate without actually examining the evidence. Notice this characteristic error in logic written by a confirmed integrationist: "Sometimes theologies are found to be in error while the findings of science stand as firm as the Copernican theory."[2] I agree that some theologies are erroneous, but to state that "the findings of science" stand *firm* reveals just how confused integrationist thinking can become. Scientific findings are in a *constant* state of flux. What is affirmed today is denied tomorrow.

For example, a scientific volume, *Science Matters*, was recently published to explain science to the general public. It promotes the concept of "the big bang" as "our best guess as to the origin and evolution of the universe."[3] The *same day* the book was announced in the media, astronomers revealed that the "big bang theory" was no longer an acceptable scientific explanation for the dispersion of matter throughout the universe! Within a few days, other scientists disputed the second opinion with a third opinion.

The purpose of *Science Matters* is to help average people

achieve "scientific literacy," yet the authors seem unable to recognize their own built-in contradictions. In Chapter 1 they write that science is "guided by one overarching principle: the universe is regular and predictable. The universe is not random."[4] Yet in Chapter 17 they write, "Many scientists believe that millions of years of random mixing and shuffling of molecules culminated in the appearance of one living cell—an object that could consume surrounding chemicals to make exact copies of itself."[5]

In order to explain variation in species, they write, "Random variations and chance mutations occasionally lead to advantages, which are preserved as *non-random* evolution."[6] The Bible describes such foolish double-talk in Romans 1:22: "Although they claimed to be wise, they became fools." Unwilling to admit their own faith, such writers set aside creationism as a mere religious belief. This sort of intellectual dishonesty is representative of much of the scientific establishment.

The same delusion is evident in psychology. Freud's "scientific findings" have been increasingly discredited by new findings. Thousands of competing psychotherapeutic systems claim to have new findings to support their conclusions. But each new system produces a new finding which contradicts the prior findings.

In infinite contrast, the psalmist writes, "Your word, O LORD, is eternal; it stands firm in the heavens" (Psalm 119:89). Jesus said, "Heaven and earth will pass away, but my words will never pass away" (Matthew 24:35). Peter proclaimed, "The word of the Lord stands forever" (1 Peter 1:25).

The Definition of Science

To see how miserably psychology fails the test of science, we need to know what science is. Simply stated, *science* is the systematically arranged knowledge of the material world which has been gathered in a four-step process: 1) observation of phenomena; 2) collection of data; 3) creation of a hypothesis or theory by inductive reasoning;

and 4) testing of the hypothesis by repeated observation and controlled experiments.

Following this fairly standard definition of science and the scientific method, one should ask several questions. Do psychiatric and psychological studies follow rigid controls? Are the findings carefully tested by verifiable experiments? Are the hypotheses drawn from the data with rational impartiality? According to some knowledgeable insiders, the answers are no.

Lack of Scientific Standards in Psychology

Dr. Alfred M. Freedman, a psychiatrist with impressive credentials, was interviewed by journalist Martin Gross. Freedman, formerly the president of the American Psychiatric Association, said, "There are a number of assumptions in psychoanalytic theory that have never been adequately tested. The consequences of childhood experience, including the Oedipus complex, may not be of the order we think."[7]

Gross documents the statements of several other prominent psychiatrists. Dr. Jules H. Masserman has stated that "psychoanalytic reports are too often based on uncontrolled theoretical and clinical preconceptions."[8] Dr. R.R. Sears headed the Social Science Research Council, which issued a report on psychoanalysis. The report stated, "Psychoanalysis relies upon techniques that do not admit to the repetition of observation, that have no self-evident or denotative validity, and that are tinctured to an unknown degree with the observer's own suggestions."[9]

The point is that human thinking and behavior *cannot* be categorized scientifically because each human is unique and one's reaction to events, circumstances, and other stimuli cannot be predicted or tested using the scientific method. Most psychotherapeutic theories cannot be empirically tested and verified. It is impossible, for example, to scientifically examine the Freudian concepts of the id, ego, or superego.

No scientist can accurately quantify percentages of rage. No one can scientifically observe the child, parent, and adult of Transactional Analysis. Science cannot be applied to prove the existence of unconscious motivations. Psychologists are in error to state as fact that humans use less than a given percentage of their total mental capacity. It is misleading for psychologists to claim that they scientifically examine minds, emotions, beliefs, values, and behaviors. A major writer of integrationist materials admits that "it is difficult to use scientific standards to study emotions like love and hope, the behavior of street gangs, the religious experiences of churchgoers or the effectiveness of psychotherapy."[10] Still, he believes that psychology is scientific.

Psychologist Larry Crabb has stated that psychology cannot be classified as science. He writes:

> [M]any admit now that the scientific research method is inherently inadequate for the job of defining truth. Science can provide neither proof nor meaning. In another paper, I pointed out that modern philosophers of science confess the incurable impotency of science to ever say anything conclusively. Science can assess probability but can take us no further. To reach certainty demands that we go beyond (not deny) reason and exercise faith. Humanistic optimism that man is sufficient to solve his problems has crumbled under the weight of science's inability to clearly assert that any single proposition is true. We need proven universals. Science cannot provide them. We must in faith reach beyond ourselves to get what we need.[11]

Psychology rarely deals with established facts or truths but with subjective opinions and interpretations of uncontrolled observations. Psychology is not dealing with the consistent interactions between chemicals that can be carefully controlled in the laboratory, but with analyses that are tainted by the unique free wills of the subjects and the mindset of the researchers.

How Psychology Achieved Scientific Status

If the answer to the question "Is psychology really a science?" is negative, then how have psychologists managed to convince the general public that their field is scientific? There are several factors in this major sociological and spiritual deception.

Statistical Illusions

Psychologists use statistics frequently in their writings to create the illusion that their statements are based on solid scientific research. One prominent Christian psychiatrist writes, "I fully demonstrated and documented my belief that approximately 85 percent of our behavior patterns and attitudes are firmly entrenched by age six."[12]

Consider these examples of unscientific statistical statements used to support psychological dogma: "In fact, 75 *percent of depressives feel they will never recover.*"[13] "Probably 98 percent of the things we worry about never come true."[14] "If the patients are not maintained following a course of ECT [electroconvulsive therapy, or shock treatment], between 30 and 40 percent of the cases will relapse within a year."[15] By attaching mathematical figures to unprovable statements, psychologists often shore up their claim of scientific inquiry.

A Christian psychiatrist states:

> During my residency in psychiatry, I did a categorical survey of the types of patients I had during a six-month rotation on the psychiatric ward. These findings were obtained:
> * 30%—Hysterical trends, personality or neurosis
> * 20%—Depression/anxiety
> * 10%—Drug-related problems
> * 15%—Psychotic[16]

What sort of vital information was obtained from this statistical study? The author says, "Conclusions are difficult to draw from such a small sample of a patient population (approximately 40), but one can conclude with certainty that individuals with emotional conflicts are in search of help. One may also conclude that being a Christian does not necessarily free one of emotional turmoil."[17]

I appreciate this writer's candor in admitting that the sampling was small. But consider for a moment: Was a statistical study really needed to conclude that "individuals with emotional conflicts are in search of help" or that "being a Christian does not necessarily free one of emotional turmoil"? Aren't those facts rather obvious?

I cite these examples of psychological "findings" because they are fairly representative of psychological "science." Many studies are performed on a small group of people and the subjectively interpreted facts are then projected upon the general population.

The Limitations of Science

Let us turn to the question of science itself. Many people assume that something is scientific if a scientist states it as fact. Freud, who spawned most of the psychological belief systems, was deeply influenced by Charles Darwin's doctrine of evolution, and the philosophical connection between the two is significant. Evolution, like psychology, has been proclaimed as a scientific fact when in reality it is merely a philosophical and religious theory. J.W.N. Sullivan writes in *The Limitations of Science*:

> The beginning of the evolutionary process raises a question which is as yet unanswerable. What was the origin of life on this planet? Until fairly recent times there was a pretty general belief in the occurrence of "spontaneous generation." ... But careful experiments, notably those of Pasteur, showed that this conclusion was due to imperfect observation, and it became an accepted doctrine that life never arises

except from life. So far as actual evidence goes, this is still the only possible conclusion. But since it is a conclusion that seems to lead back to some supernatural creative act, it is a conclusion that scientific men find very difficult of acceptance.[18]

So difficult, in fact, that many scientists regularly contradict scientific laws in their writings to support evolutionary theory, and to dismiss creation as a laughable relic of the past. In spite of the fact that life never comes from nonlife, the authors of *Science Matters* still cling to their unscientific faith. Hazen and Trefil write, "Life seems to have arisen in a two-step process. The first stage—chemical evolution—encompasses the origin of life from nonlife. Once life appeared, the second state—biological evolution —took over."[19]

No scientist has ever observed life arising from nonlife, and all evidence points away from such a conclusion. Though such scientists must be aware that they are teaching physical, chemical, and biological error, they continue to deceive the public with their "scientific" pronouncements.

In a similar way, psychologists and psychiatrists have successfully convinced the general public that their professional systems are based on hard scientific evidence. Scientists themselves are often deceived by the rhetoric of their peers. Psychologist Ray Jurjevich writes, "[Scientists] are just as suggestible to authority figures as humans in any other profession. Physicists and chemists, biologists and geologists, psychologists and psychiatrists have uncritically bought a lot of nonsense from the elders in their professions."[20]

Hazen and Trefil's statement about the general illiteracy of scientists is particularly revealing:

Intense study of a particular field of science does not necessarily make one scientifically literate. Indeed, it has been our experience that working scientists are often illiterate outside their own field of professional expertise. For

example, we recently asked a group of twenty-
four physicists and geologists to explain to us
the difference between DNA and RNA a basic
piece of information in the life sciences. We
found only three who could do so, and all three
of those did research in areas where this knowledge was useful.... The fact of the matter is
that the education of professional scientists is
just as narrowly focused as the education of any
other group of professionals, and scientists are
just as likely to be ignorant of scientific matters
as anyone else. You should keep this in mind
the next time a Nobel laureate speaks *ex cathe-
dra* on issues outside his or her own field of
specialization.[21]

The readers of *Science Matters* should also keep in mind
that Hazen and Trefil's pronouncements are no more trustworthy than those of the scientists they regard as illiterate,
for when they speak authoritatively about the origins of life,
they are out of *their* field. The origin of life is outside the
realm of scientific inquiry and should be left to philosophy
and religion. In the same way, the statements of psychologists and psychiatrists must also be examined carefully, for
they are as prone to error as other "experts" who make self-
confident assertions based on personal opinion and subjective interpretations of flawed observations.

Scientific and Medical Rhetoric

The use of scientific and medical terminology is another tool used to convince the public that psychology is
scientific. Psychologists and psychiatrists use terms such as
"controlled studies," "clinical research," and "statistical
indications" to convey the alleged scientific nature of their
field. They connect psychiatry with medical science by the
use of terms like "diagnosis," "patients," "therapy," "treatment," and "cure." Because psychiatrists are also medical
doctors, people are convinced.

Having established their position as scientific and medical, the psychotherapeutic industry proceeds to create new technical terms. They speak of "identity crisis," "self-actualization," "Oedipus complex," "paranoia," "schizophrenia," "transference," "sublimation," "coprolalia," "buffoonery psychosis," "ergasiomania," and a multitude of other labels designed to impress the layman.

Psychiatrist E. Fuller Torrey says that psychological labels "are impressive and convey to the uninitiated that we know what we are talking about. Unfortunately, this is not the case."[22] The media, however, portray psychotherapists as infallible scientists who produce an endless succession of scientific findings.

> *Self* and *science* have established a powerful psychological partnership. Its major products are its claims: truth and cure. Psychology's truth is in its thousands of *findings* about sex, marriage, mental health, personal attitudes, child raising, learning, aggression, which have been discovered by a professional. They cascade all around us in journals, newspapers, magazines, and on television, all labeled as "scientific evidence."[23]

By linking psychiatry and psychology to scientific disciplines, the public is convinced that the "findings" are accurate and true. Unfortunately, often they are not.

The Perceived Need for Experts

Our generation has great confidence in "experts." The rapid increase of knowledge in the twentieth century has forced professionals to specialize in their chosen field. Specialization has occurred not only in the hard sciences and medicine, but is evident also in the pseudosciences of psychology and psychiatry. Now we are told that we need experts to help us with every problem of living.

"America is probably the most specialized and professionalized society on earth. We have more experts in more

areas than does any other country.... Our culture is dominated by professionals who call us clients, tell us what our
needs are and how to satisfy them."[24]

We have "experts" to tell us how to lose weight, stop
smoking, raise our children, have happy marriages, and be
cured of every mental disorder. There are "grief experts"
who tell us how to deal with the loss of a loved one, and these
specialists advertise their services in mailings to *pastors!*
(Think about that.) The universal acceptance of specialization has intimidated many pastors into accepting a
secondary role in the ministry to souls.

One should ask, however, whether psychologists truly
have deeper insights into the soul of man than the average
person does. Because the human mind and soul are so
complex, there is little reliability in the interpretation of
individual behavior. "A dozen psychoanalysts listening to
the same material are likely to formulate a dozen different
estimations of its unconscious meaning."[25] Does this indicate that professional counselors are more capable than
laymen to interpret behavior and to help people to change?
If not, why are we so confident in the experts? Zilbergeld
offers this explanation:

> Our belief in the superiority of specializa-
> tion and our predilection for solutions and
> perfection pushes us to depend on experts.
> Even if we have some competence in a given
> area, we know there are others who know
> more. Our own efforts seem amateurish and
> inefficient. Why not let someone with special
> training do it or at least help us do it? The
> modern view is well expressed in a recent book:
> "The key to a successful adult life lies in sur-
> rounding yourself with experts, a master per-
> son for every need."[26]

Because Americans have accepted the need for experts,
we have also accepted their interpretations of human needs
and behaviors. Research has confirmed what common

sense knew all along: that most personal problems can be solved merely by talking with someone and by taking personal action. Why is it that most psychologists reject this rational point of view? There are at least three reasons: First, their professional training has convinced them of the "expert" myth; second, if they accept the validity of lay counseling, the legitimacy of the psychological profession becomes questionable; and third, if people realize they can get equal results from nonprofessional counseling, the personal income of psychologists will be jeopardized, for they depend upon a continual stream of paying clients.

Jeffrey Masson, a former psychoanalyst, reports that psychoanalytical training does not prepare a person to be a better counselor. He testifies that after five years of intensive analysis on himself and his patients he did not understand "emotional problems of living" better than people with no training.[27] Masson's thesis is that all professional therapy is unneeded and long years of intensive psychological study are a waste of time: "I spent eight years in my psychoanalytic training. In retrospect, I feel I could have learned the basic ideas in about eight hours of concentrated reading."[28] What an amazing confession from a secular therapist!

In spite of the evidence that laymen are equally or sometimes even more effective counselors than psychiatrists or clinical psychologists, the "experts" still insist that they are essential in the treatment of major problems.

Belief in Universal Madness

Why has psychology been allowed to intrude into nearly every area of our lives? As incredible as it sounds, many psychologists tend to view most humans as mentally ill:

> In New York City, a ten-year study, *Mental Health in the Metropolis,* claimed that approximately 80 percent of adults showed some symptoms of mental illness, with one in four actually impaired.
>
> In 1977 the President's Commission on

Mental Health confirmed these dire diagnoses. It concluded that the state of our psyches is worse than believed, and that one-quarter of all Americans suffer from severe emotional stress. They warned that up to 32 million Americans are in need of professional psychiatric help. A National Institute of Mental Health psychologist even portrays universal madness as a statistical certainty. "Almost no family in the nation is entirely free of mental disorders," he stated in a recent federal study. The NIMH psychologist estimates that in addition to the 500,000 schizophrenics in hospitals, there are 1.75 million psychotics not hospitalized, and *up to 60 million Americans who exhibit deviant mental behavior related to schizophrenia.*[29]

The only sane ones, it would seem, are psychologists, psychiatrists, and other accredited mental health experts. It reminds one of the old joke about the two psychiatrists who were discussing the general condition of the world. One said to the other, "Everybody in the world is crazy except you and me, and sometimes I'm not even sure about you."

Importance of the Issue

Even at this point, some would ask, what difference does it make? Why make such a big deal over counseling philosophies?

Because the consequences of this issue are *enormous*. It determines for many people their ultimate source of truth and authority for daily living. Rather than turning to God and His Word for solutions for the problems of life, today's Christian is being taught that he must turn to psychology. Instead of consulting with his pastor, the church member is convinced that his problems are too severe for biblical counsel, and that they require the special insights of those trained under secular-based philosophies.

In an article in *Christianity Today,* Tim Stafford writes:

> In the past, conservative Christians have tended to avoid using the mental health system, but over the past three decades psychology has become more acceptable with evangelical circles. As the influence of respected leaders like Clyde Narramore, James Dobson, Frank Minirth, and Paul Meier has broken down the resistance, the number of evangelicals seeking psychological counseling has grown. A survey conducted last year, for example, found that 29% of *Christianity Today* readers had gotten counseling for themselves or a relative within the past three years and three times as many of them went to a professional counselor or psychologist as went to a pastor.[30]

Christian pastors have also succumbed to the incessant barrage of psychological messages coming from Christian books, magazines, film series, radio, and television. Having refused to accept evolutionary theory as scientific truth, many Christians have dropped their guard and been deceived by another scientific pretender.

■ ■ ■

Two weeks passed and still Cliff couldn't get Annette Pearson out of his mind. It was not her alluring beauty that caused Cliff to see her face in his mind time and again. His own wife, Miriam, was also beautiful and the love of his life. No, the reason she kept plaguing his mind was the unsettling question she had raised about his entire philosophy of ministry.

His conversations with John Kryer and Bryan West had only made his guilt seem worse. Cliff determined to do some research on his own. He drove to the Baptist Seminary in town and spent several hours in the library searching for books from both sides of the counseling debate. He chose a book on Christian psychiatry by Frank Minirth, a book on biblical counseling by Larry Crabb, one about sexual abuse by Dan Allender, an apologetic for psychology by Gary Collins, a fiery critique by Martin Bobgan, and a large counseling manual by Jay Adams.

The more he read, the more confused he became. Each author seemed so reasonable and...so right! One day he stopped by a favorite shop, a used bookstore, to see what they carried. There was a whole section dedicated to psychology, with literally hundreds of books to choose from. As he searched through the dusty shelves, he found some startling titles, considering that the books were written by secular authors.

He picked up a volume by journalist Martin Gross called *The Psychological Society*. It detailed many of the abuses of psychiatry and psychology. Then he found a book written by psychiatrist E. Fuller Torrey called *The Death of Psychiatry*. As he began to look specifically for secular critiques of psychology, he located several more: *The Shrinking of America* by Bernie Zilbergeld, *The Crisis in Psychiatry and Religion* by Mowrer, *The Reign of Error* by Coleman, and *The Myth of Psychotherapy* by a professor of psychiatry, Thomas Szasz.

When he got home, he was almost afraid to show Miriam the pile of books he had bought. "Good grief, Honey," she said in amazement when she saw him carrying books in both arms. "When are you going to find time to read all of those?"

"I know it looks like a lot," Cliff admitted, "but I've got to sort this issue out. I haven't had any peace since Mrs. Pearson came in for counseling. Anyway, I got these with my book allowance from church."

He carried the books into his home office. As he skimmed them, Cliff was amazed that secular writers seemed to doubt psychology more than Christian authors did. Several hours later, after reading Torrey's book, Cliff phoned Bryan West.

"Cliff, old boy!" Bryan answered cheerfully. "Did you get your questions sorted out?"

"Not entirely, Bryan. As a matter of fact, I was wondering if you could refer me to a Christian psychiatrist in the area."

"Wow!" Bryan responded in surprise. "Is this for therapy or to discuss counseling philosophy?"

"I want to see what kind of answers a psychiatrist has for some specific criticisms I've read about."

"Let me guess," Bryan said with a hint of sarcasm, "Adams or Bobgan?"

"Neither," Cliff answered. "I've found some pretty serious accusations made by a journalist and a fairly substantial number of psychiatrists. And they aren't Christians, so far as I can detect."

"Well, yeah, I guess I can give you a number to call," Bryan said in a reluctant tone. "Why don't you contact Dr. Vance McCall?" His voice suddenly warmed as he said, "In fact, if you wouldn't mind, I'd like to tag along and hear what he has to say."

"That would be great, Bryan!" Cliff said enthusiastically. "Since you know Dr. McCall, why don't you make the appointment for both of us?"

"Consider it done! I'll call you back."

Less than ten minutes later the phone rang. It was Bryan West.

"It's all set up, Cliff. Next Tuesday morning, 9:00. I told him a little about our conversation and the questions you're having, and he felt it was important that we get together right away."

The following Tuesday at 8:30, Cliff drove into the parking area at Bryan West's office. He looked at the impressive building with a measure of envy and was immediately ashamed of himself. Still, he had to admit the feelings were there. He got out of his eight-year-old Chrysler and walked inside. *There's nothing cheap about Bryan West,* he thought as he took in the rich wood tones and brass accents in the waiting area. The receptionist buzzed Bryan, who soon appeared, pulling on a suede jacket.

"Let's go, Clifton! I'll drive." They went out and got into Bryan's bright red sports car. Just before 9:00 they zipped into the parking lot of Dr. Vance McCall's Greenway Counseling Services. Inside, Cliff was impressed with the beauty and richness of the offices. "Man! This business really pays, doesn't it?" he said to Bryan.

"Well, it's important to have a nice environment for counseling," Bryan said a bit defensively. "Just because we're Christians doesn't mean our places should look cheap. In fact, I think we dishonor the Lord if we don't do everything with the highest quality. You remember the passage that says, 'Whatever your hand finds to do, do it with all your might'?" Cliff shrugged his shoulders and nodded.

A few minutes later, a secretary ushered them into Dr. McCall's office. Bryan led the way and introduced Cliff to Dr. McCall. "Cliff and I were in school together at Dallas Seminary, Vance."

"I'm delighted to meet you, Cliff!" the psychiatrist said with a warm smile.

"I appreciate your taking time to meet with us," Cliff said as they shook hands.

"Have a seat, and tell me what's on your mind," Dr. McCall said. He certainly didn't fit Cliff's image of a psychiatrist. McCall was about six-foot-four in height and looked younger than his 50 years. There was an air of authority in the way he conducted himself, but his spontaneous smile and charming personality put Cliff at ease.

Cliff recounted his experience with Mrs. Pearson and of the inner turmoil which that event had produced in his own mind. "I visited another pastor who does a lot of counseling, to get his perspective." Cliff noticed that Bryan and Vance's eyes met for a split second before returning to him.

"Oh?" Dr. McCall said casually. "Would I know him?"

"I doubt it," Cliff said. "He comes from an entirely different point of view. His name is John Kryer. He's a pastor over at Faith Evangelical."

"I know about Reverend Kryer," Dr. McCall said as he shifted in his chair. Bryan crossed his legs and pushed himself further back in his chair. "He's got some pretty strong opinions of my line of work, doesn't he?"

"Yeah, I suppose so," Cliff said evasively. "But the criticisms I want to ask about don't involve him so much. I need some answers for the ones that have come from secular sources."

"Well, fire away! What are your questions?" Dr. McCall said pleasantly.

"I've tried to organize the objections into a few main categories," Cliff said as he took out some written notes. "The first is that psychiatry claims to be based on the medical model when in reality, the critics say, it is neither scientific nor medical in practice, but is actually more of an educational procedure in which medical training is unnecessary.

"A second criticism is the abuse of psychiatric power, in that psychiatrists have the authority to commit a person against his will to a mental institution where that person can be forced to submit to drug therapy. According to Coleman, Zilbergeld, and Szasz, there is incredible potential for political and social repression, as was evident in Russia during the Communist reign."

Dr. McCall sat quietly with pursed lips as he said, "Mm-hm. Go on."

"Torrey, Zilbergeld, and Gross point out that psychiatry does not and cannot follow scientific methods in dealing with human minds and that society's unquestioning trust of psychotherapy is unwarranted."

"Mm-hm. Is that all?"

"Not quite. Several writers criticize the practice of returning to the past to try to heal the present. And the last question is whether psychiatry and psychology are subtle enemies of Christianity rather than partners, as Minirth and Narramore seem to suggest."

Bryan uncrossed his legs and sat forward again. Dr. McCall cleared his voice and leaned back in his leather desk chair. "Those are excellent questions, Cliff, and I can see why these issues would concern you. First, let me tell you a little about these critics. Do you know anything about them?"

"Not really. Just what I've read."

"Well, I do. In every profession, there are those who belong to the lunatic fringe. Some psychiatrists have indeed experimented with bizarre therapies and have brought criticism on all of us. Not unlike what some televangelists have done to you preachers." Cliff nodded in agreement and wrote on his notes.

"Now let's take Szasz, for example. Were you aware that a New York State official tried to have Szasz removed from the teaching faculty of the University of New York at Syracuse for some of his extreme statements? You should question the credibility of a man who has been rejected by so many of his own peers.

"Then there's Lee Coleman. Though he criticizes the use of expert psychiatric testimony in court, he has testified in more than 100 trials himself." Cliff was taking notes as fast as he could write. "Many of the critics of psychiatry appear to me to be more concerned about making a name for themselves than in correcting the supposed abuses they write about. Doesn't it seem hypocritical to you that Szasz says that psychiatry is phony while at the same time he teaches that very subject at a major university?"

"Yeah," Cliff laughed. "That did occur to me."

"You mentioned Martin Gross. He's a professional critic. He put out a book in the late sixties called *The Doctors,* in which he criticized medicine, and his book was roundly denounced by the American Medical Association. I would take him more seriously if he were a medical doctor, but he's merely a journalist out to sell books."

Cliff nodded his head as he wrote. He was glad he had come. *Now I'm getting somewhere!* he thought.

McCall continued, "One of the most vitriolic critics of Christian psychology is Jay Adams. He doesn't even have a doctorate in counseling, last I knew. I believe he got his doctorate in speech or communications. At any rate, he's no expert on psychological counseling. Then there are the Bobgans with their accusations of psychoheresies. I think they have a personal vendetta against some of the most respected Christian leaders in America simply because they're psychologists. It's like a witch hunt!"

Dr. McCall pulled himself close to his desk. "Enough about the critics. Let's get to the real core of your questions: Can psychology and the Bible be integrated to form a counseling system that is both scientifically sound and theologically orthodox? To answer that, we need to take a quick look at the four basic counseling positions." Cliff noticed that Bryan had taken out a pad and pen and was also writing notes.

"The first is the humanistic, nonreligious or non-Christian system. This view is actually antagonistic to Christianity and tends to view believers as mentally ill by definition.

"The second is the spiritualized view, which argues that all mental problems are the result of the violation of biblical principles. Some call this the nouthetic position and it is represented by Adams. He's only been noticed because he has written so many books, all of them saying exactly the same thing: 'Nothing but the Bible, nothing but the Word!'

"The third position is what some of us call the parallel view. This is a system where the psychologist is a believer and knows the Bible, and is also well-trained in psychological truths. He uses both the Bible and psychology independently of one another as the needs arise. He doesn't integrate the two. This position is preferable to either of the first two, but is still lacking.

"The fourth system is the integrated position, which does not view the Bible and psychology as operating in two unrelated spheres. Psychology is seen as one form of natural revelation—that is, truth found in nature—while the Bible is seen as special revelation from God. The integrated psychologist is able to join these two sources of truth in a harmonious way. Perhaps they should be seen as the two eyepieces of a single microscope. Singly, the view is two-dimensional, but together, the two lenses present a clear, three-dimensional image. When properly understood, psychology and the Bible do not conflict, but actually cooperate to form a more complete system."

Cliff looked up from his notes with a smile. "That makes sense." Then his brow wrinkled with another thought.

"I see a lingering question on your face, young man," Dr. McCall observed in a teasing tone of voice.

"Well," Cliff said hesitantly, "it still appears to me that pastors are virtually obsolete. If all I can present is the Bible, and by your own description, that is a second-rate view, I'm cheating my people. If they need additional truth that I can't give them, how can I in good conscience ask them to pay me a salary?"

"Don't sell yourself too short, Cliff," Dr. McCall cautioned. "Pastors still perform a much-needed function. Most problems are simple enough for a pastor to handle. But for deeper, more complicated mental problems, psychological training is a must." Cliff detected the hint of a satisfied smile on Bryan's face that suddenly faded when Dr. McCall concluded, "And for the most serious mental disorders, the final court of appeal is the psychiatrist."

Dr. McCall stood to his feet, indicating that time was up. "I hope that has answered some of your questions, Cliff," he said with a smile, shaking Cliff's hand. "I'd like you to attend the monthly breakfast meetings we offer for pastors in the area. We deal with common counseling problems. I think you would find some helpful information."

"Thanks, Dr. McCall," Cliff replied. "I'll think about it."

As Bryan and Cliff walked out to the car, Cliff said, "Well, I guess we got put in our places, didn't we?"

"What do you mean?" Bryan asked tightly.

"I think Dr. McCall made the professional pecking order fairly clear. You, Bryan, are just one peck above a preacher!" Cliff snickered.

"Real funny, Cliff," Bryan retorted without humor.

"Well, now you see how I feel, Bryan. All kidding aside, I really wonder if I can justify continuing in the ministry if all I'm good for is to put a bandage on minor spiritual scratches."

"You're missing the point entirely, Cliff! Preachers have a unique function—to point people to heaven."

"But for real problems of living, we're not much good, are we?"

They got in Bryan's car and drove back to his office. Neither spoke most of the way. Bryan drove up next to

Cliff's car and parked. Shutting off the engine, he looked at Cliff and asked, "So what are you thinking?"

"I'm thinking that maybe it's time I reevaluated my ministry. Maybe I need to go back to school and get a counseling degree. All I know is theology, and that seems pretty inadequate for the problems of modern living."

The Psychological Counselor

Many benefits can come from therapy, in spite of its weaknesses. According to one review of the research, therapy can help people feel better.

The Biblical Counselor

Of course therapy can make people feel better— temporarily. But does it truly change them? Does it help them solve their problems? Do they become more like Christ? Are they led into Christian maturity? Are their thought and behavior patterns brought into conformity to God's Word? Those should be the tests of effectiveness for Christian counseling.

The Word of God

You have a fine way of setting aside the commands of God in order to observe your own traditions.
—Mark 7:9

C H A P T E R

3

The Myth
That Psychology
Is Effective

A woman, age 31, complains of chronic depression and low self-esteem. She has been under psychiatric care since she was a teenager, but has not improved. A fed-up husband is ready to call off his marriage because of the perpetual expense of his wife's psychiatric sessions, which are producing no positive results. A young woman has been diagnosed as schizophrenic and has been given strong psychoactive drugs which temporarily mask her symptoms.

The majority of experienced pastoral counselors have met many such clients of psychological counseling.

You might be tempted to ask, "Why would anyone submit to psychological counseling if it never helps anyone?" Few serious critics of psychology go so far as to say that *no one* is *ever* helped through psychological counseling. A better way to ask the question might be, With its claims of superiority over pastoral counseling and its high expense, why is psychological therapy so relatively ineffective?

One Christian psychologist lists five major reasons that psychology produces disappointing results: 1) unrealistic expectations by counselees, 2) inaccurate assumptions about the ability of psychology to explain human behavior,

3) wrong motivations for seeking counsel, 4) unfounded faith in psychological "experts," and 5) undelivered promises by the "experts."[1]

These causes of failure in psychology can apply to any counseling system, secular or Christian. People often enter counseling with the mistaken belief that the counselor will solve their problems. The truth is that counseling success in any system depends more upon the motivation of the counselee to change than on the insights of the counselor.

Psychopromises

Some psychologists, in an attempt to explain why therapies often fail, point out that patients often come with unrealistic expectations of being set free from all anxiety and achieving perpetual happiness. Ironically, psychiatric hospitals and psychological counseling services aggressively advertise their services on radio and television implying that such goals *are* possible...with their help.

A one-third-page newspaper advertisement for Adolescent Behavioral Health sponsored by a large hospital shows a teenage boy with his arm around his girlfriend. They are dressed in punk outfits. The ad says, "Young people frequently choose hairstyles and clothing to express *healthy adolescent rebellion*. But how is one to tell whether his teenager's behavior is OK or self-destructive?"[2] (emphasis added). The answer is obvious: "The professionals at the Behavioral Health System...are here to assist you in answering this crucial question.... We will help you.... Call someone you can trust." The ad implies that parents are simply unable to understand their teenagers without the professional insights of mental health workers. And who better to trust than those who see some teenage rebellion as "healthy"?

With such glowing results promised by the mental health industry, it is no wonder that Americans have come to expect instant solutions for all their needs, desires, and problems. Our modern generation refuses to accept the fact that suffering is an inevitable part of human existence.

Harmful Therapies

The unpleasant truth is that psychology is not only relatively ineffective in changing thought and behavior patterns, but in many cases is also actually harmful to its clients. Most laymen are unaware of Hans Eysenck's 1952 study, which demonstrated that recovery from neuroses is unrelated to whether a patient receives *any* form of psychotherapy. Some researchers have challenged Eysenck's conclusions and have stated that there is general agreement that psychotherapy is at least better than no therapy.

Additional research indicates the very opposite. To prove his point, Eysenck did a second study in 1965, and according to Martin Gross, Eysenck's revision was—

> a more extensive survey of published studies, with still more damaging results for psychotherapy. He now claims that psychotherapy is a general failure by the very nature of its being unessential to the patient's recovery. "We have found that neurotic disorders tend to be self-limiting, that psychoanalysis is no more successful than any other method, and that in fact all methods of psychotherapy fail to improve on the recovery rate obtained through ordinary life-experiences and nonspecific treatment," Eysenck states.[3]

Eysenck's research is an explosive revelation that psychotherapy is a failure and is absolutely unessential. It is not surprising that many psychologists hotly dispute Eysenck's conclusions. Gross points out that "the mere act of testing the art's effectiveness has raised a ground swell of anger within the profession. . . . This defensiveness is a professional trademark in the Psychological Society."[4]

As a result, Eysenck's work has been reexamined. A review of Eysenck's research by Truax and Carkhuff claims to validate his conclusions.[5] They go even further when they state, "The evidence now available suggests that, on the average, psychotherapy may be harmful as often as helpful, with an average effect comparable to receiving no help."[6]

If it is true that standard psychotherapy is superior to biblical counseling, how does one account for the Cambridge-Somerville Youth Study reported in *American Psychologist* in 1978? The 30-year study revealed that the men who had received an average of five years of psychotherapy as boys were in worse shape, in view of alcoholism, criminal behavior, and mental disorders, than those who had not undergone psychotherapy.[7]

In spite of the evidence that psychotherapy fails to change people's hearts and can even increase their "dysfunctions," seminaries continue to insist that pastors need psychological training to help people with their problems. How can this be when there is no scientific evidence that one form of psychotherapy is superior to other forms or is more effective in achieving results? Why should pastors or parishioners have confidence in *any* therapeutic system? And if long-term treatment does not achieve superior results, as research indicates, what possible justification is there for prolonged psychotherapeutic sessions?

Professional Versus Lay Counseling

The psychological industry has successfully concealed its ineffectiveness from the general public. Pastors, churches, and the laity have been brainwashed into believing that only psychologically trained professional counselors are competent to deal with serious problems. Christian colleges and seminaries have bought into this incredible deception and now enthusiastically encourage Christians to submit to the insights, methods, and findings of secular psychology.

Even when forced to admit the failure of psychology, Christian mental-health experts insist that professional counselors are surely more effective than untrained laypeople in helping to relieve psychic distress. The evidence, however, does not support their claim.

Psychologist Gary Collins reports an important study done by J.A. Durlack entitled "Comparative Effectiveness of Paraprofessional and Professional Helpers":

[The research] reviewed forty-two studies
that compared professional counselors with
untrained helpers. The findings were "consistent and provocative. Paraprofessionals
achieve clinical outcomes equal to or signifi-
cantly better than those obtained by professionals.... The study, on the whole, lent no
support to the major hypothesis that...the
technical skills of professional psychotherapists produce measurably better therapeutic
change."[8]

Collins reluctantly admits, "Clearly there is evidence
that for most problems, laypeople can counsel as well as or
better than the professionals." But he hastens to ask, "Is
their success rate as good with the more serious problems?"[9] Professional counselors, in an understandable
defense of their livelihood, say that inexperienced or untrained counselors can easily be fooled by counselees, while
trained professionals are more likely to detect and understand complex and abnormal behavior.

If so, one would rightly expect that their diagnoses of
mental disorders would be consistently accurate and that
they would readily perceive when someone is faking a mental illness. Dr. E. Fuller Torrey and Dr. Judi Striano,
in separate books, describe an experiment at Stanford
University that revealed just how inaccurate psychiatric
diagnoses can be and how easily the experts can be fooled.
A psychologist by the name of D.L. Rosenhan, a professor
of psychology and law at Stanford University, had eight
"perfectly sane people" (Rosenhan "himself, one graduate
student, three psychologists, a pediatrician, a psychiatrist,
and a woman who was a homemaker")[10] admitted to 12
different mental hospitals. The attending psychiatrists
were told that these "patients" were hearing voices.

Otherwise, these normal people, mostly
graduate students, gave completely truthful
histories to the psychiatrists. They were all

diagnosed as "schizophrenic," except one who was diagnosed as "manic-depressive." Once admitted, they acted perfectly normally; yet were held for 7 to 52 days (the average was 19) and were given over 2,100 pills total. The true patients on the wards often recognized them as pseudopatients but the staff never did. Once labeled, the staff's perception of them was apparently so profoundly colored that normal behavior was seen as part of their psychosis.

In an even more damning postscript to the experiment, Rosenhan told one hospital what he had done. He then told them that he would try to gain admission for another pseudopatient there within the next 3 months. Ever watchful for the pseudopatient who was never sent, the staff labeled 41 of the next 193 admissions as suspected pseudopatients; over half of these were so labeled by a psychiatrist. The experimenter concluded: "Any diagnostic process that lends itself so readily to massive errors of this sort cannot be a very reliable one."[11]

In his succeeding pages, Torrey cites several other experiments which underscore the low reliability of psychiatric diagnostic techniques.

Contradictions in Psychotherapy

Even in the face of secular criticisms, one Christian psychologist states that it is "irresponsible to dismiss psychotherapy as a pseudoscience riddled with contradictions and confusion," and that such a conclusion is "clear bias, not supported by research."[12] Yet the question remains, How could psychological counseling be anything *but* confusing when there are more than 250 competing and contradictory psychological systems in America alone?

In their book *The Psychological Maze*, Otto and Miriam Ehrenberg list just a few of the more prominent psychological systems: Freud and Psychoanalysis, Adler and Individual Psychology, Jung and Analytic Psychology, Reich and Vegetotherapy, Rank and Will Therapy, Horney and the Cultural Approach, Sullivan and Interpersonal Relations, Rogers and Client-Centered Therapy, Existential Analysis, Gestalt Therapy, Lowen and Bioenergetic Therapy, Janov and Primal Therapy, Transactional Analysis, Ellis and Rational-Emotive Therapy, Family Therapy, Child Therapy, Group Therapy, Encounter Groups, est, Hypnotherapy, Behavior Therapy/Behavior Modification, Sex Therapy, and Medical Treatment (psychoactive drugs, electric shock, psychosurgery, and orthomolecular psychiatry).[13]

If this list is not confusing enough, remember that there are subgroups within the major systems. For example, Torrey writes about psychoanalytic therapies:

> There are several different schools within this general group, including orthodox Freudian, neo-Freudian, Jungian, and Adlerian. Each of these schools is further broken down into subschools, e.g., the neo-Freudians are divided into followers of Karen Horney, Erich Fromm, Harry Stack Sullivan, and Frieda Fromm-Reichmann. Many of these schools and subschools have their own training institutes. The outcome is a panorama of parochialism and provincialism not seen since medieval Europe.[14]

A Christian psychologist and dean of the Graduate School of Psychology at Fuller Theological Seminary admits being embarrassed by some of the antics of psychology. "At times I felt ashamed to be identified with a profession that merely used psychotherapy as a cover for carnality," he writes. "Every professional convention I attended contained booths showing pornographic movies—under the guise of 'sexual therapy.' Many private gatherings of therapists reeked of marijuana's pungent odor." Feeling it necessary to defend his profession, he concludes, "Fortunately, this has all passed."[15]

However, it has *not* all passed. While professional associations may have clamped down on their peers and psychological conventions may have banned the porno stalls, weird psychotherapies still abound.

Thomas Szasz, well-known to the psychological establishment for his intense criticisms of psychotherapies, is a professor of psychiatry at the University of New York at Syracuse. He has documented surrogate sex therapy, nude therapy, divorce therapy, dance therapy, poetry therapy, shopping therapy, scream therapy, rib-cage stimulation therapy, camping therapy, pet-facilitated therapy, sailing therapy, skydiving therapy, hydrotherapy, thumb therapy, and many other unusual techniques which are recognized by the psychological establishment as legitimate treatments.[16]

Therapies can become even more bizarre. Torrey points out that virtually any activity can be labeled as therapy so long as a psychologist or psychiatrist thinks of it. These include treatments such as money-management therapy, punching therapy, kinky sexual therapies, and more. "One common element is that they are all labeled as 'psychotherapy.'"

Szasz refers to a *Newsweek* article to illustrate this point:

> Sandi Enders, an attractive brunette of 26 who intends to become an occupational therapist, is earning her way through San Jose State University by working as a sexual therapist. She charges $50 for a two-and-a-half-hour session—including love-making—in her sensuously decorated apartment with its incense burner and heated water bed.[17]

By relabeling her trade as a therapy, Ms. Enders made her prostitution acceptable. I ask then, is it "irresponsible to dismiss psychotherapy as a pseudoscience riddled with contradictions and confusion"? Not according to the research —or common sense.

Listen to this statement, which is representative of the unscientific and almost desperate approach that psychologists often take in supporting their findings: "Many benefits can come from therapy, in spite of its weaknesses. According to one review of the research, therapy can help people feel better."[18] *One* review? And the astonishing conclusion of this research? That therapy "can help people feel better."

Of course therapy can make people feel better—temporarily. But does it truly change them? Does it help them solve their problems? Do they become more like Christ? Are they led into Christian maturity? Are their thought and behavior patterns brought into conformity to God's Word? Those should be the tests of effectiveness for Christian counseling.

Though most people believe that professional counselors are more effective in dealing with people's problems than untrained laymen, studies have shown that laymen are often more effective than professionals. One does not need to study psychology to help other people find God's solutions for problems of living, for it is not as hard to diagnose a person's problem as the professionals would have us believe.

There are only a few essential qualifications for a competent counselor. One must have an extensive knowledge of the Scriptures (Romans 15:14), a good measure of divine wisdom (experience and common sense under the illumination of the Holy Spirit) (Colossians 3:16), goodness (consistent, righteous lifestyle with a humble attitude) (1 Peter 5:5), an ability to relate to others (Colossians 4:6), an ability to communicate (Titus 2:8), and a genuine desire to help others (1 Thessalonians 5:14).

A word of balance at this point: One must be careful not to lump *all* psychologists under the label of pagan incompetence. Merely having a psychological credential does not automatically disqualify one from being a biblical counselor, though it should throw up a warning flag to the discerning believer. In any case, Christians would do well to carefully examine the counseling philosophy of *any* therapist before accepting his or her advice.

No competent biblical counselor would state that psychologists have *never* helped *anyone*. In God's providence, there are psychologists who rely more upon biblical truths and common sense than psychological theory to guide their clients. Some psychologists who have a genuine faith in Christ will doubtless give better advice than the average secular therapist. Yet the fact remains that while there may be an occasional trustworthy psychologist, Christians cannot uncritically trust a counseling system that is based upon nonbiblical foundations.

■ ■ ■

Psychiatrist Vance McCall arrived for a luncheon appointment at the Country Fork with Charles Duncan, one of the counselors at Arvada High School.

"I'm so glad you were able to come, Mr. Duncan. I've heard such good things about your work at the high school!"

"Really?" Charles replied, genuinely surprised. "I try to do a good job, but I'm not aware of any special accomplishments."

"Oh, you're much too modest," McCall said warmly. "Whenever I hear about a Christian counselor in our school system, I get really excited! There aren't many, you know."

"How well I know!" Charles agreed. "To tell you the truth, I don't know of more than one or two others in the entire district."

"Well, let's order!" McCall suggested. "It's on me, so have whatever you like."

They chatted amiably until the food came. As they ate, Charles finally asked, "Was there something special you wanted to talk about, Dr. McCall? I don't often get invited out by a psychiatrist."

McCall laughed heartily. "We're not such a bad lot, you know!"

"I didn't mean it that way," Charles replied sheepishly.

"Of course not, Mr. Duncan. I was just teasing. Yes, there is a reason I wanted to get together with you. You see, I feel that with all of the emotional problems that are evident in today's young people, there needs to be more Christian input. Don't you agree?"

"I certainly do!" Charles said with a smile.

"Good!" McCall smiled with a nod of his head. "The problem is, there aren't enough qualified Christian counselors, psychologists, and psychiatric facilities to meet the need. So, far too often, you counselors are not able to refer your students to qualified Christian care, and consequently, they end up in secular institutions. Right?"

"I guess so," Charles said hesitantly, not sure where McCall was headed.

"I'm visiting with as many counselors as I can to tell them about our new psychiatric hospital, Mount Haven, near Broomfield. It is an outstanding facility with only the most qualified personnel. Unfortunately, since we're so new to the area, not very many counselors know we're available. So here's what we're doing. Rather than spend hundreds of thousands of dollars on advertising, we want to make financial contributions back to the counselors who refer clients our way. They can use that money to upgrade their own facility or to take professional seminars, or however they feel is most appropriate."

Charles cocked his head slightly and sat back in his chair. "If I didn't know better, Dr. McCall, I'd say that you're offering me a kickback."

"Not at all!" McCall said smoothly. "Kickback is such an ugly word and it totally misrepresents the intent of my offer, which is to professionally assist deserving counselors."

"And it's all aboveboard?" Charles asked further.

"Absolutely! To avoid any appearance of illegal or unethical conflicts of interest, we ask each participating counselor to join with us as a consultant," McCall explained.

"What would I be expected to do as a consultant?"

"Basically, we want to be able to ask your advice in meeting the needs of students and parents at your school. As an official associate of our practice, there would be no problem with your receiving compensation."

Charles nodded as he considered the proposition. "I see. Would I be able to visit the hospital before I make a decision?"

"Absolutely! I would want you to be thoroughly acquainted with our philosophy of practice. Do you think you would be interested in becoming part of our professional group?" McCall asked, trying to close the sale.

"Possibly," Charles responded. "I'd like some time to think about it. And I probably should run it by the administration as well."

McCall coughed nervously and took a sip of iced tea. "I'd be careful who you share this opportunity with and how you explain it. Your first reaction of calling the arrangement a kickback shows how easily it can be misunderstood. And the fact that the checks would come directly to you and not through the school might precipitate some professional jealousy, if you see what I mean."

"I'm afraid I don't really understand," Charles said, feeling increasingly uneasy about the arrangement. "Why wouldn't the checks go through the school?"

"Because you are acting as an independent contractor. Let me give you an example. When your principal is invited to lecture on educational management at some civic group or college, he is paid an honorarium. That doesn't go through the school accounting system, does it?"

"No, I suppose not."

"Of course it doesn't, because he is acting as an independent consultant. That is precisely what we're offering you."

"Are there restrictions as to how the money is to be used?" Charles asked.

"No. We feel that you are in the best position to know how to make good use of the funds. You can purchase educational materials, take in counseling seminars, sponsor your students to attend special events, or use the money in any way you see fit, even if it is of a personal nature."

Charles looked at his watch and pushed away from the table. "Well, it sounds very attractive and I'll give it some thought. I've got to get back to the school. Thanks for lunch, Dr. McCall."

McCall stood to his feet and extended his hand. "You're so very welcome, Mr. Duncan! I hope we can work together in the future. Do you have any idea how soon you might have an answer for me?"

"I think I might be able to let you know in a few days. Why don't you call me next week?"

"You can count on it!" McCall smiled warmly. "I think you'll be glad if you decide to work with us. There are so many hurting people in this world, and if we don't reach out and help them, who will?"

Charles returned to his office at the high school and shut the door. He sat thinking for a few moments, then picked up his phone and dialed a number from memory. "Sarah? Charlie Duncan! How are you?"

"Fine, Charlie," Sarah replied. "Are you calling about the Sunday school material for the singles class?"

"Well, no, I needed to talk to John," Charles replied. "But now that you mention it, did the books come in?"

"Yes, they did. UPS delivered them this morning."

"All right! I'll stop by the church office on my way home. Is John in? I really need to talk to him for a minute."

"He's in a counseling session right now, Charlie. Can I have him call you?"

"Would you please, Sarah? It's kind of urgent."

"If it's an emergency, I can buzz Pastor," Sarah offered.

"No, that won't be necessary. Just ask him to call me before 3:30 if possible."

"Okay, Charlie. I'll let him know you called."

In between counseling sessions, John returned Charles Duncan's call. "Sarah said it was urgent, Charlie. What's up?"

"Thanks for calling back, John. Listen, I had an unusual offer made to me at lunch today, and I'd like to get your opinion."

"Go ahead," John replied.

Charles looked out his office-door window nervously as he saw kids standing around waiting to talk with him. "I'd rather talk with you in person, John, if possible. I'm done here about 3:30. Do you have even a few minutes to see me?"

John leaned back in his chair and rubbed his eyes. "I'm going to be tied up straight through till 5:00, Charlie. But if you want to come then, we can talk for a while."

"Thanks, John!" Charles said gratefully. "I'll be there right at five and I promise to keep it as short as possible!"

Charles arrived at the church office just before 5:00 and waited in the reception area. A few minutes later a tense-looking couple emerged from John's office and walked out silently. John came out a few moments later and held out his hand in warm greeting. "Charlie! Come on back!"

They walked back to John's office and sat down. Charles looked at John and said sympathetically, "You look really tired. I'm sorry to add to your burden."

John smiled and waved off Charles' apology. "Everybody's tired! You look tired yourself! Tell me what's so urgent."

Charles told him about his lunch with Dr. Vance McCall and the offer he had made. "The thing is, John, it seems to me to border on unethical conduct. I mean, isn't it a conflict of interest for me to be tied in with a psychiatric center?"

"Tell me what makes you say that," John replied.

"Well, I can see how a counselor who is being paid for referrals could easily be tempted to encourage parents to commit their teens for psychiatric evaluation. You can't believe how desperate and vulnerable most parents are! They don't have a clue when it comes to discipline or building close relationships with their kids. So many of our teens are already on drugs and alcohol and come from incredibly abusive environments. Their grades are down and many of them are so distressed and burned out that they consider suicide as an easy way out."

"Do you feel psychiatric treatment is in their best interest?"

"John! You know how I feel about psychiatric care in general! But, I'll admit, there are some extreme cases, such as suicide potentials, that may need restraint and some intensive therapy. Dr. McCall says his center is truly Christian, and if that's true, I'd certainly feel more inclined to refer people to him. What bothers me is that if I were getting paid for these referrals, I'm sure I would be tempted to push psychiatric treatment when it is not really necessary."

"How much did he offer you?"

"He didn't state a figure. I didn't let it go that far. I wanted to check with you first."

"I'm glad you did, Charlie," John said as he opened his file drawer and searched through the folders. He found an article and pulled it out. "Did you see this article in *U.S. News & World Report* about mental-health scams?"*

"No. What does it say?"

"Well, it says insurance payments for mental health and substance abuse treatments grew during the eighties when for-profit psychiatric hospitals decided to take advantage of a seemingly endless source of revenue. Problems have been growing, however, because," John said as he pointed to the article, "'the industry was overbuilt and insurance firms, alarmed by exploding costs, began scrutinizing payments more carefully.' It goes on to say that 'the result is that "private hospitals that once made a great deal of money are now desperate for patients"' and 'that desperation has opened the door for fraud.'"

"What kind of fraud?" Charles asked as he leaned forward, looking at the magazine article.

"It lists patients being abducted by 'bounty hunters,'" John replied, "and people hospitalized against their will until their insurance runs out, diagnoses and treatments that are dictated by insurance payments rather than actual illnesses, kickbacks for recruiting patients, unnecessary treatments, and gross overbilling." He handed the magazine to Charlie.

"Do they give any actual examples?" he asked as he glanced through the article. His eyes opened wide and he whistled as he said, "They name specific hospitals! Here's a private psychiatric hospital in San Antonio that paid

---

* "Health Care Fraud," *U.S. News & World Report*, Feb. 24, 1992, pp. 38-42.

private security agents a bounty for each patient brought in. It says that the doctor who signed the admission papers had falsified his own credentials. This is just the tip of the iceberg, John. The article states here that 12 other Texas facilities and at least three national hospital chains are currently under investigation and that similar charges have been made against hospitals in New Jersey, Florida, Alabama, and Louisiana. It says that other probes are underway in more than a dozen states."

"Isn't it incredible?" John said as he shook his head sadly.

"There's more, John. Dr. Duard Bok, who ran the chemical dependency unit at the Psychiatric Institute of Fort Worth, sued the hospital. He alleged that, and I'm quoting here, 'the hospital routinely gave financial support to doctors, social workers and even local high-school guidance counselors for referring patients.'"

Charlie laid the magazine on John's desk and sat back in deep thought.

Finally John asked, "What are you thinking, Charlie?"

"I'm just wondering what counseling is coming to, John. I mean ... I got into counseling because I really want to help young people. But it seems to me that counseling has become an industry ruled more by financial considerations than compassion."

The Psychological Counselor

[The "selling of therapy"] isn't blatant manipulation. Most therapists probably haven't even noticed what they are doing. Subtly, however, they convince people that their lives could be better, that therapy will help them and that "a few more sessions" would be a wise investment in their future happiness and stability. Soon people who aren't sick are willingly paying to get better.

The Biblical Counselor

Remember, these are the "experts" trained to uncover the hidden motivations of clients. They know what they are doing.

The Word of God

Why spend money on what is not bread, and your labor on what does not satisfy?
—Isaiah 55:2

4

The Myth That Psychology Is Motivated by Compassion

The popular image of the money-grubbing fundamentalist preacher has grown in recent years due to the excessive lifestyles of some televangelists. Most people should be aware, however, that the average pastor is on the low end of the professional pay scale. His weekly responsibilities include sermon preparation, business administration, committee meetings, hospital visitation, staff leadership, long-range planning, teaching, preaching, and a host of other tasks. In addition, his parishioners call on him for comfort, help, and advice. Rarely does he charge extra for counseling, though people often expect him to schedule sessions during evenings or weekends. Yet people are heard to whisper as the offering plate goes by, "All the church wants is my money."

In sharp contrast, psychiatrists and psychologists seldom pass the plate for a freewill offering. Their fees are set, and if the client expects continued service, he had better pay, and pay promptly. The patients are expected to take time off from work and come for counseling when there is an opening in the doctor's schedule. Yet the stereotypes persist that psychotherapists are motivated by compassion, while pastors are greedy money-vacuums.

The High Cost of Psychotherapy

Psychology is big business. A glut of psychiatric hospitals compete with one another for patients, fees, and insurance payments. Pastoral counselors encounter church members who have spent thousands of dollars on therapies which have failed to produce the results so enthusiastically advertised.

A woman recently drove nearly a thousand miles to consult with me about her mental condition. She had spent five months at a Rapha center at a cost of more than $100,000 and another month at the Minirth-Meier Clinic at a cost of over $20,000, and she was as confused as she had been before seeking treatment.

Newsweek magazine reported that several for-profit Christian psychiatric centers have begun franchising their services. "These groups are growing because they can make money," said psychiatrist David Larson of the National Institute of Mental Health.[1] The article reported that Christian clinics like LifeCare, Rapha, and the Minirth-Meier Clinic charge up to $1200 per day for therapy.

According to one report, Americans pay more than $17 billion annually for psychological therapies. A 30-minute consultation with a psychiatrist can cost as much as $150, with the average psychiatric fee reaching $90 for a 55-minute session. Psychologists are cheaper; they charge around $60 an hour.[2] Few surveys list what a pastoral counseling session would cost, but it is fair to say that it is considerably less. Often the cost is nothing.

Though I am critical of the exorbitant fees for psychological therapy, I am not opposed to a reasonable charge for counseling. It is true that people take counseling more seriously if they have to pay something. Those who pay nothing feel that the counseling is worth just that much. With that in mind, in our church counseling service we ask for a minimum donation of $50 per session, which often runs as long as two hours. Members of our church are not charged, but those who are referred by other pastors or who come by word of mouth sign a contract. They have this choice: Either they will attend our church during the time of counseling, or they will have to pay the fee. If they miss a session without calling to cancel with a legitimate reason, they must pay the fee for that session. If they miss a service prior to a given session, they must pay the fee. Those who come from other Bible-teaching churches are charged the fee, since we do not require them to attend our services. If they are unable to pay the full fee we ask their church to pay one-half, but we insist that the counselees pay the other half so that they will be fully committed to the counseling process.

Our purpose in the fee structure is not to generate huge sums of money, and indeed it does not. We want counselees to become involved in the regular instruction of the Word of God and in the fellowship of the body of believers. As they take part in the life of the church, they can begin to learn how to solve the problems of life biblically, supported by the prayers and encouragement of other believers.

Fees and Competence

You might ask, "Do the clients of psychotherapy get what they pay for?" If therapeutic results are indicative of relative worth, the answer clearly is no. Psychiatrist Bernie Zilbergeld reports that when it comes to the common problems people bring to psychotherapy—"confusion, depression, low self-esteem, distressed relationships or inability to form a relationship, difficulties in decision-making, and so on—you can expect about the same results regardless of which therapy you choose."[3] The Ehrenbergs tell us that psychiatrists charge more than other mental-health professionals because they work under a medical label, not because their counsel is superior. "The size of the fee is not necessarily a measure of competence."[4]

Justifying high psychiatric fees for ordinary psychotherapy is like saying one should pay—for the same repair job—more to a mechanic who has a college degree than to one who does not have a degree. But it is foolish to pay more for *any* service simply because the "expert" has a credential, if the results are not superior. Personally, I want a mechanic who knows how to fix my car, and the one with dirty fingernails and no degree may be the best choice.

As Striano says, "Some therapists with less thorough academic work and fewer years training or no formal education might be better therapists for you because they have a natural talent for the work or healthier personalities or they're just right for you."[5]

The Marketing Strategies of Psychotherapy

One Christian psychologist reveals a questionable part of the whole psychotherapeutic industry which he calls "the selling of therapy."[6] He is speaking of psychiatric hospitals and counseling services that use television, radio, newspapers, and magazines to bring clients through the doors. It is strange that he defends the motives of psychologists who use such sales techniques:

> This isn't blatant manipulation. Most therapists probably haven't even noticed what they are doing. Subtly, however, they convince people that their lives could be better, that therapy will help them and that "a few more sessions" would be a wise investment in their future happiness and stability. Soon people who aren't sick are willingly paying to get better.[7]

In my opinion this *does* constitute blatant manipulation! I find it difficult to accept the notion that "most therapists probably haven't even noticed what they are doing." Remember, these are the "experts" trained to uncover the hidden motivations of clients. They *know* what they are doing, and the fact is that psychologists and psychiatrists have no built-in incentive to quickly resolve a client's problems, for the longer a person continues therapy, the more money the therapist receives.

Susan Sturdivant, Ph.D., is developing a company in Dallas to help psychologists market their services. She speaks of marketing "as an integral part" of psychotherapy. She encourages therapists to "readjust our attitudes so that we can say that this [is] an ethical and professional thing to do." She teaches her colleagues how to market their services by inviting "clergy or a PTA group to come and talk about what worries them." She says that "the trick is to do something we know how to do very well, which is to be nondirective and simply encourage people to talk."[8]

A strategy she suggests is to send newsletters to "medical professionals, community groups, former clients" approximately every three months. "This provides reinforcement." What is it that Sturdivant seeks to reinforce? The concept that psychotherapy is needed. "The prevailing attitude is that private practice is a step-child and therapists should strive for an unattainable goal of being an academic scientist and clinician."[9]

Read her statement again carefully. Finally a therapist admits that psychologists face "an unattainable goal of being an academic scientist and clinician," and that a primary purpose of psychotherapy is to sell itself to the public. "Running a private practice is the same as running a small business,"[10] she advises her readers.

The Social Costs of Psychology

Psychology is costing our nation dearly. Sexual abuses, medical fraud, crime, intense unhappiness with day-to-day living, and consistent decreases in educational scores throughout the nation can be partially traced to the psychological industry's pervasive influence in today's society—an influence that impacts average citizens in a variety of ways.

Educational Costs

Columnist Thomas Sowell criticizes educational psychologists and counselors for draining the educational system of financial resources.

Barely more than half the people employed by the New York City Board of Education are teachers.... Moreover, one-third of the money that trickles down to the school goes for psychologists and counselors alone.... What has gotten better in American schools after we flooded them with psychologists, counselors, "facilitators" and the like?...

Academic performance certainly hasn't improved. We have yet to see test scores as high as they were 30 years ago. Maybe students are happier, healthier or something. But statistics on cheating, theft, vandalism, violent crime, venereal disease and teen-age suicide all say no.

Educators are uncomfortable even discussing actual results. They are at their best talking a good game, full of lofty buzzwords and puffed-up jargon. As long as we keep buying it, they'll keep selling it....

You cannot subsidize irresponsibility and expect people to become more responsible. Many of those who say otherwise, who are urging us to throw more money at social problems, are among the organized hustlers out there to intercept it if we do.[11]

The costs of psychotherapy must be measured not only in terms of dollars but also in terms of the damage done to family life, justice, and society in general. Two primary psychological doctrines are largely to blame: the emphasis upon self and the denial of personal responsibility.

Judicial Costs

Hardly a day passes without newspapers carrying a story of psychiatric testimony given on behalf of a mass-murderer or other sociopath with the consistent message that "he isn't an evil man; he's a sick man." Rapists, torturers, child-molesters, and a host of other criminals are all too often protected from justice by the psychological doctrine that no one is responsible for his own actions.

Columnist Charles Krauthammer relates the story of a 17-year-old Milwaukee girl who stole another girl's leather jacket and then murdered her. Her lawyers argued that she should not be put in prison, but rather should undergo psychotherapy. Their basic argument was that a brutal crime is, in itself, evidence of insanity. Krauthammer writes with disgust about "this trivialization of the law by psychiatry," and he offers a reason that it has happened: "Some of these newfangled psychiatric syndromes are so elastic that one can always find an expert witness willing (for a fee) to pin an extenuating diagnosis on just about anybody."[12]

He argues that insanity should not be grounds for acquittal. "It is absurd to permit the heinousness of a crime to become self-acquitting. That sets up a perverse standard: The more terrible the crime, the crazier, therefore the less culpable, the criminal. The man who commits incomprehensible torture is acquitted. The father who steals bread to feed his children is convicted."[13]

The American Medical Association has accepted the concept of "mental illness" and fully recognizes the implications of such a definition: "The concept of mental illness is . . . important, for legal reasons, in determining whether a person can be held responsible for his or her actions."[14]

Taxpayers are required to pay outrageous sums to maintain vicious criminals in mental institutions and prisons until overcrowding in the prisons forces early releases, and soon these offenders are back on the streets stalking new victims. I truly grieve for the criminals who grew up in harsh and abusive environments. Of course, they have also been victimized by others in their past. But they are still responsible for their choices, and I put forth the proposition that appropriate punishment is far more compassionate in the long run for the victim *and* the criminal.

Severe and swift punishment is a statement of compassion for the victims of brutal crimes. Why should a young girl have to fall asleep each night in terror that the rapist will return as he promised? Why should a family who loses a husband and father also have to pay the very taxes used to maintain his murderer in jail or the psychiatric hospital?

Certain punishment is also compassionate toward those who become criminals. If there were absolute assurance that crime would be punished severely, there would be an eventual decrease in the crime rate. I am aware that this phenomenon has been hotly debated for years; many studies claim to demonstrate that punishment has no effect on crime rates. Yet those studies may be as faulty as the other unscientific psychological reports which have been carefully tailored by their authors to support their sociological theories.

One such study in Colorado said that longer prison sentences did not help to lower the crime rates there. But an editorial in the *Rocky Mountain News* sheds light on the debate:

> Just because the violent-crime rate has not declined in the past 10 years is hardly reason to conclude that long sentences are pointless. In the first place, society doesn't imprison people merely to reduce crime rates. It also does so to make a moral statement—to balance the scales, if you will....
>
> By keeping [violent criminals] in prison, society undoubtedly averts other crimes....
>
> Once [criminals have turned to violence] the choice is clear. Lock them up for a long time where they can't hurt people—or claim that imprisonment is no deterrent and set them free to prey on yet more of the innocent.[15]

Go to Singapore and see how the certainty of punishment has made it one of the cleanest and safest places on earth. Ask how many Americans import illicit drugs into Turkey, where punishment is certain and harsh for such a crime. Yes, it is far more compassionate to inform a person ahead of time that if he commits a crime, he will be punished. Deterrence *is* a compassionate act.

Yet humanistic philosophy continues to wring its hands in misplaced sympathy as it objects to appropriate punishment for serious offenses. How then can we expect criminals to take their actions seriously when we excuse them from personal responsibility?

Family Costs

Families are suffering from the psychological doctrines being spread in both secular and Christian media. Women are taught that biblical submission to their husband's authority is a chauvinistic concept that must be reinterpreted in the light of Paul's Jewish culture. The emphasis upon self has caused husbands and wives to turn their backs on loving sacrifice for one another. The current word is, "It's time I finally did something for myself." In the search for self-esteem and self-fulfillment, the security and stability of marriage begins to crumble, and divorce is the common result.

Christians who once lived in the freedom of God's forgiveness and healing are being dragged back into their former cesspools in order to "work through their past." Victims of child abuse are never allowed to recover, but are instructed in the philosophy of permanent victimization. Husbands who had no part in the childhood sexual abuse of their wives are now told that they have become the "surrogate abuser" because they have not "entered into the pain" their wives experienced.

The tentacles of psychology have also reached into the parent-child relationship. Social workers have nearly unlimited power to remove children from homes for virtually any cause to "protect them from psychological harm." Parents are afraid to discipline their children for fear a schoolteacher might report them as abusive. Children have picked up on this power and threaten their parents: "If you spank me, I'll report you." Genuine abusers, however, are not afraid to beat and torture children without mercy because they can always plead temporary insanity.

Eternal Costs

There are eternal costs connected with psychological counseling. When people are told that the Bible cannot guide them in their day-to-day problems of living, they have every reason to doubt that it can lead them to eternal life. When we accept the doctrine that we need more information than God has given in His Word, we open the doors of our hearts and minds to the god of this age, who is at work filling us with his lies.

Only in eternity will we fully grasp the impact of the pagan philosophies which have swept into the church in the guise of Christian psychology by way of books, magazines, tapes, films, radio, and psychological counseling services. As shipwrecked saints struggle helplessly against the raging tides of despair, instead of throwing out the lifeline of God's eternal Word, we tell them to climb into the leaking rubber rafts of psychology. Why are we amazed, then, when they slowly sink beneath the waves?

■ ■ ■

Cliff Chase's church had sponsored a 12-step self-help group for several years. After the events of the preceding weeks, Cliff decided to visit the group as an observer. That night, a group of hurting people formed a circle in a large adult classroom at the church, learning how to apply the 12 steps to their particular ailments. Cliff tiptoed into the room and sat in a darkened corner at the back, where he could listen without being observed.

He couldn't help noticing that the leader, Larry Soderstrom, began the discussion without prayer. Then he remembered a conversation they had shared before the group was launched. "Cliff, I don't want you to get mad when you hear we don't pray in the 12-step group," Larry had said. "Is that going to bother you?"

"I guess not," Cliff had replied. He had been a bit surprised, but not overly alarmed, since he knew Larry was a sincere Christian. "But, out of curiosity, I'd like to ask why you don't pray at the group."

"Cliff, Cliff," Larry had said almost condescendingly, "you have to remember that we're dealing with dysfunctional people. They aren't ready for prayer. They have so much anger and pain they have to work through before they can even consider God. Trust me, Cliff. I know what I'm talking about."

"Oh, I know. I was just asking."

The room came back into focus as Cliff returned to the present. About 15 people had gathered in a circle and had already begun their discussion.

"My husband really couldn't help himself," a white-haired lady said sorrowfully. "He came from a dysfunctional family. And what's even worse, I'm an enabler." Everyone knew what she meant and nodded sympathetically. She continued to describe the problems she and her husband were experiencing.

When she was done, Larry said, "Thank you, Edith. You've been very open with us. Who would like to share next?"

A woman on the other side of the circle looked years older than her probable actual age. Dark circles drooped in bags beneath her eyes. She leaned forward. "I'm an adult child of an alcoholic," she said. "My life is forever scarred by the abuse I've endured. Though I don't drink, I have all the mental and social symptoms of alcoholism. I just can't seem to help myself. I'm always so depressed that I just feel like giving up. To tell you the truth, I sometimes feel mad at God for putting me in this position."

"That's all right, Barbara," Larry said. "God's a big boy. He can handle your being mad at Him." The group giggled nervously. "Who's next?"

The woman next to Barbara was wearing heavy makeup to cover some ugly bruises, but the swelling around her cheeks and nose revealed that she was a battered wife. "I hate my husband! I don't know why I can't leave him. He treats me like dirt. I mean, he beats me all the time. I've recently found out that I'm codependent."

"Sometimes, the first step toward real healing is to let yourself hate your husband, Carol," Larry said. "Don't fight it. Get in touch with your feelings. You have to fully embrace your pain before you can overcome it." The group murmured in agreement. "Okay, folks, someone else."

An attractive, neatly dressed woman about 40 years of age sat quietly, staring at the floor as she rotated her wedding ring with her thumb. She looked up with tears filling her eyes. "My husband doesn't understand. My pastor doesn't understand. No one understands what it's like to be an abused person. They expect me to go on with life as though nothing ever happened. They refuse to enter my grief with me, to go back and comfort that 16-year-old innocent child who was seduced by a trusted authority figure." Cliff was glad the group hadn't noticed him sitting quietly in the back.

"I know just what you mean, Sharon," said a little man who sat twisted uncomfortably in a wheelchair across from her. "My family doesn't understand that I have the right to expect their financial support since I'm a handicapped person. And when they do finally give me some money, strings are always attached. They'll pay my rent *if* I let them move me to a one-bedroom apartment instead of two. And *if* I'll let them bathe me once a week, and so on!" he snarled bitterly.

The man next to Sharon told his story of a downward spiral. He finally concluded, "I've been sober now for eight years, but I know I'm still an alcoholic. I always will be."

"My problem is cocaine," a 28-year-old businessman admitted softly. "I heard about this 12-step group meeting at your church and hoped you would have some spiritual answers for me. But I'm afraid I feel even more hopeless now, listening to all of you. It seems as though I'm doomed to always be an addict, no matter what I do. Isn't there a permanent cure anywhere? Will I always be chained to my substance abuse?"

They all nodded sadly. Larry finally spoke. "You'll learn like the rest of us that you have to gain victory one day at a time. The moment you drop your guard and think you've finally been fully delivered, watch out!"

Cliff tiptoed out quietly and went directly to his office to call John Kryer at his home. "John? Cliff Chase again."

"Yes, Cliff! What can I do for you?"

"John, I just came from our 12-step self-help group at church, and I need to get your insights on some questions that came to mind. Can you fit me in again?"

"Of course, Cliff. I'm all booked up tomorrow, but I can see you on Thursday at 10:00."

"Thanks, John. I'm sorry to be such a bother, but I've got to get a handle on this thing." Cliff hung up, a bit embarrassed, but at the same time he felt relieved.

On Thursday, Cliff sat in John's office once again. "Thanks for taking time for me, John," he said gratefully.

"I'm always glad to see you, my friend," John responded warmly. "You sounded upset when you called. What's up?"

"Well, like I told you when I called, I sat in on our church's 12-step program, and I was concerned by some of the things I observed."

"Like what?"

"I guess the biggest problem to me was how little emphasis was put on God's power to change people's lives. One man actually said that he felt more hopeless after the session than when he had come. So I'm starting to understand your concerns about psychology in general. But I still have some questions about your counseling philosophy, too."

"Well, ask away," John said cheerfully.

Cliff hesitated for a moment, then said, "I was surprised that you readily admitted to being a nouthetic counselor when I last came to see you."

"Why does that surprise you? It isn't a dirty word, is it?" John laughed pleasantly.

"Well, to hear some of my seminary professors, you would think so. It's just that the common stereotype of nouthetic counseling is—"

"Wait, let me tell you," John interrupted, putting on his reading glasses and pulling them forward to the tip of his nose. "We nouthetic counselors supposedly look down over our horn-rimmed glasses at cowering counselees and scold them mercilessly for living such pathetic lives. We don't listen to their hurts or consider their feelings. We just quickly find the biblical principle they have broken and tell them to knock off the sinning and everything will be fine. Is that pretty close?" John asked as his eyes twinkled with amusement.

Cliff chuckled sheepishly as he scratched his head. "That's the picture that was painted for me, all right."

"Well, I think some of the stereotype might be deserved for some so-called nouthetic counselors. There's usually a bit of truth in every caricature, don't you think? Some pastors do handle their counseling in a very sloppy and uncaring manner and deserve the censure of their peers. It is easy to arrive at a premature diagnosis without carefully listening to the counselee, and if we misunderstand the problem, of course we give the wrong solution."

"But if the stereotype is so distorted, wouldn't you be better off using a different label?" Cliff asked.

"I don't advertise as a nouthetic counselor, Cliff. People don't understand the term. Remember, you asked me if I was a nouthetic counselor and I simply agreed. I prefer to call myself a *biblical* counselor because the Bible is my source of authority and information. Unfortunately, there are many counselors who also call themselves biblical who rarely open the Scriptures to help the people who come to them for advice. Labels are a funny thing, Cliff."

"But you use labels, don't you, John? Don't you call those who want to mix psychology with the Bible 'integrationists'?"

"Yes, I do. I don't mind labels so long as they are accurate. Integrationists openly declare their intention to take the best of both worlds and integrate them into a hybrid system. They compare it to what they call "spoiling the Egyptians.""

"I kind of like that concept," Cliff admitted. "Why *shouldn't* we use what the world offers if it doesn't compromise our faith?"

"But that is the precise issue, Cliff. I contend that psychology does *exactly* that. It compromises our faith in the power of God, in the truth of His Word, and in the work of the Holy Spirit in the lives of God's children. We aren't merely taking gold and silver and jewels from the Egyptians. We are importing their pagan idols, religious beliefs, and humanistic philosophies. There's a world of difference."

Cliff sat thinking with his fingertips pressed together in a classic pose of meditation. "That helps," he finally said, looking up. "I know I've taken a lot of your time, John. Before I go, I wonder if you would explain a comment I saw in your brochure."

"Sure, Cliff. Which comment?"

"Well, it's been a while since I read it. I think you said something like you don't believe in categorizing people as 'mentally ill,' 'addicted,' 'abused,' 'handicapped,' and other such names. In our self-help group I visited the other day I heard the people refer to themselves with various labels. I take it you wouldn't agree with that."

"You're right about that, Cliff," John agreed.

"Why do you feel that way?"

"Because, once again, the labels are inaccurate. They communicate the idea that a person *is* what he has done or experienced. It is a summary statement—the bottom line. If a man says 'I *am* a handicapped person,' that is what he becomes. It's totally different from the statement, 'I *have* a handicap.' Do you see the difference?" John asked earnestly as he leaned forward.

"Yes, I think I do," Cliff replied. "It's similar to a child who is told over and over again that he is stupid or ugly. He begins to think that the chief characteristic of his existence is stupidity or ugliness. He doesn't see his other potentials and talents—just his weaknesses."

"That's it! A woman who sees herself as an abused person focuses every detail of her life around that central fact. It becomes her whole life. Every thought, every action, every response to others is colored by her identity as an abuse victim."

"But you wouldn't deny the fact of her abuse, would you?" Cliff asked.

"Of *course* not. The abuse *happened*. It's a *fact*. But that fact must not be allowed to remain the *determinative* event of her entire life. The more she concentrates upon her tragedy, the less she is able to focus her mind, heart, and will to produce fruitful thoughts and actions."

"How do you help someone like that? What do you suggest as an alternative focus?" Cliff asked with growing interest.

"I help her to focus her attention..." John paused for emphasis "...on Christ. The more she learns about the Lord, His love, His character, His power, and His plan for her life, the freer she is to become a healthy and joyful child of God. And that is no simplistic solution, Cliff. It takes great patience, wisdom from the Holy Spirit, and knowledge of the Word to apply His truths effectively to each individual."

"What label would you suggest instead of 'abused person'?" Cliff asked as he prepared to leave.

John set his glasses on the desk, smiled, and said, "I would suggest she start identifying herself as a 'child of God.'"

The Psychological Counselor

Labels help us to understand ourselves, so we can manage our problems. Unless you know what the disease is, you can't treat it.

The Biblical Counselor

Do we understand the human heart better now that we have created hundreds of labels? ... No, and I suggest that our ignorance of the human heart will increase in direct proportion to new discoveries and findings of the mental health experts.

The Word of God

Do you not know that the wicked will not inherit the kingdom of God? ... And that is what some of you were. But you were washed, you were sanctified, you were justified in the name of the Lord Jesus Christ and by the Spirit of our God.
—1 Corinthians 6:9-11

5

The Myth of Psychological Labels

All around America are self-help groups that meet to provide mutual support for hurting people. Many of these groups meet in churches. One common factor in their discussions is psychospeak, a vocabulary composed by psychological experts and taught in books, magazines, radio, and television. Psychospeak uses labels to describe every human behavior. The labels are often presented in noun form: "an ill person," "an adult child," "an abused person," "a handicapped person," "an addict," "an alcoholic," "an enabler," a "codependent," "a kleptomaniac," "a psychotic," "a foodaholic," "a schizophrenic," "a nymphomaniac," and an endless selection of other designations. In common conversation, these terms are often preceded by the confession "I am..." as a person accepts his assigned role in our "dysfunctional" society. The labels produce more confusion than solution.

"Untrue!" the indignant shout will come from those dedicated to psychospeak. "Labels help us to understand ourselves, so we can manage our problems. Unless you know what the disease is, you can't treat it."

But that's just the problem. By avoiding the *real* issues, suffering people are prevented from finding an eternal cure.

Why are people drawn to psycholabels? Herbert Fingarette of the University of California, a critic of the concept of alcoholism as a disease, says, "Life is so puzzling and mystifying and obscure that giving something a name seems to give it clarity and power."[1] As Fingarette and others observe, however, psycholabels communicate two extremely serious and mistaken concepts: 1) the belief that anything short of perpetual happiness is a medical ailment that needs professional treatment, and 2) that since these disorders are actual illnesses, the individual bears no responsibility for their existence or solution.

Psycholabels do not reflect a consistent regard for scientific inquiry or professional integrity. As Goode suggests, one additional motivation for creating mental-illness categories is that "a new diagnosis gives doctors one more condition to treat."[2] Psycholabels are built upon personal observations of behavior and attitudes which are interpreted according to the biases of psycho-experts. Just because a psychiatrist or psychologist coins a new term does not prove that such a condition actually exists. As Bryna Siegel, a psychologist at the University of California, San Francisco, observes: "People need to realize that these categories are not given by God."[3]

"What's the harm in labeling behavior as illnesses?" some people sincerely ask. There are at least four major problems with psycholabels.

The Excuse Label

The first problem is that psychological categories under the heading of "mental illness" provide crippling excuses for sinful behavior.

Dr. Thomas Szasz has said, "It is customary to define psychiatry as a medical specialty concerned with the study, diagnosis, and treatment of mental illnesses. This is a worthless and misleading definition. Mental illness is a myth."[4]

In reply, integrationists ask, "Is mental illness really a myth? Is it a mind game that allows professional counselors to believe in 'the myth of psychotherapy' and gives their counselees an excuse to avoid responsibility while doing nothing about the problems of living?"[5]

Many observers on the outside would say yes. "What about physically caused abnormal behavior?" integrationists retort. "Distorted thinking, emotional disturbances, unusual behavior and many of the other symptoms we call 'mental illness' can and often do have a physiological basis."[6]

Critics of psychology recognize that fact. Biblical counselors realize that there are complex interactions between the physical and spiritual aspects of human beings. We are aware that brain tumors, neurochemical imbalance, mercury poisoning, poor nutrition, hypoglycemia, fatigue, pain, and a host of other physical disorders have an impact on the thinking processes of human beings. Nouthetic counselors do not suggest that all mental and emotion problems are the result of sinful thinking or behavior.

The real debate is not over organically caused problems. William Glasser describes the prevailing concept of mental illness:

> Those who believe in mental illness assume incorrectly that something definite is wrong with the patient which causes him to be the way he is. [This leads people] into the false belief that the doctor's job is to treat some definite condition, after which the patient will get well. This attitude was graphically illustrated by a patient whom I treated some years ago, an imposing woman who sat down, looked directly at me, and stated in all sincerity, "I'm here, Doctor. Do psychiatry!"[7]

What then is wrong with the term "mental illness"? It is wrong because it communicates the inaccurate concept that the mind is synonymous with the brain. It reduces mental and spiritual processes to electrical/chemical inter-actions between the neurons of the brain. Psychiatrist Fuller Torrey writes: "The very term [mental "disease"] is nonsensical, a semantic mistake. The two words cannot go together except metaphorically; you can no more have a mental 'disease' than you can have a purple idea or a wise space."[8] He goes on to say that a "'mind' is not a thing and so technically it cannot have a disease. 'Mind' is shorthand for the activity and function of the brain. It is thinking, remembering, perceiving, feeling, wishing, imagining, rea-soning, and all the other activities of which the brain is capable."[9]

Some would argue that Torrey is exaggerating a minor semantical mistake. He says, however, that "the mistake is important. We must be very clear on what we mean by a mental 'disease' because our language shapes our thoughts. If we forget that 'mind' is only a metaphor, then it will shape our thoughts and determine our course of action."[10] Tor-rey points out that there are diseases of the brain such as tumors, meningitis, neurosyphilis, and epilepsy, but "the mind cannot *really* become diseased any more than the intellect can become abscessed"[11] (emphasis in original).

The Alcoholism Label

The reason this part of the debate is so important is that the medical model of mental disorders has determined society's attitude toward mental/emotional/behavioral prob-lems. The current attitude toward alcoholism is a case in point. Herbert Fingarette writes in *Heavy Drinking, The Myth of Alcoholism As a Disease*:

> What is the "classic disease concept of alco-holism"? First proposed in the late 1930's, it goes like this. Alcoholism is a specific disease to which some people are vulnerable. Those who are vulnerable develop the disease if they take up drinking . . . those afflicted by the disease *inevitably* progress to uncontrolled drinking because the disease produces a distinctive

disability—"loss of control," a loss of "the power of choice in the matter of drinking"[12] (emphasis in original).

Fingarette, a consultant for the World Health Organization, states that "*no* leading research authorities accept the classic disease concept. One researcher puts it quite baldly: 'There is no adequate empirical substantiation for the basic tenets of the classic disease concept of alcoholism.'"[13]

In spite of the fact that alcoholism has not been proven to be a disease, "Almost everyone outside the scientific community still takes it for gospel that there is a scientifically proven, uniquely patterned drinking history peculiar to a disease called alcoholism."[14]

The reason that alcoholism has been promoted as a disease is that a huge industry has grown up around the concept. Public hospitals and private clinics harvest more than one billion dollars per year in tax-supported payments and insurance claims for the treatment of alcoholism. The industry spends huge sums protecting their territory through public relations and legislative lobbying.

If the disease concept of alcoholism is incorrect, why hasn't the public been alerted? Fingarette suggests a chilling answer:

> Intimidation should not be discounted. The classic disease concept remains the cornerstone of traditional treatment and public opinion, the central premise of media coverage and social debate, such that anyone who publicly doubts or challenges the disease concept is likely to be ignored, dismissed, or ostracized... truthfulness can threaten, block, or ruin the truthteller's career.[15]

Professional intimidation is not the only factor in keeping this information from the public. Self-serving greed must also be taken into account: "A second factor is that all program staff, paraprofessionals and professionals, have a stake in their organization's financial survival. So in turn they have a stake in persuading government, private funders, and potential clients and families of the truth of the organizational doctrine."[16]

The Disease Label

Fingarette's assessment of the disease model for alcoholism applies equally to the mental illness model, and the consequences are enormous. As the public becomes convinced that they are suffering psychic diseases, the mental health industry can reap immense sums of money from insurance payments, government subsidies, and client fees.

And since the psychotherapeutic industry has labeled nearly every possible behavior as a disease, everyone is a potential patient needing their services. As Torrey notes:

> [I]f we were to follow logically the medical approach, almost everybody would be mentally "ill." The present official classification of psychiatric "diseases" is already so broad that there is a real question whether anybody can claim to not fit into at least one category. To do so, one would have to be free of everything from anxiety, depression, suspiciousness, and hostility, to ulcers, asthma, and hives, to tics and disorders of sleep, to acute alcohol intoxication. In short, all you have to do to qualify as "normal" under the present system is to be a bowl of Jello.[17]

The public is a willing accomplice to the charade of the mental illness medical model. After all, if alcoholism is a disease, how can we hold a drunk responsible for the crime he commits? If a person has "multiple personalities" and murders someone, he must receive psychiatric treatment, not punishment. As Glasser says, "Deviant behavior is considered a product of mental illness, and the patient should not be held morally responsible because he is considered helpless to do anything about it."[18]

Garth Wood writes, "The concept of 'neurosis' has not helped the plight of 'neurotics.' For in truth, neurosis is the word we use in an attempt to explain the condition of those who have chosen to make a mess of their lives, to live unsuccessfully and to experience semi-permanent psychological pain."[19]

The Addiction Label

All obsessive behaviors can be relabeled as addictions in order to include them in the medical model. Samuel Janis has determined that prostitution is an addiction.[20] An Australian doctor treats jealousy with a drug.[21] Incest, multiple lovers, mate-swapping, rape, and sexual assaults can all be defended under the heading of sexual addictions. There is even a National Council on Sexual Addiction. Gambling and overeating are now officially recognized as addictions over which the victims have no control.

Lawrence Frank has suggested that our entire culture "is sick, mentally disordered, and in need of treatment.... The conception of a sick society in need of treatment has many advantages for diagnosis of our individual and social difficulties and for constructive therapy."[22] There certainly are financial advantages for the mental health industry!

Some Christian psychologists seem to believe that bad habits are signs of mental illness. They say that such things as "perpetual procrastination, nail biting, overeating, masturbation, lustful thoughts, worry, overusing credit cards" may be caused by reasons that are "neither physical nor spiritual."[23] For the integrationist, the problems are psychological. One prominent Christian psychologist writes, "Perhaps many of the personal problems which people bring to counselors are completely unrelated to spiritual issues."[24]

To understand such reasoning, you must remember that integrationists view the mind as a reality distinct from the spirit. Thus only psychologists and psychiatrists are qualified to treat it. This is the great divide between biblical and psychological counselors. Psychologists view destructive habits as behavior that is unrelated to spiritual matters, while biblical counselors view such things as procrastination, lustful thoughts, masturbation, uncontrolled spending, and overeating as sinful choices that can be corrected by obedience to the Word of God.

"Aha! You finally said it!" an integrationist is sure to shout gleefully. "You have simplistically and naively reduced *all* dysfunctions to sin."

That simply is not true. As I have carefully stated, there are physically caused disorders that we readily recognize. But *choices* are mental and spiritual matters. The unproven psychological theories of unconscious drives over which a person has no control are simply mechanisms for excusing irresponsible, immature, and undisciplined behavior and thinking.

Victimization

A second major problem with psycholabels is perpetual victimization. When one accepts his label, he is forever categorized. Every experienced pastoral counselor has heard these ideas expressed: "I am an alcoholic . . . so it's not my fault" or "I am a codependent . . . so it's not my fault" or "I am an abused person . . . so it's not my fault" so many times that it requires great personal discipline to keep from screaming, "Accept responsibility for what you once *were* and rejoice in what you now *are* in Christ! If you are in Christ, you are a new creation! The old things have passed away! All things have become new!" (2 Corinthians 5:17).

Two of the most liberating truths of the gospel of Christ are that God forgives us for our sins and we no longer have to remain slaves to the past! We *can* experience cleansing and total healing through the unlimited power of God.

It is troubling to know that many Christian counselors cling tenaciously to the labeling concept and consequently make their counselees slaves to the past. It is encouraging, by contrast, to discover that some secular counselors are coming to the conclusion that one does not have to remain a victim forever. William Glasser, a secular psychotherapist, rejects the concept of mental illness and the importance of past events and unconscious drives. In his practice, he says:

> We do not accept the concept of mental illness ... we do not get involved with the patient's history because we can neither change what happened to him nor accept the fact that he is limited by his past.... We do not look for unconscious conflicts or the reasons for them. [Glasser refuses to allow a patient to excuse] his behavior on the basis of unconscious motives.[25]

It is plain, then, that nouthetic counselors are not alone in holding to this opinion. So far as I am aware, therapist Garth Wood makes no claim to being a Christian, yet he believes that a troubled person must assume responsibility for past choices and make appropriate choices to change his behavior. He writes:

> The unsuccessful person with his low self-esteem can, like the sinner, return at any time to the correct path and can be helped to do so. But he will not be helped by a denial of his problem or by reassurances that he does not really have one, or again that if he does have a problem it is through no fault of his own.[26]

God has promised that for His children there is no such thing as a drive over which a person can have no control. He says, "No temptation has seized you except what is common to man. And God is faithful; he will not let you be tempted beyond what you can bear. But when you are tempted, he will also provide a way out so that you can stand up under it" (1 Corinthians 10:13).

Some might argue that this verse does not apply to serious disorders and addictions, but merely to normal temptations that mentally healthy people experience. But the context shows that Paul *is* writing about obsessions, abuse of alcohol, overeating, and sexual "addictions": "The people sat down to eat and drink and got up to indulge in pagan revelry. We should not commit sexual immorality, as some of them did" (1 Corinthians 10:7,8).

Forever Children

A third result of psycholabeling is that it stunts the development of mental, social, and spiritual maturity. Some of the characteristics of childishness are an unwillingness to accept change, pouting or crying at disappointment, a preoccupation with self, a tendency to lie, shirking of responsibility, shifting of blame, demanding instant gratification, throwing temper tantrums, and a host of other symptoms that coincide with the labels of psychological disorders, such as "infantile regression."

Psychologists tell middle-aged men and women that they are the "adult children of _____" (you fill in the blank). The theory is that since they suffered genuine torment at the hands of their parents or other authority figures, they must bear their psychic scars forever. The best they can hope for is to learn to cope. They can never be whole because they were eternally damaged. This is supposed to explain why they never learn to say no to alcohol, food, or drugs. Who can blame them if they become sexually promiscuous or if they get into extreme debt? It is to be expected that they too will abuse their children and perpetuate the cycle of violence. After all, they're only children in big bodies.

Yet Paul wrote, "When I was a child, I talked like a child, I thought like a child, I reasoned like a child. When I became a man, I put childish ways behind me" (1 Corinthians 13:11). With the power of God, no matter how horrible one's childhood may have been—and I do *not* discount the incredible horror inflicted upon millions of children—one can experience genuine healing of wounded hearts and grow into full maturity in Christ.

The commands of God—His invitations to joy—are given to every human, whether one grows up in a loving Christian home or in a cesspool of hell. Thank God, Jesus did not make this offer only to those who had healthy childhoods: "I have come that they may have life, and have it to the full" (John 10:10). He makes that offer to everyone regardless of his past.

Endless Therapy

A fourth result of psycholabeling is endless therapy. If a person is forever a child in need of the guidance of a mental health professional, there will be an endless source of revenue for therapists. If he is now and always will be an alcoholic, he will need to continue his meetings at AA without break until he dies. Otherwise, he will inevitably slip back into drunkenness and destruction. If one is a schizophrenic—never mind that no one really knows what that means—he must continue swallowing powerful drugs to control his bizarre behavior. If he is an abused person, he must go back into the dark and frightening past, rip open his emotional wounds, and embrace his hurts—realizing that life will always be painful.

Few people ever address one reason that standard psychotherapy takes so long: Therapists often don't have a clue as to what the real problems are. The moment one dismisses accountability to God and discards His Word, therapists are left to their own subjective guesses as to what a person's root problems are. We could hardly fault the psychologist for not knowing what lies in the heart of his patient were it not for his claims to godlike knowledge.

The client, feeling temporarily relieved by a verbal confession to his secular priest, believes that therapy has helped. He returns to long-established habits of thinking and acting in the hours and days that follow and within a week needs another psychic fix. Some clients finally awaken to the fact that having invested hundreds or even thousands of dollars in psychoanalysis or other forms of counseling, the ones primarily benefitting are the therapists themselves.

New Labels

The mental health industry is seldom at a loss to create a new label for "abnormal behavior." Erica Goode says that in 1917 only 59 distinct forms of mental disorders were recognized by the American Psychiatric Association. When the APA first published its *Diagnostic and Statistical Manual of Mental Disorders* (DSM) in 1952, the number of official labels had grown to 106. The third edition (1980) lists 292 specific disorders—a veritable smorgasbord to choose from —including "nicotine dependence," "Self-Defeating Personality Disorder," and the titillating "Hypoactive Sexual Desire Disorder."[27]

Are these categories scientifically determined? Goode writes that—

> psychiatric diagnoses rest mostly on description of symptoms. And deciding which diagnoses to include, and how to define them, has historically been a judgment call. Cynics question how heavily such decisions are influenced by factors that have nothing to do with science —for example, social mores, psychiatrists' wish to be seen as "hard" scientists, economic motives or the idiosyncratic views of prominent experts. As one psychologist says, "It's a very political process."[28]

The rankness of such political influence became apparent in 1973 when homosexuality was removed from the manual as a disorder, since society had accepted the prevailing view that it is merely an alternative lifestyle.

Do we understand the human heart better now that we have created hundreds of labels? Has the general condition of psychic health improved noticeably now that we have the APA's DSM to explain PMS?[29] I hardly need to answer that question.

Christian Psychological Labels

Some people may be surprised to discover that the four basic temperaments presented by a popular Christian writer are not found in the Bible. The writer admits that he is aware of the problems associated with such labeling. He says, "There is danger in presenting these four types of temperaments; some will be tempted to analyze their friends and think of them in the framework of, 'What type is he?'" He tells his readers that the temperaments are to be used for self-analysis only.

Biblical Labels

I would suggest that instead of studying modern psycholabels we look to the Word of God. In the previous section I pointed out four problems generated by psycholabeling. Now I would like to suggest five biblical labels that have set millions of suffering people free from psychic bondage.

Child of God

The first is "child of God." Jesus says in John 1:12, "To all who received him, to those who believed in his name, he gave the right to become children of God." Paul emphasizes this truth in Romans 8:14 when he writes that "those who are led by the Spirit of God are sons of God."

What a contrast to the enslavement of forever remaining a child victim of an abusive parent! Paul says that a Christian is "no longer a slave, but a son; and since you are a son, God has made you also an heir" (Galatians 4:7). In spite of the depraved environment one may have grown up in, we are told that we "may become blameless and pure, children of God without fault in a crooked and depraved generation, in which you shine like stars in the universe" (Philippians 2:15). What wonderful news this is for "adult children" who have been handcuffed to their tortured past!

Redeemed Person

A second joyful biblical label is "redeemed person," in direct contrast to the psycholabel of "abused person." I have personally watched people who for years enjoyed a clean and whole life in Christ but then allowed themselves to be led back into the bondage of their past sufferings. I watched a beautiful, victorious Christian woman, who in her childhood had been sexually molested by her father and brothers, turn into a bitter and hateful victim all over again under the guidance of a Christian psychiatrist. I watched a loving marriage disintegrate as a wife, who had been seduced in her teen years, was led back to "work out her past" according to the theories of a Christian psychologist who labels husbands who disagree with his therapy as "surrogate abusers."

How I wanted to ask these suffering people, Why have they chosen to feed in the troughs of psychology when they have the pure milk of God's Word available? When I hear Christians say, "I am an abused person," I quickly remind them that they once *were* abused persons, but now they are *redeemed* persons! Isaiah promises that "the ransomed of the Lord will return. They will enter Zion with singing; everlasting joy will crown their heads. Gladness and joy will overtake them, and sorrow and sighing will flee away. I, even I, am he who comforts you" (Isaiah 51:11,12).

I am reminded of the old gospel song that says, "Redeemed—how I love to proclaim it! Redeemed by the blood of the Lamb! Redeemed thro' His infinite mercy, His child, and forever, I am."

Forgiven Person

In addition to being a child of God who is redeemed from the clutches of hell, the Christian can assume the label of a "forgiven person." David wrote, "He forgives all my sins and heals all my diseases" (Psalm 103:3). No matter what is in one's past, God can cleanse and forgive. Whether one was abused or the abuser, "If we confess our sins, he is faithful and just and will forgive us our sins and purify us from all unrighteousness" (1 John 1:9). The victim of incest who mistakenly assumes that he or she must have deserved such treatment need not spend years in therapy to sort out blame or to comprehend why something so awful took place. A biblical understanding of man's sinful nature removes much of the mystery.

Healing begins to take place when the victim learns to rest in God's glorious love. Understanding God's unlimited forgiveness for the sins he truly has committed can free an abused person to forgive those who sinned against him.

And what of the abuser? Because of the awfulness of what he has done to others, he may well assume that there is no possibility of forgiveness for him. The best he can do, according to the standard psychological view, is to undergo years of therapy so that he will never repeat his crimes. But psychotherapy will not change his heart, and the psychologized rapist, when released from jail, may well repeat his abuse whenever possible.

Compare that with the biblical view, which says that God loves the abuser, who can genuinely repent of his unspeakable wickedness, receive the cleansing forgiveness of God through Jesus Christ, and thereby have his heart radically *changed.* How can we know if someone has truly repented and is changed? Two indications will be his desire to ask the forgiveness of the ones he so viciously ravaged and his willingness to submit himself to close supervision and strict accountability.

New Creation

Is it possible for any thoroughly depraved person to be permanently transformed? Yes! The fourth biblical label that has freed so many people from their inner sufferings is "new creation." Before Paul became a believer in Jesus Christ, he was guilty of incredible abuse of men, women, and children. What he did was so awful that he called himself "the chief of sinners" (1 Timothy 1:15 KJV). Yet under the inspiration of the Holy Spirit he wrote, "If any man is in Christ, he is a new creature; the old things passed away; behold, new things have come" (2 Corinthians 5:17 NASB).

You cannot truly reform a person through therapeutic techniques. What is needed is the miracle of *transformation* that is performed by the Holy Spirit. This process, called regeneration, is described by Ezekiel: "I will give you a new heart and put a new spirit in you; I will remove from you your heart of stone and give you a heart of flesh" (Ezekiel 36:26). Titus calls it "the washing of rebirth and renewal by the Holy Spirit" (Titus 3:5). Anything short of this supernatural work of God will fail.

Victor

A fifth and final biblical label I suggest—a label that is an alternative to psychovictimization—is "victor." We live in a victimized age. We are all casualties, to a greater or lesser degree, of a sin-cursed world. Whether you suffered at the hands of an alcoholic father, a drug-crazed rapist, a bitter stepmother, an unfaithful wife, or a violent husband, you have been victimized.

I want you to know that God cares about your suffering and is full of sympathy for your pain. Matthew quotes a portion of Isaiah that gives us a hint of Jesus' compassion for the suffering: "A bruised reed he will not break, or a smoldering wick he will not snuff out, till he leads justice to victory" (Matthew 12:20). Are you a bruised reed who has been trampled on by those around you? Jesus cares. Do you feel like a smoldering wick in a lamp nearly out of fuel? Take heart, my friend. Jesus understands.

You can choose to remain a victim the rest of your life, or you can choose the path of victory by following One who was abused as no other. We are told that Jesus was beaten nearly to the point of death, was spat upon, humiliated, dragged bleeding through the dirty streets of Jerusalem, and hung naked on a Roman cross. Yet Jesus did not curse those who tortured Him so cruelly or walked by laughing at His suffering. Instead, He prayed for them, "Father, forgive them, for they do not know what they are doing" (Luke 23:34).

How could Jesus love His abusers? By faith in a loving God. We are reminded in Romans 8:35-37 that nothing can separate us from God's love. Not "trouble or hardship or persecution or famine or nakedness or danger or sword." Though we suffer in a cruel world, "in all these things we are more than conquerors through him who loved us."

That sounds wonderful in theory, doesn't it? But how do we make it real? John says, "Everyone born of God overcomes the world. This is the victory that has overcome the world, even our faith" (1 John 5:4). You can become a victor instead of a victim as you live by faith in the Lord Jesus Christ.

Perhaps you're rolling your eyes, shaking your head in irritation, and muttering, "Another nothing-butterist is dispensing his simplistic solutions by quoting Bible verses." Think what you will, but God's holy Word has given you the key to your liberty.

I am not suggesting that it will be easy, for it involves a paradox: Living by faith is hard work, but the reward is unbelievable freedom and joy.

Living by faith doesn't mean that you believe real hard so that nice things will happen magically. Living by faith means that you saturate your mind, soul, and heart with the living truths of the Scriptures. Then you submit to those precepts in your day-to-day existence. Living by faith simply means walking with our loving heavenly Father in humble, childlike trust and obedience, as stated in the old gospel lyric: "Trust and obey, for there's no other way To be happy in Jesus, But to trust and obey."

How can we be so foolish as to trade our glorious labels in Christ for the pathetic labels of secular psychology? We must never forget that we "were once darkness, but now you are light in the Lord. Live as children of light" (Ephesians 5:8).

■ ■ ■

Terri Cummins hurried into the classroom at the Baptist Seminary and sat down just as the bell rang. She was working on her master's degree in counseling with the goal of setting up a counseling center in the church where her husband, Bill, was pastor.

She had been so excited when she began her course of study. She felt that her background as a nurse, coupled with a counseling degree, would enable her to minister to some of the dysfunctional people in their congregation.

Lately, however, she had been having some doubts about the philosophy of counseling being taught. Her questions began after her husband had come home from a pastor's meeting where John Kryer had been the featured speaker.

"At first he made me mad," Bill had admitted to Terri. "I couldn't believe he was critical of the counseling programs being taught in conservative seminaries. But the more I thought about what he said, the more I began to see his point."

Terri had been very defensive, she recalled. When Bill showed her the notes from Pastor Kryer's lecture, she actually threw them in the trash. "That's where they belong, Bill!" she had said loudly as she paced back and forth. "He makes it sound like there is a conspiracy among the seminaries to undermine orthodox faith. I know the professors at the seminary. I know they love the Lord. They would never do anything to turn people away from the Scriptures! It's not right for John to slander good people!"

"Well," Bill had replied, "John wasn't exactly slandering the therapists, or the seminaries either, for that matter. He was careful to say that he believes they are sincere people trying to do the best they can. He just thinks they're sincerely wrong."

Since that time Terri had listened more carefully in classes and some nagging questions were forming in her mind. She had decided she would get some answers today.

Dr. Paul Ballard called the class to order. "Today we are going to continue our study in recovery from sexual abuse. We are fortunate to have one of the foremost authorities on this subject residing here in Denver. I had hoped that he would be our guest lecturer for this topic, but unfortunately his extensive seminar schedule prevents that. So we'll have to be content with his book *The Wounded Heart*. I'd like some reactions to what you've read."

A hand went up at the back of the classroom. Dr. Ballard pointed. "Yes, Mr. Allen."

The class turned to view Chad Allen as he said, "I'm a bit confused over the author's view that a woman is not to be held accountable for any part of a sexual relationship if the man has any significant power over her. He has stated that opinion in his seminars without sufficiently qualifying it. It doesn't seem to matter what the age of the female. I'm concerned that this might remove all accountability for her part of the relationship."

There was an instant hum of discussion in the class. One woman raised her hand.

"Yes, Ms. Tolliver?" Dr. Ballard said as he pointed to her.

"I'd expect that sort of reaction from a man!" she said hotly. "Unless you've been a victim, you have no idea how powerless a woman feels around a trusted authority figure."

"I can see how that would be true of a young girl," Chad Allen replied, "but doesn't a woman have the responsibility to cry out for help at some point? And if the affair had some aspect of mutual agreement, to the degree that there was voluntary involvement, don't both parties bear some responsibility?"

Terri raised her hand.

"Ah, yes, Mrs. Cummins," Dr. Ballard said with a smile as he sat on the front edge of his desk.

"I know this may not be considered politically correct," she began timidly, "but I guess I'd have to agree with Chad to some extent. Just because a person is a woman shouldn't remove all responsibility from her. I also question how long a woman can cling to victim status. In some way it seems as though counseling is designed to give people an excuse to continue in defeat and bitterness."

"I'm not sure I follow you," Dr. Ballard said, standing to his feet.

"Well, it seems to me, as I've been thinking through these issues for the past several months, that Christian counseling doesn't offer much more hope for dysfunctional people than secular counseling. In fact, I honestly don't see much difference."

"What kind of difference were you expecting, Mrs. Cummins?" Dr. Ballard asked.

"Well, I expected that we would be taught how to open the Scriptures and help guide people to God's solutions for the problems of living. Instead, we've been told not to pray with our clients because that would be threatening to them, and we aren't supposed to quote Scripture to them because it only adds to their guilt."

"I think I explained my positions on those matters, Mrs. Cummins. It isn't that I discount prayer or the Bible. It's just that so many church counselors make the mistake of projecting a spiritual dimension onto every problem, when in reality most dysfunctions are psychological in nature. And I have not said that counselors are *never* to pray with their clients. It is just unethical to try to press our own spiritual convictions on clients who have come to us for help at their most vulnerable state."

"But, I . . ."

Dr. Ballard waved her off and said, "You are getting us off the subject, Mrs. Cummins. I'd be happy to discuss this further with you after class."

"Oh, I'm sorry," Terri said. "But could I make a suggestion?"

"Certainly. What sort of suggestion?"

"I would really enjoy seeing a discussion between yourself and someone from a different counseling philosophy on the topic of what makes biblical counseling biblical."

"I see. And do you have someone in mind?"

"Actually, I do," Terri answered. "There is a pastor in the north suburban area who is very critical of our seminary's counseling position. His name is John Kryer. Are you familiar with him?"

"I've heard of him," Dr. Ballard answered. "If I understand correctly, he takes the nouthetic approach to counseling."

A voice from the other side of the classroom laughed and said, "Oh, a Jay Adams disciple! Wonderful!"

"I'm a bit disappointed, Mrs. Cummins," Dr. Ballard said. "I thought you were suggesting that a serious therapist should join us for a discussion. I doubt I could get clearance for someone like the Reverend Kryer."

Chad Allen interjected, "Why should we discount a pastor simply because he follows a conservative theory? I've read some of Adams's books, and though I don't agree with every point, I have found some of his arguments to be very persuasive."

"I'm sure you have, Mr. Allen," Dr. Ballard said, "but it is that sort of counseling that has given pastoral counselors a bad name."

A hand was raised near the front of the class.

"Yes, Miss Chavez?"

"I don't agree with Adams's philosophy, but I would like to hear firsthand from a nouthetic counselor."

"Yes, so would I," someone said from the back of the room.

"Me too!" said another.

Dr. Ballard seemed somewhat taken back by this turn of events. "Well, I don't know," he said hesitantly.

"Surely, Dr. Ballard, you can't deny us hearing from a nouthetic counselor when we have been required to attend seminars led by John Bradshaw," Chad Allen said.

"All right, class," Dr. Ballard finally agreed. "I'll try to arrange for Pastor Kryer to come. Now can we get back to our original subject?"

The discussion returned to recovery from sexual abuse, but Terri didn't hear much. She began writing down some of the questions that had been troubling her since her husband had first brought John Kryer's notes home.

After class Dr. Ballard stopped Terri as she approached the door. "Mrs. Cummins, may I speak with you for a moment?"

Terri followed him to his desk as the other students filed out of the classroom.

"I wish you would have asked me privately about inviting Reverend Kryer to our class. I felt you really put me on the spot," he said.

"I'm sorry, Dr. Ballard. I hadn't planned on asking at all. The idea just came to me in class, and I thought it would be helpful for us to see the difference between integrated counseling and what you have described as simplistic biblical counseling."

"Well, I'm going to leave it up to you to contact Reverend Kryer. I'd like him to come two weeks from today, if possible."

"I'll contact him as soon as I get home," she promised.

That evening she was able to reach John Kryer at home. "I'm sorry for calling you at home, Pastor Kryer, but my husband said it would be okay."

"That's perfectly all right, Mrs. Cummins," John said. "What can I do for you?"

Terri quickly explained what had happened in class. "When I asked if we could have someone represent a more conservative approach to counseling, your name popped into my head. I guess it's because my husband showed me your handout on integrated counseling. I must admit I didn't like what I read, but the more I've thought about your criticisms, the more I'm beginning to see that they were true. Would you be willing to come lecture our class on your views?"

"I'm surprised that I would be allowed at the seminary, considering my criticisms. But I'd be delighted!" John replied. "I'd love to explain to sincere seminary students why I believe psychology cannot be trusted."

The Psychological Counselor

Does it follow, however, that the modern disciple of Christ and reader of Paul's epistles should throw away psychology books and reject psychology because it was not used centuries ago?

The Biblical Counselor

His error is found in the phrase "because it was not used centuries ago." That is not the reason psychology should be discarded. When it was used has no bearing on its validity. Paul would not have rejected it on the grounds that it was modern, but because it is "another gospel."

The Word of God

I am astonished that you are so quickly deserting the one who called you by the grace of Christ and are turning to a different gospel—which is really no gospel at all. Evidently some people are throwing you into confusion and are trying to pervert the gospel of Christ.
—Galatians 1:6,7

6

The Myth
That Psychology
Is Trustworthy

Can a Christian *trust* psychology? This is the essential question one must consider in evaluating the mixing of psychological concepts and Scripture in Christian counseling.

The Contrived Medical Model

William Kirwan presents his case for integrating psychology and theology in his book *Biblical Concepts for Christian Counseling.* He believes that psychology is "the science of mental processes and behavior."[1] If psychology is a science along the lines of medicine, one could expect a fair amount of agreement within the trade. Indeed, newcomers normally view psychology, psychiatry, and other forms of counseling as a rather unified discipline. Those who have studied the field, however, know that there are literally hundreds of distinct and contradictory therapeutic approaches to counseling—with thousands of conflicting techniques—all claiming to cure the human psyche.

Gary Collins quotes F.H. Garrison, who wrote in his 1921 *Introduction to the History of Medicine*: "Whenever many different remedies are used for a disease, it usually means that we know little about treating the disease."[2] Psychology can't even agree on the diseases, let alone the cures.

Medical doctors study physical ailments, diseases, injuries, and remedies. Generally speaking, when a treatment for a given illness is found to be successful, most doctors use that technique until a more effective one is discovered. There is general agreement among doctors regarding human physiology. Most medical doctors agree on the functions of the heart, liver, kidneys, or lungs. You may travel the globe from Mexico to Mauritania and not find significant medical disagreement about the purpose of the pancreas or the lymphatic system. Medical students from the time of Hippocrates have dissected cadavers and found the same physical human organs regardless of race, culture, continent, religion, or economic condition.

Dealing with the human mind and soul, however, is an entirely different matter. No one has yet observed a mind or dissected an emotion. No X-ray scan has ever detected the soul. Psychologists are not even sure how to define the mind. Is the mind synonymous with the brain? The following statement on psychology is revealing.

> Psychology [is the] science or study of the mind. Such a definition, however, without an accompanying adequate description of what is meant exactly by mind is without meaning, and as yet there is no agreement among psychologists upon any single definition of mind. By some, for example, mind is considered a definite thing apart from the body and as such virtually synonymous with soul. Others, although they establish mind as distinct from body, bind it to body by the interaction held to take place between the two. Still others, in an attempt to do away with this separation, tie mind closely to the brain, making the one a function of the other. Others, however, deny

existence of mind altogether, basing their
conclusion on the belief that human behavior
can be adequately described without the use of
any such vague and indefinable term.[3]

Isn't that amazing? According to *The Columbia Encyclopedia,* psychology is the study of something that cannot be defined, and the term *mind,* lacking a clear definition, is "without meaning," and according to some, the mind does not exist at all. Is there any wonder that psychology is confused and confusing?

The Questionable Use of Psychoactive Drugs

Though psychologists cannot adequately define the entity they presume to cure, they want us to trust their judgment and place ourselves in their care. In so doing, we can actually jeopardize our health—especially now that the psychological establishment has reduced all negative human emotions and behaviors to diseases instead of sin, and now that its natural conclusion is to treat those ailments with drugs. For example, prostitution is now being described as an addiction,[4] and if so, it must be treated psychotherapeutically. The misconception that sin is a psychic disorder is precisely why Christians need to question the use of psychotherapeutic drugs as a normal part of counseling.

Most counselors have encountered people who use the medical model as an excuse for their behavior. After all, who can be blamed for having a "disease" that requires medication? There is the question of whether psychologists and psychiatrists haven't merely redefined old behaviors as new "disorders." For example, I hesitate to accept Attention Deficit Disorder (ADD) as a genuine malady unless it is caused by biological problems such as brain or nervous-system damage or infant addiction to substances carried by the mother during pregnancy. Sometimes ADD is merely undisciplined behavior.

There is another serious question about therapeutic drugs: Can they lead to addiction? The answer clearly is yes, and that fact alone should be cause for deep concern in a potential counselee. Dr. Lee Coleman, a practicing psychiatrist, writes in his book *The Reign of Error* that psychoactive drug dependency is actually fostered by psychiatry: "Millions of patients are now told by their doctors to stay on psychoactive medications for years or even a lifetime."[5]

Zilbergeld says that "common anxieties are also treated with drugs" and that "there are dangers, addiction to the medication being one of the worst. Antianxiety medications are highly addictive for some people, as easy to get hooked on and as hard to withdraw from as heroin."[6] One of the "mental illnesses" commonly treated with drugs is schizophrenia. While it is true that those who have biologically caused symptoms sometimes improve with drug therapy, "there are debilitating side effects with long-term use of these medications."[7]

Lithium is a case in point. It is often prescribed for patients who have been diagnosed as having a manic-depressive or bipolar disorder. Some clients have been led to believe that they are suffering from a lithium deficiency. Coleman reports:

> So many patients have told me similar stories that I now know that psychiatrists and family doctors are disseminating a great deal of misinformation about lithium. Authorities advocate that patients be "educated in the concept that lithium is a perpetual preventive much like insulin." These authorities also repeatedly call lithium a "simple, naturally occurring" substance. It therefore comes as no surprise that many patients consider lithium to be like a new vitamin. Unfortunately they are wrong: Lithium is a very toxic substance whose side effects include permanent kidney and thyroid damage, as well as other potential complications.[8]

Side effects of psychoactive drugs are a legitimate cause for concern. A patient should be informed of the potential dangers a drug presents, and he should understand that the doctor is actually experimenting on him, for the doctor cannot reliably predict how a given patient will react to a particular drug. Harold M. Silverman, a doctor of pharmacology, writes, "*Every* drug has side effects. Your chances for developing a specific side effect depend on the drug, how much of it you are taking, the frequency of the specific effect, your age, your metabolism, and unpredictable responses to drugs known as 'idiosyncratic reactions.'"9

Some drugs may actually *increase* the symptoms they are supposed to cure. Xanax, a drug used to treat anxiety, has been known to create depression or to make existing depression even worse in some patients. It is now recognized as habit-forming. Its common side effects include clumsiness, drowsiness, and dizziness. In some patients it can cause hallucinations, irritability, confusion, and depression.

Antipsychotic drugs such as Haloperidol are used to restore emotional calm in people who suffer extreme anxiety, agitation, or other "psychotic" behavior. It is not completely understood how these drugs work, but one theory is that they inhibit the action of dopamine—that is, they short-circuit nerve-impulse transmission in the area of the brain believed to control the emotions.10

The "natural, expected, and unavoidable drug actions" of strong tranquilizers include drowsiness, lethargy, blurred vision, dryness of the mouth, impaired urination, constipation, and transient drop in blood pressure.11 In addition, there are other potential side effects, such as skin rashes, loss of hair, anxiety, agitation, heart palpitation, jaundice, Parkinson-like disorders, muscle spasms affecting the jaw, neck, back, hands or feet, eye-rolling, muscle-twitching, convulsions, photosensitivity, hallucinations, impotence, and depression. There is the danger of interaction with over-the-counter allergy medications, drugs which control internal eye pressure, antihypertensive drugs, and especially with methyldopa, which can cause "serious mental and behavioral abnormalities."12

Tricyclic antidepressant drugs, such as Norpramin, are used to treat emotional depression by affecting those areas of the brain controlling moods and emotions. Again, scientists are not entirely certain how tricyclic drugs work. It is believed that "the drug slowly restores to normal levels certain constituents of brain tissue (such as norepinephrine) that transmit nerve impulses."[13] The potential side effects are similar to those of Haloperidol. This drug can have adverse effects upon the liver, bone marrow, heart rhythm, and more.

Some of my counselees have been treated with antidepressants. One had been incorrectly diagnosed as a schizophrenic and another had been in psychiatric therapy for more than 14 years, without cure. In both cases, the cause of their problems was deep anger and bitterness. Drugs were not the solution.

Though many exaggerated claims are made for psychotherapeutic drugs, it is clear that a large percentage of patients in one study recovered without *any* treatment, counseling, or drug therapy.[14]

Psychotherapeutic Drugs and Christians

One Christian psychologist suggests that the reason many Christians resist taking psychotherapeutic drugs is that they "believe that drug use is a sign of spiritual weakness."[15] He then asks, "If the Lord has allowed us to discover new chemical tools to counteract the biological bases for human problems and to help us cope temporarily with the stresses of life, are these necessarily wrong? ... Psychotherapeutic medications can help us relax so that we can think more clearly."[16]

If the problems are genuinely biological in nature, pharmaceuticals may be justified. But if the problems are caused by wrong actions or thinking, the Bible teaches that we are to learn new ways of acting and thinking by renewing our minds rather than by anesthetizing them. Psychotherapeutic medications often "relax" a person so much that they prevent clear thinking.

Psychiatrists do not always explain the potential side

effects of psychoactive drugs. Thus I strongly recommend that before a counselee takes any prescribed psychoactive drugs he consult with a biblical counselor who is literate about such drugs.[17]

Counselors should also inform older people that they are especially vulnerable to misapplied drug therapies. Their bodies are more sensitive to tranquilizers and psychoactive drugs. Silverman writes:

> Increased tissue sensitivity is a particular problem for seniors taking tranquilizers and other psychoactive drugs. The response to psychoactive medicines is definitely enhanced as the years pass. This means then, unless the dosages of these medicines are reduced, seniors run the risk of being overmedicated and developing unwanted side effects. : . . . Some studies have shown that seniors experience as many as seven times more side effects than do younger adults given the same medication. Although the numbers vary somewhat, the trend is always the same: the older we get, the more likely we are to suffer from the medicines that are supposed to cure our ills.[18]

I am not suggesting that there is no legitimate purpose whatsoever for psychotherapeutic drugs. For those mental/ emotional problems which have biological causes, there may indeed be medical and pharmacological solutions. But it would seem that these should be the *last* resort rather than the first. And remember, the patient has a right to know what effects a drug may have before it is administered.

If there is no actual biological or chemical deficiency, Christians should learn how to handle their feelings of anxiety and depression by renewed thinking (Romans 12:1,2) and changed behavior (Ephesians 4:17-32) rather than by dulling those emotions with drugs.

The Pretense of Divine Approval

Integrationists often defend their use of secular psychological concepts by insisting that psychology is a God-given scientific field of knowledge. This belief assumes two things: 1) that God has given the information, and 2) that the information is actually scientific. Let us look at the first assumption.

Gary Collins admits that Jesus would not have needed to use psychology even if it had been available in His day, because "his knowledge of human behavior was infinite and perfect."[19] And the apostle Paul knew that ultimate truth could not be found in worldly philosophies. "Instead, he built many of his arguments on Scripture and insisted that the scholars of his time repent. Surely the apostle would have presented a similar message to psychological scholars if they had existed when Paul was alive."[20] I agree.

Collins then commits a monumental error in his next paragraph: "Does it follow, however, that the modern disciple of Christ and reader of Paul's epistles should throw away psychology books and reject psychology because it was not used centuries ago?"[21] His error is found in the phrase *"because it was not used centuries ago."* That is not the reason psychology should be discarded. *When* it was used has no bearing on its validity.

Paul would not have rejected psychology on the grounds that it was modern, but because it was "another gospel." Responding to a similar issue, Paul wrote, "I am astonished that you are so quickly deserting the one who called you by the grace of Christ and are turning to a different gospel—which is really no gospel at all. Evidently some people are throwing you into confusion and are trying to pervert the gospel of Christ" (Galatians 1:6,7).

Integrationists defend their position with the logic that if Christians have accepted other modern advances such as the radio, the microphone, antibiotics, computers, and cars, we shouldn't reject the advances of psychology. The error of this apples-and-oranges comparison is that psychology is not dealing with *material objects* but *spiritual issues*. It deals with the very issues discussed in the Bible, but it does so from an opposing platform.

Paul vehemently denounced Christians who would mix light with darkness. He wrote:

> Do not be yoked together with unbelievers. For what do righteousness and wickedness have in common? Or what fellowship can light have with darkness? What harmony is there between Christ and Belial? What does a believer have in common with an unbeliever? What agreement is there between the temple of God and idols? For we are the temple of the living God. As God has said: "I will live with them and walk among them, and I will be their God, and they will be my people. Therefore come out from them and be separate, says the Lord. Touch no unclean thing, and I will receive you" (2 Corinthians 6:14-17).

An increasing number of informed believers are questioning the mixing of biblical truth with psychological theory. Unfortunately, these critics of integrationist counseling are commonly stereotyped as incompetent reactionaries. But the truth is that many are thoughtful professionals who refuse to buy the party line that psychology and the Scriptures together are better than the Bible alone.

Integrationists seem to believe that there are counseling issues about which the Bible is silent and which therefore require psychological insights. It is true that the Bible does not specifically speak about cocaine addiction, but it deals with the principles of substance abuse (Proverbs 20:1; 23:21; 26:11; Daniel 1:8; Romans 6:12; 13:13; Ephesians 5:18). The Bible does not specifically address pornography, but it does deal with mental and spiritual purity (Psalm 119:9,11; Matthew 5:27,28; Ephesians 4:19; Colossians 3:5; 1 Thessalonians 4:3-7). There is no single mental/spiritual issue upon which the Bible is silent.

Still, the integrationist asks plaintively, "Could it be...
that psychology is a God-given field of knowledge?"[22]
It could be, but *is* it? Historical evidence shows that the
founders of modern psychology attempted to define and
interpret human behavior in purely natural terms without
reference to God. Wilhelm Wundt, who established the
first psychological laboratory in Leipzig in 1879, divided
the mind into three basic structural elements (sensations,
images, and feelings),[23] but left out the soul or spirit. He is
commonly honored as the founder of modern psychology,
but there is no evidence that he credited God for his "discoveries."

William James, the founder of the first American psychological laboratory, was "strongly influenced by the
evolutionary principles of Darwin,"[24] and saw human
behavior in terms of function, or the interaction between
mind and body. He wrote a landmark work entitled *Pragmatism: A New Name for Some Old Ways of Thinking*, which
held that an idea is true if it "works." Nothing indicates that
James was given his theories by God, even though his
relativistic doctrine had major implications for religion.

Behaviorist John B. Watson saw human behavior simply
in terms of response to stimuli. He was not even sure that
the mind existed. "An avowed materialist, he objected
to concepts such as mind, consciousness, volition, and
emotion, stating that psychology should be the science of
directly observable behavior."[25] B.F. Skinner, another behaviorist, offered "a systematic and scientific program to
alter the nature of Man,"[26] though it did not include God.

Psychoanalysis was formulated by Sigmund Freud, who
theorized that man is under the control of unconscious
urges that originate in childhood traumas and inner conflicts between the *id, ego,* and *superego.* He had a "profoundly low opinion of human nature...referring, on
several occasions, to the majority of human beings...
as 'worthless.' [Freud had] two deeply held sentiments,
which were characteristic of the man: a bitter antagonism to
religion and all forms of religious authority, and a hatred of
America."[27]

In his book *The Future of an Illusion,* Freud ridicules religion. Carl Jung, Erich Fromm, and most of Freud's other successors carried the same fanatical hatred of religion that Freud revealed in his writings.

These men are fairly representative of the general attitude which psychologists have of scriptural authority and validity. Literally thousands of branches of psychotherapies have sprung from these early roots, which grew from the seeds of rebellion toward God.

No, psychological counseling is not a God-given field of knowledge. It is a system of beliefs that originated in the minds of men who were godless rebels. Romans 1:22 says of such men, "Although they claimed to be wise, they became fools."

Psychological counseling is darkness masquerading as light. It is built upon a foundation of sand, and as the storms of life crash upon it, the psychological system crumbles into ruin.

Is Modern Life More Complex?

A second question is whether psychology "might be an academic and practical discipline enabling us more adequately to help people who live in a society permeated with change and complexity unknown in the days of Jesus and Paul."[28] To help people more adequately than what? The Scriptures? Jesus? Paul? Though integrationists clearly state that "psychological conclusions, psychotherapeutic practices, counseling principles, psychiatric theories—all these, like every other area of study, must be examined carefully under the probing light of Scripture,"[29] they also believe that modern life is simply too complex to be handled by the principles of Scripture alone.

In his defense of integration, one Christian writer compares psychology with other "modern methods" such as homiletics, education, and medicine.[30] Yet the two greatest preachers who ever lived, Jesus and Paul, had nothing to learn from modern homiletical techniques; modern education can hardly boast of its successes over the older systems; and medicine deals with physical conditions rather than the spiritual matters invaded by psychologists.

The writer cites "stress management" and "coping methods" as examples of psychological techniques unknown to man before the development of psychology. The Bible, however, dealt with those issues centuries before Wilhelm Wundt, William James, or Sigmund Freud came on the scene. The Scriptures offer many solutions for stress in passages such as Matthew 6:25-33, Philippians 4:4-9, and 1 Peter 5:7. Rather than telling us to learn how to cope, the Bible tells us to walk by faith (2 Corinthians 5:7) because we have a trustworthy God (Psalm 118:8; Proverbs 3:5; Isaiah 26:4) who loves us (Psalm 32:10) and will give us inner peace (Isaiah 26:3). We are told that if we are in darkness we should "trust in the name of the LORD" (Isaiah 50:10), but we are not told to seek psychological insights.

I take issue with a representative integrationist summary: "I doubt that Jesus or Paul would be likely to throw away psychology—as some contemporary Christians might hope. As a formal discipline, psychology was not available in Bible times; but it is available now and can be used by believers, with thanksgiving."[31]

On the contrary, psychotherapy *was* available in Bible times. As Thomas Szasz writes:

> In the history of the cure of souls, no less than in the history of civilization itself, Jesus Christ occupies a unique place. Indeed, in the Continental Reformation, He is represented first and foremost as a physician of the soul....
>
> Jesus' role as psychotherapist is important on several counts, not the least among them being His disagreements with the established practices of the then officially recognized physicians of the soul, that is, the rabbis.... Jesus not only departed from established practices of soul-healing, He also castigated and condemned the counseling establishment itself in the strongest terms....
>
> Jesus' role as reformer could not be clearer. Similarly, He might now warn people to beware

of psychiatrists who like to go about in the
white coat of doctors, and to receive government grants and the best seats in the theater.[32]

A Substitute for the Holy Spirit

One of the dangers of the integrationist approach is that
it substitutes psychological techniques for the work of the
Holy Spirit. Collins reports that—

> a respected Christian psychologist . . . argued
> that the fruit of the Spirit . . . could all be
> produced by psychological techniques alone.
> There was no need to wait for the Holy Spirit to
> develop these. . . . They could all be duplicated
> by any competent psychologist . . . in his opin-
> ion, spiritual maturity and psychological health
> are really the same thing. They can be pro-
> duced either psychologically or spiritually.[33]

That Christian psychologist speaks for many of the
Christian psychological establishment who believe that
there is little actual difference between the theories, goals,
and results of psychotherapy and the gospel of Christ.
According to them, both systems seek happiness, fulfill-
ment, relief from suffering, self-esteem, meaning, and
purpose for their followers. Note that the "respected Christian psychologist" did not even require that the therapist be
a Christian—only competent.

Many Christian writers accept the idea that Christian
maturity is somehow dependent upon psychological methods. A psychiatrist writes in *The Christian's Handbook of
Psychiatry*, "We assume that because we are now possessed
by the Holy Spirit somehow this magically protects us from
psychological or emotional problems. In fact, however, this
is no more the case than that being a Christian protects us
from getting mumps or measles."[34]

Yet just a few pages further the author says, "[The true
Christian's] belief in the divine inspiration of Scripture helps
him to become 'perfectly fit and thoroughly equipped for

every good enterprise' (2 Timothy 3:17 Williams)....
Christian moral character and mental health are mani-
fested by these graces and are made possible in the believer
because of his vital union with Christ."[35]

Which *is* the author's real position? Does the Christian
have no more protection from mental and emotional woes
than from catching the mumps? Or is mental health made
possible by a vital union with Christ? His confusion stems
from trying to mix two opposing systems.

Other Christian psychologists make the same dangerous error. Crabb believes that one cannot become
mentally and spiritually mature until he digs back into the
past, exposes his unconscious drives, and embraces his
hurts.[36] Schuller teaches that the Christian cannot experience mental health or Christian maturity until he learns to
love himself.[37] Allender insists on the need to reclaim sub-
merged memories.[38] Minirth says that one must deal with
his defense mechanisms on the subconscious level.[39] Narramore believes that it is a medical responsibility to determine if someone is mentally ill[40] and that "counseling
with the emotionally and mentally ill is of special psychological and psychiatric concern."[41]

Carter writes in an essay about Christian therapy entitled "Maturity" that "many non-Christians show varying
degrees of behavior and attitudes similar to the fruit of
the Spirit," and that "an individual may develop his humanity (the God-given divine image) by utilizing the principles of psychology and mental health, with or without
the aid of a therapist, to become a more mature, healthy,
self-actualized person."[42]

Where does God or His Word fit into this model? Psychology offers a system that replaces the role of God and
the Scriptures in producing real change.

The Struggle to Define Mental Health

In one form or another, most psychologists tend to
define mental health in terms of the highest characteristics
of human functioning. They use different descriptions,

such as "healthy personality," "maturity," "self-actualized personality," "transcendent personality," and "authentic personality."

At the same time, psychological "experts" vary on the number of characteristics that a mature personality will exhibit. Rogers lists ten essential traits; Maslow contends that there are fourteen characteristics.[43] The Menninger Foundation has developed a table of seven criteria of emotional maturity.[44] Allport cuts the list to six.[45] J.D. Carter condenses the necessary attributes to five: "(1) having a realistic view of oneself and others; (2) accepting oneself and others; (3) living in the present but having long-range goals; (4) having values; (5) developing one's abilities and interests and coping with the task of living."[46] Another writer boosts the essentials back to ten.[47] Yet the truth is that these respected psychologists have not added any knowledge by their new labels and categories. To the contrary, the more they categorize, the more confused and confusing they become.

Psychology has found it nearly impossible to define mental health. If it is relatively good adjustment, then relative to what? If mental health consists of "feelings of well-being," does that include criminals who feel good about themselves? If one does not fulfill his "expected role" in his society or group, does that mean that he is mentally unhealthy? By that definition, Jesus surely was as insane as his brothers diagnosed when "they went to take charge of him, for they said, 'He is out of his mind'" (Mark 3:21).

The question is, *Who* are we going to trust for a proper definition of mental health? Psychologists or the Bible? The right to define mental health immediately places great power in the hands of the definer. The practical implications of this power may not be immediately apparent to a casual observer, but the dangers are incalculable. For example, children are being removed from their parents on the basis of the psychological opinions of social workers. Sincere religious parents are being charged with child abuse for exercising their faith. As Thomas Szasz has noted,

"Classifying human acts and actors is political, because the classification will inevitably help some persons and harm others."[48]

Torrey warns about the inherent dangers of the psycho-pathological model of mental health when he writes:

> Certainly the most serious criticism which can be leveled at preventive psychiatry is that it leads logically to psychiatric fascism. If the problems referred to ... are all really mental "diseases," then psychiatrists should be given increasing amounts of power so that these "diseases" can be "cured." Eventually they would be given control over almost every phase of human life and it would all be justified by the medical model.[49]

Torrey relates a chilling statement from G. Brock Chisholm, who once directed the United Nations' World Health Organization and was President of the World Federation for Mental Health: "If the race is to be freed from its crippling burden of good and evil, it must be psychiatrists who take the original responsibility.... With the other human sciences, psychiatry must now decide what is to be the immediate future of the human race. No one else can. And this is the prime responsibility of psychiatry."[50]

Psychiatrists like Chisholm are going to decide the future of the human race? It may not bother integrationists that the psychological society wants to determine the course of humanity, but it bothers me immensely.

Psychiatrists' self-proclaimed "original responsibility" to free the human race exhibits not only delusions of grandeur, but misidentification with deity.

An Untrustworthy Understanding of Spiritual Maturity

Just as general mental health is impossible to define, so integrationists believe that there is no "universally accepted" definition of Christian maturity and therefore

Christian maturity and mental health do not necessarily go hand in hand. One Christian psychologist says, "It may be possible for believers to mature spiritually and remain psychologically unhealthy, but this seems rare and unlikely."[51]

I agree that one cannot equate spiritual maturity with psychological health, nor would I want to. Psychological definitions of mental health are subjective interpretations of thought and behavior patterns by the unregenerate standards of unbelieving men.

God has given us *His* standard of normalcy in Jesus Christ (Ephesians 4:13-16). He has listed the inner characteristics that humans must develop to be truly mature: "love, joy, peace, patience, kindness, goodness, faithfulness, gentleness and self-control" (Galatians 5:22,23). He has told us the three-step method of therapy that will change a person: "Put off your old self . . . be made new in the attitude of your minds . . . put on the new self created to be like God in true righteousness and holiness" (Ephesians 4:22-25).

I am not arguing that all unbelievers are to be categorized as "mentally ill," since I question that very term. Furthermore, not even Christians can be accurately classified as spiritually mature, since we all fall short of God's standards (Romans 3:10,23). Instead, we need to understand that Christians are in the process of being conformed to the image of Christ (Romans 8:29) and that even though we fail in many ways, we can be confident that "he who began a good work in [us] will carry it on to completion until the day of Christ Jesus" (Philippians 1:6).

Complete Christian maturity cannot be achieved in this life, yet we recognize that there are those who have spiritually matured beyond the average Christian. Christians who are walking in the Spirit (Galatians 5:16), in obedience to God's eternal laws (Mark 12:28-31; Galatians 5:14), according to the principles of His Word (2 Timothy 3:16,17; 2 Peter 1:3), will produce the fruit of the Spirit (Galatians 5:22,23) and will exhibit the characteristics commonly described as mental health.

■ ■ ■

As Cliff Chase continued to wrestle with the biggest philosophical question of his ministry, his preaching began to suffer. He would catch himself doubting Bible verses as he prepared his sermons. He was amazed at how omnipresent psychological concepts were in everyday life. He couldn't pick up a newspaper or magazine without finding a reference to the latest psychological discovery. Psychologists frequently appeared on news programs as expert consultants on everything from sexual dysfunctions to child-rearing to spiritual experiences.

One morning, as he sat on the back porch reading his Bible and praying, another doubt flooded his heart. *What if all of this religion stuff is a hoax? What if there really is no God?* He couldn't believe he was even thinking such thoughts, yet there they were.

A few days later, as Cliff was sorting papers at the church office, Walter Harrison stopped by. "Hi, Pastor," Walt said nervously. "Do you have a few minutes to spare?"

"For you, Walter, I have all the time in the world," Cliff responded with a smile. Walter was one of Cliff's favorite parishioners, perhaps because Cliff had personally led him to the Lord soon after arriving at Evangelical Bible Church. Walt had come from a hard background scarred by alcohol and abuse. Cliff remembered the glorious changes that had taken place in Walt's life as he learned more and more about the Christian walk. Everything about him had changed—his language, his habits, his marriage, even his face. He seemed to radiate a glow of enthusiastic joy wherever he went. Not today, though.

They went into Cliff's office and shut the door. "What's the problem, Walt? You look absolutely exhausted."

"I am, Cliff. I've hardly slept all week."

"Well, what's going on?"

Walt looked down at the floor for a few moments and then spoke quietly. "I don't really know where to start." Tears welled up in his eyes and he wiped them away, ashamed. Finally he spoke again. "Ellen and I have been having trouble lately."

"What kind of trouble, Walt?" Cliff asked gently.

"Well, it started out sorta strange," Walt said in a raspy voice. "A few months ago, Ellen stopped by the Christian bookstore to look for a birthday present for me. She ended up buying a book for herself on healing the past. Ever since then, we've had nothing but problems."

"What kind of problems?"

"Every kind! I mean, she won't let me touch her, she yells at me, says I'm insensitive to her needs and if I only understood how wounded her heart is, I'd be a lot better husband." He paused, shaking his head in frustration. "Now she's going to a psychologist for counseling to help her resolve all the pain from her past."

"Is there a major problem in her past?" Cliff asked.

"Well, when we first started going together, she told me her dad had been really bad to her. I found out later that he had abused her for years when she was a child."

"What kind of abuse was it?" Cliff asked, already knowing.

Walter swallowed hard. "He raped her. Since she told me, I've tried really hard to be careful with her, you know, not demanding sex all the time and stuff like that."

Cliff nodded, "Go on."

"Our first five or ten years were pretty rough. We almost divorced twice. I started hitting the bottle pretty hard. You knew that. But when we came to Christ, our whole world changed. I felt so clean, and for the first time in my life I understood what it meant to be loved and how to love others. Ellen felt the same way. Our marriage turned around and we felt we had found heaven on earth."

Cliff smiled. "I remember the changes, too."

"Well, Preacher, everything has gone downhill these last few months."

"Tell me how it happened, Walt."

Walt leaned back in the chair and took a deep breath. "Ellen went back East to visit her sister, Carol. She was abused by their dad, too. She had been seeing a psychologist who specializes in sexual abuse, and he taught her that to be healed of all her inner pain, she had to go back into her past and reclaim it. I don't understand it, Cliff. She went out there happy but came back full of anger. I mean, if going back into her past was supposed to heal her, it sure failed."

"How has she acted toward you?" Cliff asked.

"It's like she thinks *I'm* the one who abused her! She's even called me a 'surrogate abuser' and told me she doesn't think I understand her pain at all. Look, Cliff, I had a pretty sorry childhood too. My dad was an alcoholic and used to beat me pretty bad. I know what pain is. I know what abuse is. And I've never abused Ellen in any way!"

"What have you done to try to solve the problem?"

"I asked her to come talk with you. I said I'd come too, but she said you weren't an expert in sexual abuse and you'd only give her some Bible verses to read."

Cliff's mouth got dry and he sighed wearily. "Is the psychologist she's seeing a Christian?"

"Yeah. She called the office here and your secretary gave her the name of a psychologist, a Dr. West. She started seeing him a couple of months ago. Goodness, Cliff! It's costing us a fortune! He charges $90 a session and that's for less than an hour. He makes her come once a week. I don't have an extra 360 bucks to throw around each month," Walt said glumly. "You've probably noticed that our giving has gone down."

"No, I don't know what our people give," Cliff said, shaking his head. "But, in view of what you're paying, I imagine you've seen some improvements in Ellen. Has she gotten better since going to Dr. West?"

"Not really. In fact, she seems madder now than ever. She says she can hardly stand to look at a man, let alone have one touch her. I tell you, Cliff, I don't know how much more of this I can stand!" Walt leaned forward and held his head like he had a pounding headache. "What should I do?"

Cliff had dreaded this moment. *O Lord, give me an answer!* he prayed silently. But nothing came to mind. He opened his mouth to speak, but then stopped. He licked his lips as his eyes darted from book to book on his shelves, seeking a quick suggestion. Still nothing.

Walt lifted his head and looked Cliff in the eye. "Cliff, what would the Lord have me do?"

Cliff looked at his Bible longingly. A few weeks ago he would have opened it eagerly to point out some of his favorite passages. But now those verses seemed so simplistic. He knew he needed the insights of psychology for guidance in moments just like these. He shrugged his shoulders helplessly as he said, "I don't know, Walt. I simply don't know. I guess my best advice is to listen to what Dr. West has to say and to try to help Ellen deal with her past as gently as you can."

The Psychological Counselor

Through the use of imagination, the counselee endeavors to recreate the painful memory and actually visualize it as it once took place. . . . A child or teenager might ask God to heal her of a terrifying or damaging experience that has emotionally crippled her.

The Biblical Counselor

Often, returning to past suffering, failure, and pain can reignite the hatred and bitterness that God has already dealt with and reopen the wounds that Christ has already healed.

The Word of God

Forgetting what is behind and straining toward what is ahead, I press on toward the goal.
—Philippians 3:13,14

7

The Myth
That Psychology
Can Heal the Past

According to widely accepted psychological theory, humans are captives of their past. Many Christian writers use the term "adult children" to describe people who were damaged in their youth by divorce or emotional or physical abuse. They generally believe that we must return to the past in order to experience healing in the present. One Christian psychologist says, "We are as much our past as we are our present and our hopes for the future. To cut off the past is to erase part of our story, our journey, our self. The reclamation of the past involves the courage to be all that we are so that we can be all that we will be in our relationships to others."[1] He lists three purposes for the journey into the past: "removal of the denial, reclamation of the self, and movement toward real change."[2]

While I agree that we should not deny the facts of the past, I find no scriptural command to return to it or to reclaim one's self in order to accomplish real change in the present. Instead, I find the command to *deny* ourselves and to take up our cross daily to follow Christ (Mark 8:34,35).

Another prominent Christian psychologist concurs with the current psychological concept of "the inner child."

153

In order to heal this inner being, he suggests that you "use your memories as the key to understanding your past and the influence your inner child has had on your emotions and reactions as an adult."[3] He recommends the use of your imagination to free you from your past.[4]

Inner Healing and Imagination

Collins points out some of the legitimate concerns believers have with occult practices that often appear in the garb of psychology: "biorhythms, reincarnation, astrology, ESP, Eastern meditation, altered states of consciousness" and more.[5] As a result, he says—

> some writers have condemned visualization, self-talk, the healing of memories and other frequently used therapeutic methods. These have been labeled "occultist," and even their Christian advocates are described as misguided and deceived. These are serious allegations. If they are true, then psychology is indeed a more dangerous force than most people suspect.[6]

To integrationists, "visualization, imagination and guided imagery are related words that describe the use of mental pictures to bring increased understanding, relation or self-confidence."[7] For example, visualization takes place when an athlete mentally reviews each move he is about to make or when a speaker imagines the positive reaction his audience will give him. It sounds innocent enough. So what's the problem?

Dave Hunt writes in *The Seduction of Christianity*:

> So in the name of the latest psychology we are being led back into primitive paganism/ shamanism, which then enters the church because psychology is embraced as scientific and neutral. Tragically, this is often done by sincere Christian leaders who imagine that they are bringing a revival to the church.[8]

Is Hunt overreacting? I don't think so. A book entitled *Self-Talk, Imagery, and Prayer in Counseling* makes several observations about how the mind processes thoughts with images. I agree with some of the statements about the effect of one's thought life upon behavior and emotions. For instance, the author says:

> In this type of counseling, we encourage the individual to engage in self-observation, to become sensitive to what he or she is saying inwardly. Scripture teaches this. "Search me, O God, and know my heart! Try me and know my thoughts! And see if there be any wicked way in me, and lead me in the way everlasting!" (Psalm 139:23,24).[9]

I do not disagree with the writer's conclusions about the importance of the thought life. Note, however, that the passage he quotes asks *God* to search the heart. *Self*-observation can lead to self-*deception* unless done under the intense spotlight of the Scripture. This is because man's nature is so wicked that "every inclination of the thoughts of his heart was only evil all the time" (Genesis 6:5). We are warned that "the sinful mind is hostile to God. It does not submit to God's law, nor can it do so" (Romans 8:7). Paul warned the Colossians that an "unspiritual mind puffs [a person] up with idle notions" (Colossians 2:18). He told Titus that "the minds and consciences" of impure people "are corrupted" (Titus 1:15).

The author of *Self-Talk* explains his concept of the healing of memories:

> Through the use of imagination, the counselee endeavors to recreate the painful memory and actually visualize it as it once took place. Then he prays, asking God for the kind of help he needed in that situation. A child or teenager might ask God to heal her of a terrifying or damaging experience that has emotionally crippled her.

In our minds we can walk back in time with Christ in order to minister to the hurting person. This does not change the event that occurred, but God can release the hurt and the damage.[10]

An Unproven Theory

There are at least three weaknesses with the increasingly popular healing-of-memories theory. First, the theory itself is unproven. Not only is there no solid scientific evidence that mentally repeating an event aids in healing, but there is also no scriptural warrant for the practice. Instead of looking backward in time, we are encouraged to look *forward*. Paul said, "One thing I do: Forgetting what is behind and straining toward what is ahead, I press on toward the goal" (Philippians 3:13). I am not implying that memories must be repressed, but grace, forgiveness, and the power of God are sufficient to heal memories without deliberately ripping old scars open.

Often, returning to past suffering, failure, and pain can reignite the hatred and bitterness that God has already dealt with and can reopen the wounds that Christ has already healed. One woman told me that she went to a supposedly Christian counselor who insisted that she return to her past for healing. Instead of experiencing freedom and joy, she felt violated and defiled. "Pastor," she said, "at the end of the counseling, I felt so dirty all over again. Does a person really have to go through all of her pain over and over?" Her forehead was creased with anxiety and concern. When I shared some biblical concepts of God's forgiveness and healing, peace began to appear in her face once again.

Inaccurate and Selective Memories

A second weakness to the healing-of-memories theory is the fact that memories are inaccurate and selective. Psychologists and psychiatrists who lead their clients back into the past can actually create memories of events that never took place. Memories can become distorted with time so that the recollection of an event may bear only a hazy resemblance to reality.

Growing Doubts About the Accuracy of Memories

One of a series of articles by journalist Bill Scanlon was headlined "Incompetent Therapists Are Turning Patients' Fantasies into Repressed Reality, Some Experts Are Saying." The article questions the validity of delving back into the past for repressed memories. "Increasingly...a vocal number of psychologists and researchers question whether repressed memories are memories at all. Instead, some experts believe, they often are fantasies coming from overactive imaginations fired by incompetent therapists."[11]

The potential harm is incalculable. "Twenty-eight percent of the cases of reported incest are based on repressed memory, according to a survey by the Kempe National Center for the Prevention and Treatment of Substance Abuse. Elizabeth Loftus, a psychologist and memory expert at the University of Washington, says there is no way of knowing how many of those accusations are true."[12] Who knows how many innocent people are accused of abuse on the basis of questionable memories? It seems that there are many. "It's very painful, these stories I hear," Loftus said. "Everywhere I go, it's amazing. I'll give a talk about memories, and two or three people independently will come up to me and tell me a story about someone in their family who thinks they've been wrongly accused—a repressed-memory story."[13]

How are suppressed memories resurrected? "The commonality seems to be the therapist, not the person. They go to therapists who believe that a huge amount of women have been sexually abused and a lot of them don't remember it."[14] According to Scanlon's article, therapists often suggest the existence of hidden memories: "The line of questioning goes this way, Wakefield said: 'Have you ever been abused? No. Are you sure? Let's talk about it, let's explore it . . . maybe you were. Let's help you get the memories back.'"[15] The theory is, if you can't remember any specific sexual abuse, but have a vague feeling or suspicion that it might have happened, it probably did.

The media and publishing industries have helped to foster the concept of repressed memories. According to the article, one can find more than 200 books on incest, recovery, and repressed memories at The Tattered Cover Bookstore in Denver. Incest-recovery books are hot sellers, but their scientific reliability is doubtful.

"'It's probably possible you can repress something,' Loftus said. 'But whether whatever comes back 20 or 30 years later is an authentic version of reality—there is no proof of that.' Memories, she believes, are unreliable."[16]

Dr. Martin Orne, a psychiatrist at the Institute of Pennsylvania Hospital, also disputes the concept that painful memories are frequently repressed:

> "Typically, memories of horrible things are not forgotten," Orne said. "People who were in concentration camps, who were treated horribly and saw people die before them—they know exactly what happened."
>
> Orne and the other skeptics say there is a crucial difference between people who have always remembered the abuse they suffered as children and those who "remember" it decades later, usually after reading a book or going to a therapist.[17]

Others share Orne's skepticism:

> The idea that the brain can store traumatic memories, then produce them in exquisite detail in a flashback, is simply wrong, argues Dr. George K. Ganaway of the Ridgeview Center for Dissociative Disorders in Atlanta.
>
> "Reconstructed memories may incorporate fantasy, distortion, displacement, condensation,

symbolism, and other mental mechanisms," Ganaway said. "Their sum factual reliability is highly questionable."[18]

The article reports the story of a woman who was convinced by a therapist that she had been abused by her father:

> It took a prying therapist, bizarre psychological techniques and several types of medication to convince her that her father, her mother and her grandfather sexually abused her, too.
>
> Today, after three years of therapy hell, Lynn believes she was abused by a hysteria run amok, not by her parents.[19]

Many therapists have come to believe that virtually everyone is a victim of sexual abuse, and the lack of memories is cited as proof. Sometimes, however, the abuse is perpetrated by incompetent therapists.

> The therapists kept working on her memories, [Lynn] said. "The therapist insinuated and interpreted more to my relationship with my father than I remembered."
>
> She recalled to her therapist that she walked in once on her mother and father making love. And she felt bad about it.
>
> "My therapist's theory was that I felt bad because I'd caught my lover with another woman."
>
> On Dec. 3, 1986, she wrote a letter to her parents, accusing her father of abuse.
>
> "After I got away from therapy, my memories began coming back to me," she said. "Within six months, I knew my dad did not abuse me, nor my mother or grandfather."
>
> Happily, "My dad never held me accountable for those accusations. He accepted me back wholeheartedly."[20]

Christian Therapy Embraces the Healing of Memories

The theory of repressed memories has even infiltrated Bible-believing churches. A woman's tragic personal testimony of "repressed memories" was published in the magazine of a large metropolitan church in the Chicago area. It was full of psychological descriptions relating her inner battle between her "conscious mind and [her] unconscious mind." She confessed to having "repressed memories of sexual abuse," but as her "flashbacks came more frequently, [she] began to lose hold of what was real." She was finally committed to a mental hospital, where, she said, "I lost hold of the reality of God."

She said she tried to imagine where Jesus had been during the time of her abuse, and the image she conjured up was this: "I saw Him standing in a darkened corner. He was watching [as she was abused]. His face was expressionless. His hands were in His pockets and He was leaning against the wall," in seeming unconcern. The image devastated her, and she lived with that imagination for two years.

During that time, she said, "I didn't want anything to do with the Bible," and, though she continued attending church, she did not find peace. "I was afraid of being stuck in the corner forever—the little child inside me needed for Christ to move. If the little child's hope died, all of her childlike ways would perish—her spontaneity, her joy, her undying trust toward God and life. And I would be left an empty shell."

So she continued imagining Christ in His corner until she imagined Him reaching out to her and saying, "Come and let Me hold you." Instead of finding relief, "a new wave of memories" hit her, this time involving satanic ritual abuse. Then she imagined Jesus saying to her, "Imagine being on a warm beach playing in the sand...imagine being the princess of the sand castle...imagine a warm tender creature...."

She saw her defense mechanism as a gift from God to help her survive. "I went to the beach in my mind. I got away from the horror and covered the horrendous with the beach and a flying creature. And I forgot. I had found a safe place. Christ had demonstrated His love." In spite of His love, she admitted, "I still don't fully trust Him."

Her source of comfort was to return to her "safe place. He takes me there on His wings. He comes by my side and strokes my hair. He whispers to me ways in which to survive, and even thrive, no matter what happens."[21]

Do you see a problem with this woman's testimony and therapy? Nowhere in the article is it even hinted that she found Christ as He is represented in the Scriptures. Instead, she sought comfort in imaginations that in no way resembled Jesus. Is it any wonder that she still finds it difficult to trust in God?

Before publishing the above example, I contacted the church that had presented her story to see whether the article accurately reflected the position of the church.

I received a two-page response to my inquiry that only increased my concern. The unsigned paper, titled "Some Additional Thoughts on 'Borne on His Wings,'" said that "someone with an abusive past will inevitably have a distorted view of God...." It pointed out that the woman in question was "not...uninformed or biblically illiterate, but...a mature believer revisiting a deep, unresolved wound...."

The response stated that such psychic wounds, "like a physical wound, won't necessarily go away with new information. More than truth is often needed to heal such a person because more happened to her than being misinformed."

Then the letter states a commonly believed assumption of psychology: "Sometimes, like a physical infection, our emotional wound has been 'covered over' without adequately healing, and must be reopened. The wound may require 'lancing' to heal."

I do not question the sincerity of the therapists who worked with this woman. But the letter they sent powerfully illustrates my concerns. Psychologically driven systems consider it "inevitable" that those who have experienced abuse will have a distorted view of God. But the truth is that left to ourselves *all* humans have a distorted view of God.

The solution is found in His supernatural revelation about Himself, not in psychotherapy.

The letter states that healing often requires more than truth, pointing out that the woman was not biblically illiterate, but was a "mature believer." The respondent seems unaware that being biblically literate is no sign of spiritual maturity. *Obedience* to the Word is the point. The Bible isn't just "new information." It is God's own revelation to man about our woeful condition and how He can transform our hearts. It is not a matter of merely hearing the truth, but *following* it (James 1:22-25).

Why does God tell us to leave the past behind (Philippians 3:13,14) if it is necessary to revisit, reopen, and resolve a wound by "lancing" it? And *how* does one "lance" a psychic wound? For many therapists, this psychological metaphor has become an actual goal so politically correct that few question its scientific or biblical validity.

A more powerful method of healing inner wounds is to apply the two-edged sword of God's Word, which penetrates so deeply that it reveals the thoughts and intents of the heart itself (Hebrews 4:12).

The Danger of False Memories

In a column titled "Don't Always Believe the Children," Nat Hentoff reported a tragic result that shows just how twisted psychological thinking can become. Hentoff relates a 1992 *CBS News* report that a father was accused of raping and sodomizing his eight-year-old daughter, even though she had told police that a stranger had climbed through her bedroom window and attacked her. "'Her description of the intruder,' said the CBS report, 'closely resembled a convicted serial rapist. A footprint his size was found nearby. But Wade, her father—a Navy petty officer with a drinking problem—was at home when the attack took place. And the authorities immediately suspected him.'"

Hentoff writes, "Having been accused, Jim Wade was presumed guilty. Alicia was taken from her parents and assigned to foster homes and to a county therapist who, after 13 months of treatment finally heard the child say that her daddy did it."

The problem was that the father was innocent, and was exonerated by incontrovertible evidence that had been ignored for more than two years. A member of the grand jury said, "The therapist kept telling the child she'd feel better if she'd just say, 'Daddy did it.' I think the therapist was so convinced the father did it, she never listened to the child." A family was broken up and the eight-year-old girl was separated from her parents for 2½ years because a therapist had convinced a grand jury that the father was guilty.

Hentoff concludes, "In New Jersey and North Carolina, among other places... there are people serving very long prison sentences because therapists, prosecutors and juries would not listen to anyone but the children."[22]

I cite the articles above not to deny the existence of sexual abuse. It is happening with growing frequency, and the effects on the abused are devastating. But many of the reports are questionable and some are fabricated, and the effects on those who are falsely accused are devastating.

Secular Indictments of Christian Memory Therapies

Even in the cases of genuine abuse there is simply no evidence that mentally revisiting one's past abuse produces inner healing. There is no value in forcing a woman to relive the incestuous attacks of a drunken father in order to forgive him, and the therapeutic technique of imagining does not produce the inner healing so desperately desired. "Embracing one's pain" increases the agony and prolongs the cycle of despair. It does not heal the wounded heart.

The problem of therapy-induced memories has grown to ridiculous proportions. It has become so widespread that family members "who believe someone has falsely accused them or another relative of incest, pornography or even the worst of the worst, ritual sexual abuse that includes satanic or occult activity," have formed an organization called the False Memory Syndrome Foundation.[23] It is a stain on the evangelical Christian community when secular newspapers report accusations that false memory syndrome "sufferers are victims of their therapists, particularly Christian counselors who plant these ideas of past abuse in their heads."[24]

The same suburban paper related a story about "Jane," a woman whose family had been damaged by false accusations. She said that her sister "was unwilling to take responsibility for her own problem, in this case, her weight; counseling became a crutch; the charge of sexual abuse came at the suggestion of the therapist." Eventually the accusing woman was put into group therapy, and finally into a hospital psychiatric ward. There, it seems, the woman was convinced that she had also experienced satanic abuse. Jane said, "I personally believe when you open your mind up to things other than the Lord, that gives Satan an open playground to open your mind to evil powers."

Jane explains why people seem to respond to the victimization concept: "It's a nice way out.... In this generation of not wanting to take the blame, this is really convenient. And not only does the therapist have a solution, but a lifetime client at $125 an hour.... The whole thing is nuts. It's tragic. I think these counselors should be punished."[25] Though the newspaper did not endorse Jane's sensible explanation for her sister's behavior, it is amazing that *secular* publications are blowing the whistle on questionable *Christian* therapy, while *Christian* magazines are propagating this insidious doctrine!

Misplaced Focus

A third weakness of the healing-of-memories theory is that the focus is placed upon the counselee, his suffering, and his past instead of on the God of healing, His power, and our glorious future in Christ. You will not find this emphasis on the self in the Scriptures, but it certainly is found in psychological systems:

> Conventional psychiatry holds that an essential part of treatment is probing into the patient's past life—searching for the psychological roots of his problem because once the patient clearly understands these roots he can use his understanding to change his attitude toward life.... [Standard theory believes] if a

patient is to change he must gain understanding and insight into his unconscious mind.[26]

Though the concept of memory is mentioned more
than 200 times in the Bible, I have found none connected to
the healing of memories. The term *imagine* or *imagination*
is found some 40 times in the Bible, yet none of these relates
to the healing of memories. Instead, the Scriptures encourage people to remember God, His powerful deeds, and His
righteous attributes. Consider passages such as Psalm
78:35: "They remembered that God was their Rock, that
God Most High was their Redeemer"; Psalm 78:42: "They
did not remember his power—the day he redeemed them
from the oppressor"; and Psalm 143:5: "I remember the
days of long ago; I meditate on all your works and consider
what your hands have done."

David pleads with God *not* to remember his past: "Remember not the sins of my youth and my rebellious ways;
according to your love remember me, for you are good, O
LORD" (Psalm 25:7). One verse that may refer to psychic
distress is Psalm 42:6: "My soul is downcast within me;
therefore I will remember you." Even here, the healing
involved remembering *God*, not experiences of the painful
past.

Why then do psychologists insist that their patients
return to their past? Psychological interpretation of memories is based on the concept that repressed memories damage the psyche. As one Christian psychologist writes:

The reason [memories] hurt is because
they tend to be mostly buried and emerge only
when they choose. The more painful these
memories are, the more hidden and repressed
they become. They hide, as it were, in a corner
of the deepest cavern of our minds. Because
they are hidden, they escape healing.

What do you do with a painful memory?
You may try to forget it, or you may act as
though it did not occur. Trying to forget the

pains of the past gives these memories power and control over your life. . . .

How does healing occur? By facing your memories, remembering them, letting them out of their closet. Henri Nouwen said, "What is forgotten is unavailable and what is unavailable cannot be healed."[27]

Where is the scriptural support for this theory? It does not sound all that different from Freud's concept of the unconscious.

The Concept of the Unconscious

In Freud's twisted system, the mind is comprised of three distinct areas: the conscious (thoughts, concepts, and ideas a person is aware of), the preconscious (ideas that are not in the forefront of one's mind but can easily be drawn out by an act of the will), and the unconscious (ideas a person cannot be aware of due to repression). Carl Jung expanded the concept of the unconscious to include not only one's own past but also one's collective ancestral past. Is Freud's theory of the unconscious a scientifically proven fact? No, but it is a sociological belief so deeply ingrained in our culture that society accepts the concept without question.

Most integrationists teach it as truth. Christian counseling books are deeply colored with this theory, and the general Christian public accepts it as though it were scripturally based. Prosperity prophets take us a step further and equate imagination and the unconscious with faith itself. The pastor of the world's largest church writes in *Solving Life's Problems*, "Many suffer because of a negative way of thinking. . . . God works through the imagination. As long as one allows these negative thoughts to be dominant, God himself is blocked from helping that person, for imagination is even stronger than will power in controlling a person."[28]

Dealing with Memories Biblically

I am not taking issue with the statement that negative thinking can cause suffering. The biblical contrast to negative thinking, however, is not "fourth-dimension thinking," or "positive thinking," or "possibility thinking." The opposite of negative (carnal) thinking is Philippians 4 thinking:

> Rejoice in the Lord always. I will say it again: Rejoice! Let your gentleness be evident to all. The Lord is near. Do not be anxious about anything, but in everything, by prayer and petition, with thanksgiving, present your requests to God. And the peace of God, which transcends all understanding, will guard your hearts and your minds in Christ Jesus. Finally, brothers, whatever is true, whatever is noble, whatever is right, whatever is pure, whatever is lovely, whatever is admirable—if anything is excellent or praiseworthy—think about such things. Whatever you have learned or received or heard from me, or seen in me—put it into practice. And the God of peace will be with you (Philippians 4:4-9).

For emphasis, I repeat this fact: The Bible does *not* encourage us to return to the past to experience our pain all over again. Instead, it says, "*Forgetting* what is behind and straining toward what is ahead, I press on toward the goal to win the prize for which God has called me heavenward in Christ Jesus" (Philippians 3:13,14; emphasis added).

■ ■ ■

John Kryer sat at his desk with the office door closed, reading the counseling information form and session notes for his 10:00 A.M. appointment. He sighed deeply and bowed his head in prayer. "Lord Jesus," he said out loud, "You know that I'm not capable of discerning the needs of the Harrisons without Your help. Ellen has been convinced that she is a captive to her past. Help me to show her that You took care of her past when she accepted You as Savior. Give me wisdom."

His secretary's voice came over the intercom. "Pastor, the Harrisons are here for their appointment."

"Send them in, Sarah."

Walter and Ellen Harrison walked into John's office nervously. John came around his desk with a smile and held out his hand in greeting. "Hello, Walt, Ellen. I'm John Kryer. Have a seat and we'll get started right away."

Walt and Ellen sat down without looking at each other. Anger was clearly evident in both their faces. Ellen sat as far from Walt as her chair allowed, with her arms crossed and her lips closed so tightly that white lines appeared around them. Walt's nostrils flared and his jaw muscles flexed as he strained to control his temper.

John returned to his place behind his desk and sat down. He looked at both of them with gentle sadness in his eyes. He opened the file folder which contained their counseling information forms, folded his hands across them, and said, "Let's pray together." Both Ellen and Walt looked at John for a moment and then bowed their heads slowly.

"Lord Jesus, we ask You to join us as we talk together. It is obvious, Lord, that Walt and Ellen are very angry with each other, and we know this grieves Your heart. Holy Spirit, please give us wisdom as we talk and show us the truths in Your holy Word that we can apply to this situation. I pray this, loving Father, in the name of Your Son, Jesus. Amen."

He looked up at them with a warm smile. "I see from your counseling information forms that you attend Evangelical Bible Church, where Cliff Chase is the pastor." They nodded but didn't say anything. "Is there some reason you aren't counseling with him?"

"I went to see Cliff," Walt answered, "but he didn't know what to tell me. I sure don't intend to go see that psychologist of Ellen's!"

"Oh?" John looked over his reading glasses at Walt. Turning to Ellen he asked, "Are you currently seeing a psychologist?"

"Yes, I am!" she said almost defiantly, daring John to challenge her decision.

"I see," John said as he leaned back in his chair. "Do you think you've been helped by the counsel you've received so far?"

"I certainly do! I understand myself much better now that I realize I'm a victim with a wounded heart. All these years I've blamed myself, but no more!" she asserted with a tight smile.

Looking back to the counseling forms, John said, "I didn't see any notation here about your being under psychological counsel."

Raising her eyebrows, Ellen replied curtly, "I didn't see how that was any of your business."

John took his reading glasses off, and looked Ellen squarely in the eyes. "Look, Ellen, if I'm going to be of any help, I need all the information I can get. I can't read your mind and God doesn't reveal secret information to me miraculously. Another thing: I didn't ask you and Walt to come see me. *You* folks called *me*, and I don't expect you to answer me in a rude fashion when we talk. Is that understood?"

Ellen blinked in surprise. She wasn't used to being challenged so directly. "Well . . . I . . . I'm sorry," she finally said. "It's just that I'm tired of being blamed for all the problems in our marriage. I didn't want to come here, but Walt absolutely insisted, so here we are."

Turning to Walt, John asked, "How did you happen to come here, Walt?"

"Pastor Chase suggested I call you. He said he didn't know what to tell us and that you do a lot of counseling. Ellen didn't want to come because she thinks pastors can't handle deep psychological problems like hers."

Ellen half-smiled apologetically, "No offense, Pastor Kryer. It's just that I've become aware in the last year or so that my problem isn't spiritual. It's psychological."

"Really?" John asked. "And how did you discover this fact?"

"I've been listening to a counseling program on the Christian radio station. Maybe you've heard of their clinic?"

John nodded. "Well, the doctors there are psychiatrists, and they believe that pastors are really helpful with many of the ordinary problems Christians face, but when it comes to deep psychological hurts, special training is required." She looked at the diplomas and certificates on John's wall behind him. "What kind of training *do* you have?"

"I got my undergraduate training at Iowa State University in biology, a Master of Divinity at Trinity Divinity School, and my Doctorate of Ministry in counseling from Westminster Seminary."

"Those are impressive degrees, but unless I'm mistaken, none of them are psychological in nature. Are you a licensed counselor?"

"I'm not licensed by the state as a counselor, Ellen, because I do not accept the foundational presuppositions of psychology. I'm licensed by the church to minister to the needs of believers. I have been trained as a biblical counselor. I believe that the Bible provides every essential truth the Christian needs to live a successful, joyful, and godly life. It would seem that you don't accept that position."

"I used to," Ellen replied firmly, "but I have come to realize how simplistic biblical counsel can be."

"Oh? And how much biblical counsel have you received?" John asked.

Ellen shifted in her chair uncomfortably. "Well, actually, I haven't gone to a biblical counselor as such. But I have read enough to know what happens in a lot of churches. One book says that counselors who don't use psychology in their counseling merely listen until they detect a sinful pattern of behavior and then pounce on it and tell people to conform to the Bible and all will be well."

"Hmm," John smiled and scratched his head. "If what you say is true, I can understand your reluctance to come in. Of course, there's no way for you to actually know whether that caricature is correct unless you try biblical counsel, is there?"

She shrugged her shoulders and replied, "I guess not."

"Before you make up your mind, let me ask you a few questions." He took the counseling forms again, looked at them, and said, "Walt, you had a full physical about six months ago. Was there any particular reason?"

"I was having headaches a lot. The doctor said it was probably job-related stress and gave me a painkiller."

"Mm-hmm. I see it listed here." Turning to Ellen, John said, "You didn't fill out the question about your last physical exam."

"I didn't see any purpose in it. What does a physical have to do with our problem? I've got a wounded heart, not a physical problem," Ellen said with irritation darkening her countenance. She squinted and blinked her eyes for a moment as if to clear her vision.

"Our mental and spiritual processes interact with our physical condition, Ellen," John replied. "Please don't take offense. It is a standard question and it is pertinent information. So, tell me, when was your last physical?"

Ellen glanced at Walt with resentment, as though to say, *See what you've gotten me into?* She looked back at John and with an angry sigh said, "I haven't had a full exam for more than two years. I still don't see any connection!"

"There may be no direct connection between your current feelings about your past and the damaged relationship between you and Walt," John conceded, "but before I begin making major recommendations for changes in behavior or thought patterns, I want to eliminate any possible physical factors."

"Would you know how to interpret the results of a physical?" Ellen asked with a hint of scorn.

"Actually, I have done a great deal of study on those very issues. I have a fairly extensive medical library. What I'm not able to decipher, I check with a medical colleague," John answered. He looked back at the form and said, "Now, as to the medications you are taking, are the prescriptions fairly current?"

"Yes," she replied.

"So you have been to a doctor in recent months?"

"Well, yes," Ellen said as she uncrossed her arms and leaned forward to watch as John wrote in his notes.

"I see that you're taking Adapin. When did you start taking it?"

"About three months ago, I think."

"What strength?"

"Twenty-five milligrams."

"Have you ever taken a tricyclic antidepressant before?"

"I don't think so," she answered.

"Have you ever had any problem associated with diabetes, epilepsy, glaucoma, heart disease, or thyroid?"

"Not that I know of."

John continued to write on the form. "Have you noticed any side effects since you started taking Adapin?"

"Like what?" Ellen asked.

"Drowsiness, blurred vision, dryness in your mouth, constipation."

"No, not really," Ellen said hesitantly.

Walt looked over at her and said, "Wait, Ellen. You've been complaining lately that you think you need glasses because things look blurry sometimes, and you're always needing a drink of water. Right?"

"Well, yeah," she admitted.

"And you told me that you've been itching a lot lately and that you feel dizzy sometimes," Walt continued.

"Have you felt more fatigued than normal?"

"Somewhat, I guess."

"Have you felt any increase in restlessness or agitation?"

Walt nodded as Ellen said, "Yes, but I don't think it's related to Adapin. I think it's because I am finally dealing with my inner sorrows instead of pretending they don't exist!"

"Your symptoms may not be related to Adapin at all, Ellen, but those are some of the common side effects of that particular drug. I wouldn't expect that many side effects on the dosage you're taking. Did your doctor schedule periodic exams to monitor your blood-cell count, liver function, and blood pressure?"

"No," she said, "why?"

"Because a patient on Adapin needs to be monitored in those areas. How about electrocardiograms? Have you had one recently?"

"No, should I have?" she asked with concern.

"It's recommended, and I certainly want you to discuss these matters with your doctor," John instructed as he looked up from his writing. "Let's move on through your counseling form." He skimmed through the education section and highlighted in yellow the fact that Ellen had a college degree while Walt had only completed the tenth grade.

Ellen noticed the yellow mark and asked, "What have you found now?"

"It may not be significant, Ellen, but I notice that you have a college degree. Has the fact that Walt stopped at the tenth grade had any negative effect on your relationship?"

"No. I couldn't care less about that," Ellen replied, almost defensively.

"Oh, come on, Ellen!" Walt disagreed. "You've needled me plenty of times about my lack of education! You've even suggested that my ignorance might be the reason I can't understand the need for psychological counseling."

"All I meant was that you haven't studied it, and you don't have a right to judge my decision!" she explained hotly.

John put another checkmark by that item and moved to the next page. "I see you only knew each other less than two months before you got married. Was there some reason you seem to have rushed into this marriage?"

"Ellen wanted to get away from her dad and I was the only way out right then," Walt said with some bitterness.

"That's not the only reason, Walt!" Ellen objected as she glared at him.

"What else, then?" he returned with equal anger.

"You got me pregnant! Or did you forget?"

"No, I didn't forget! And I didn't do it against your will!"

Looking at John, Ellen reported, "Then he made me get an abortion because he didn't think we could afford a baby!"

"That was a joint decision, Ellen! And neither one of us was a Christian then. I've asked your forgiveness a thousand times for that!" Tears of frustration and sorrow filled Walt's eyes.

John looked up from his writing. "Is that true, Ellen? Has he asked your forgiveness?"

"Yes, he has, but that doesn't take away the pain," she said as she looked at her hands, which she opened and shut repeatedly. "You see, Dr. Kryer, we can't have children now. Complications in the abortion left me sterile."

John looked into her eyes with genuine compassion. "I'm so very sorry, Ellen. I know this must be very painful for you to even talk about, but I need all the information I can get in order to be of any help."

He moved on to the religious background section of the questionnaire. "I notice here that you were both involved in occult practices. Could you tell me a little about that, Walt?"

"Well, before we were saved, we both did a lot of drugs. During that time, we were invited to a seance that eventually introduced us to a satanist cult. We were both scared to death when we saw the animal sacrifices and mutilations, and after a month or so we never went back."

"Is there any question in your minds about the reality of Satan?" John asked.

"No," Ellen replied. "We both know that he exists and that he is evil beyond our wildest imagination." She shivered involuntarily at the memory of those dark days.

"Walt, I see from your counseling form that you are not in the Word on a regular basis. Is there some reason for that?" John asked.

Walt looked embarrassed as he said, "I don't have any good excuse, Dr. Kryer. I've just gotten lazy the last few months, and I think I've been mad at God for all that's happened in our home recently."

"Did you two ever develop the habit of family devotions?"

"At first we did," Ellen replied, "but after the initial excitement of being Christians wore off, we just let it slip."

Turning to the next page of the form, John read and marked points he considered significant. "Walt, you describe yourself as uneducated, embarrassing, hardworking, easygoing, self-conscious, sloppy, and a failure. Is that how you really see yourself?"

Walt swallowed hard and nodded. "Yeah, I guess I do."

"Ellen, do you agree with his assessment of his qualities?"

"Not all of it, I don't," Ellen said almost gently. "He's being too hard on himself. He is a hard worker; sometimes he works *too* hard. And Walt is good-natured, and kind, and he used to be fun to be with."

"Let's look at your self-analysis," John said to Ellen as he pointed to her counseling form. "You see yourself as godly, ethical, hypocritical, angry, active, self-confident, persistent, impatient, moody, often blue, and well-groomed. Is that a fair summary?"

"I think so," Ellen said.

"Walt, do you agree with her?"

"Well, I see her as angry all right, and persistent. Once she gets something in her head, she won't let go! And, yes, the last few months she's been incredibly moody!"

"Well, thank *you!*" Ellen said.

Time was getting away, so John moved ahead. "You say here, Ellen, that you're extremely angry with your father and with Walt. Who are you the most angry with?"

"Right now? I guess I'm most angry at Walt for not supporting me in my effort to resolve my past once and for all!" John wrote her statement down for part of the future agenda.

He turned the pages to the family and childhood information section. Skimming through the circled characteristics, he was able to get a fairly good picture of their childhood environments. "Ellen, you say that you came from an alcoholic, sexually abusive, yet perfectionist home that had the facade of religion, right?"

Ellen nodded her agreement.

"And Walt, your home was alcoholic, broken by divorce, repressed and abusive. Physically or sexually?"

"Physically. Dad used to beat the tar out of me, especially when he got drunk."

John quickly skimmed the rest of the forms and looked to see if both had signed the counseling agreement. Walt had, but Ellen's agreement was still blank.

"Before I can set up any further sessions with you, you'll have to sign the counseling agreement," John said firmly to her. "It says that you will either attend worship services faithfully during the time of counseling or that you will be assessed the counseling fee each time you miss. Seeing that you attend Pastor Chase's church, I will ask you to bring a signed statement from him each week verifying that you were in attendance." He slid the form over to Ellen to sign.

"I'm not ready to make that commitment just yet," she said, her jaw jutting forward a bit.

"That's fine," John said. "If you do decide to proceed with me, you can sign it then. Let me explain to you the procedure I will follow if you choose to come to me for further counsel. I expect you to be on time and to keep every appointment unless you have a legitimate excuse such as being deathly ill, having a major accident, or having actually died. Then I will excuse the absence," he said with a twinkle in his eye. Ellen smiled in spite of herself. "If you do not have an excuse, the regular fee will kick in and I will not set a further appointment until you take care of it. I also give weekly homework assignments that must be finished before you can return for another session. I take counseling very seriously, folks, and because it consumes a large part of my time, I will hold you firmly accountable. Do you have any questions?"

"No," Walt said, standing to his feet. Ellen shook her head, also standing.

John stood and said, "Let's pray before you go." Walt and Ellen bowed their heads as John prayed: "Lord Jesus, I thank You we could spend this time together. I pray that You will lead both Walt and Ellen to make the decisions You would have them make, and that their marriage will be totally healed as they learn to apply the truths of Your Word to their specific problems. Thank You for Your blessed promises! We love You, Jesus. Amen."

"Amen," Walt said. Ellen blinked back tears and turned to leave.

John held out his hand and said to them, "I'll be praying for you both. God wants to help you put your home back together and He is able to do it! Call me if you want me to be involved. And Ellen, if you do decide to come for counseling, I'll expect you to have a full physical beforehand."

"I'll think about it," she replied.

■ ■ ■

The following Sunday, as John Kryer stood at his pulpit, he was surprised to note that Walt and Ellen Harrison were sitting close to the front of the auditorium, listening intently to every word. Walt's expression was one of deep concentration, while Ellen's face was troubled.

After the service, Walt and Ellen stopped at the door to visit with John for a moment. "Dr. Kryer," Walt began, "that was such a helpful message for me! Ellen and I have agreed that we want to return for further counsel, if you can fit us in."

John looked at Ellen to see if she was in agreement. Her face revealed that she was less than enthusiastic about the prospect. "I told Walt that I'd come if he insisted," she said.

"Are you prepared to sign the agreement on your counseling form?" John asked.

"Yes," she said reluctantly. "I know that if Walt and I are going to get help, we have to be coming at our problems from the same point of reference. The one thing we still agree on is that we both believe in Jesus and the Bible. So I guess that's a start."

John smiled and said, "Have you made arrangements for a physical exam?"

"Yes," she said. "I can't get in for a couple of weeks, though. Are we going to have to wait until after I see the doctor?"

"No, I'm not quite that rigid. Call the office tomorrow and Sarah will set up an appointment."

"All right, Dr. Kryer," Walt said with a smile. Ellen shook John's hand without a smile and marched on out the door, followed by her husband. *Help them, Lord,* John prayed as he turned to the next person in line.

PART THREE

Are Psychology and Christianity Compatible?

A Professor
of Psychology

*Psychology and religion
are competing faiths. If
you seriously hold to one
set of values, you will
logically have to reject the
other.*

The Biblical
Counselor

*It is amazing to me that the
most dedicated proponents of
integrating these two opposing
world views are Christians.
The most ardent defenders of
psychological counseling are
Christian therapists, while the
most credible critics of psychotherapy are secular psychologists and psychiatrists who
have seen the damage their
own systems have produced.*

The Word of God

*How long will you waver between two
opinions? If the LORD is God, follow him;
but if Baal is God, follow him.
—1 Kings 18:21*

8

Psychology and Christianity

Having examined some of the myths of psychology, I invite you to join me in this section as we examine why Christianity and psychology cannot be successfully integrated. Before moving forward with this topic, I want to call your attention briefly to the observations of three men —a secular journalist and two professors of psychology— who contend that psychology is a religion gradually and subtly being substituted for Christianity.

Journalist Martin Gross has stated:

> *Psychotherapy is a key ritual of our twentieth-century psychological religion.* In this ritual, the impressionable patient's hope and faith are coupled with the healer's belief in his own magical powers. The combination creates a persuasive setting of suspended reality. It is industrial society's sophisticated imitation of the witch doctor's primitive healing technique.
>
> It is now obvious that most tenets of the Psychological Society, including psychotherapy,

are Western man's disguise for a new spirituality. It is the educated person's opportunity
to practice religion under the cloak of science.
It enables us to call on occult powers of healing
while appeasing our Western need for a rational underpinning. It makes little difference
that each of the psychotherapies has a different
faith[1] (emphasis in original).

Gross says that psychiatrists, psychologists, and the
mental health establishment have "sought the priestly
power once granted to the clergy he is replacing. Many
psychiatrists and therapists have developed what has been
termed 'the quest for omnipotence,' the drive to be re-
garded as a magical figure by self and public."[2]

Gross, however, is not a psychologist. Perhaps we should
consider what some of the insiders have to say about psychological religion.

William Kirk Kilpatrick, Associate Professor of Educational Psychology at Boston College, has made a strong
statement: "Psychology and religion are competing faiths.
If you seriously hold to one set of values, you will logically
have to reject the other."[3] He goes on to say, "The appeal
psychology has for both Christians and non-Christians is a
complex one. But it is difficult to make sense of it at all
unless you understand that it is basically a religious appeal.
For the truth is, psychology bears a surface resemblance to
Christianity."[4]

Kilpatrick shares his own experience of attempting to
integrate psychology and religion. His warning of the
inherent dangers are worthy of note:

I, too, was a victim of the confusion between
psychology and Christianity. My own experience may help to illustrate how it can come
about.

I began to lose interest in the Christian
faith in graduate school. That was when I discovered psychology. I didn't realize I was losing

interest in Christianity; I merely thought I was adding something on. But before long I had shifted my faith from the one to the other.[5]

As a result of his conversion to psychological faith, Kilpatrick was unable to discern between what was real and what was false:

> ...I was blissfully unaware of the discrepancy between my psychological precepts and my actual experience.
>
> I was also unaware of the growing discrepancy between my psychological creed and my religious one. The fact that such a discrepancy existed was muffled by the noise of many clerical voices lifted in praise of psychology. A priest introduced me to the writings of Carl Rogers, and a minister suggested I read Maslow and Fromm.
>
> ...I had developed a mental habit of seeing harmony in all things. I was fond of the phrase, "all knowledge is one." I sought synthesis everywhere. Religious, philosophical, psychological, and sociological ideas blended easily and conveniently.[6]

As is so often the case when one attempts to integrate psychology and the Bible, Kilpatrick found that Christianity lost out: "...whatever reconciliation I managed to effect between psychology and religion, however, was always at the expense of Christianity. The Christian view of life that had once powerfully pervaded my thinking was continually crumbling at the edges, leaving a smaller and smaller center."[7]

Kilpatrick sets forth a vital proposition:

> ...the point I wish to make here is that religion and psychology had become nearly indistinguishable for me. Freud and the church

fathers, faith in God and faith in human potential, revelation and self-revelation—all slid together in an easy companionship. As for God, He began to take shape in my mind along the lines of a friendly counselor of the non-directive school. I never balked at doing His will. His will always coincided with my own.

. . . true Christianity does not mix well with psychology. When you try to mix them, you often end up with a watered-down Christianity instead of a Christianized psychology. But the process is subtle and is rarely noticed.[8]

Kilpatrick is not alone in his concerns about psychology's displacement of Christian faith. Paul Vitz, Associate Professor of Psychology at New York University, has written a book entitled *Psychology As Religion,* in which he says, "[P]sychology has become more a sentiment than a science and is now part of the problem of modern life rather than part of its resolution. . . . [P]sychology has become a religion, in particular, a form of secular humanism based on the worship of self."[9]

These are strong words, but carefully weighed, for in his acknowledgment section he admits that "for someone who is a psychologist in a large and outstanding department writing an extensive criticism of psychology is not without hazards."[10] Yet Vitz makes some intense statements that only an insider could get away with:

Specifically, I shall argue for five theses:

1. Psychology as religion exists, and it exists in great strength throughout the United States.

2. Psychology as religion can be criticized on many grounds quite independent of religion.

3. Psychology as religion is deeply anti-Christian. Indeed, it is hostile to most religions.

4. Psychology as religion is extensively supported by schools, universities, and social programs financed by taxes collected from millions of Christians. This use of tax money to support what has become a secular state religion raises grave political and legal issues.

5. Psychology as religion has for years been destroying individuals, families, and communities. But for the first time the destructive logic of this secular religion is beginning to be understood, and as more and more people discover the emptiness of self-worship Christianity is presented with a major historical opportunity to provide meaning and life.[11]

If Vitz's charges are true, this discussion is more than a minor philosophical difference between nouthetic counselors and our integrationist brethren. This debate is not about insignificant variations of doctrine; the controversy centers on the issues of authority and the source of truth. It is not a question of mixing morally neutral techniques with Christian doctrine. The question is, "What fellowship can light have with darkness? What harmony is there between Christ and Belial? What does a believer have in common with an unbeliever? What agreement is there between the temple of God and idols?" (2 Corinthians 6:14-16).

Integrationists plead, "We do not throw out all psychology simply because some misuse it, any more than we would discard all science or education because some abuse these fields or see them as the only hope for mankind."[12] The psychology in question, however, is that which involves psychological "treatment," psychotherapy, psychiatry, and any other value-oriented counseling. These are the systems that directly challenge and contradict the Scriptures.

Many who are involved in clinical research, however, are also explicitly antagonistic to the precepts of the Word. I remember well my first day in physiological psychology class at the University of Colorado. The professor stood before a couple of hundred students and loudly challenged,

"Are there any of you here who still believe in the myths of the Bible?" *He* did not believe that psychology and the Bible could be successfully integrated.

It is amazing to me that the most dedicated proponents of integrating these two opposing worldviews are *Christians*. The most ardent defenders of psychological counseling are *Christian* therapists, while the most credible critics of psychotherapy are secular psychologists and psychiatrists who have seen the damage their own systems have produced.

■ ■ ■

Professor Ballard stood before the counseling class at the Baptist Seminary. "Reverend John Kryer has graciously consented to come to our class today to discuss his view that it is not possible to integrate psychology into biblical counseling without compromising doctrine. Actually, I should introduce him as *Dr.* Kryer, since I have been made aware that he has an earned doctorate in biblical counseling. Please welcome Dr. John Kryer as he comes to share his views with us."

John nodded to Dr. Ballard and stood at the front of the classroom. He asked a couple of men in the front row to pass out his lecture outline. "Thank you, Dr. Ballard, for this invitation. I am honored to be allowed to share my views, which are in direct opposition to much of what is being taught in our seminaries today. I commend you for asking me to come."

Dr. Ballard smiled tightly and nodded in return. He took a seat in the front row on the left side and began skimming John's notes.

"Let me begin by saying what I do not believe," John said. "I do not believe that most professors at our conservative seminaries and Bible schools are deliberately seeking to undermine a belief in the Scriptures. I do not believe that they are trying to destroy the church or to weaken pastors. Instead, I believe that most professors in our conservative seminaries are sincere believers in Jesus Christ who are trying to prepare their students to minister to hurting people in these difficult days. And I believe that most Christian counselors are trying to find solutions for the deepest problems of human experience. When I disagree with their philosophies, their writings, their seminars, and their methods, I am not generally questioning their sincerity, their motives, or their commitment to our Lord."

Opening his notes, John said, "I would like to show you why I believe that integrating psychology into biblical counseling inevitably weakens one's confidence in the sufficiency of Scripture and ultimately in God's power to transform human lives. Please take your copy of my notes and follow along with me as I quickly touch on several ways that psychology has displaced the church in the healing of souls."

Terri Cummins had intentionally sat at the rear of the class so she could see the reaction of the students as John lectured. At first, several in the class snickered as they pointed to certain statements in the notes. But as John continued to speak and demonstrated his familiarity with psychological theories and writings, their attitudes began to change. They had expected a rather ignorant, angry, backwoods fundamentalist preacher. Instead, here was a man who had clearly mastered his subject and who quoted both secular and Christian sources that raised serious questions about integrationist counseling.

As the hour sped by, John concluded his lecture. "So the question really is this: Can we successfully merge psychological theories with biblical counseling without undermining biblical doctrine? I contend that we cannot."

He looked over at Dr. Ballard. "I'll be glad to answer any questions, if that's all right with you."

Dr. Ballard raised his eyebrows, paused, and then nodded. Hands went up all over the classroom.

"Yes," John said, pointing to a young man in the third row.

"I'd like to know why you feel that psychology is displacing the church if we do our counseling *within* the church?"

"Thank you for asking that," John replied. "*Where* the counseling takes place is not the point. Location is not the

issue. What sets the church apart from any other organization—or therapeutic system, if you prefer—is its source of
authority and power. If we substitute *psychological* principles for biblical precepts, we no longer have *biblical* counseling.

"Look at it this way: If foreign agents infiltrate our
military, dress in our uniforms, speak our language without
telltale accents, and carry on their work in our headquar-
ters, does that make them part of our army? No, because
they have an entirely different mission. In the same way,
counseling in a church facility does not make the therapy
Christian. Using Christian terminology does not guarantee
that the system is Christian. Merely *calling* a counseling
system biblical does not make it so."

Terri noticed several students with angry faces. One
raised his hand. "Are you saying that we are foreign agents
infiltrating the church, trying to subvert pure doctrine?"

"I'm not saying that at all," John replied gently. "As I
said at the beginning, I do not believe that most sincere
integrationists set out with the mission to emasculate the
church. I think the destruction that follows psychological
doctrine is as surprising to the ones who introduce it as it is
to the rest of the church."

"Oh," Dr. Ballard interjected, "so you're saying that
we're naive?"

"I would hesitate to characterize integrationists as naive,
Dr. Ballard," John replied. "Being naive implies a certain
childlike innocence and a lack of sophistication. In any
system, though, there is an element of faith that one must
exercise. Integrationists tend to believe that man's nature is
basically good, though dysfunctional. The Bible doesn't
picture man that way. It says that man is a rebel at heart and
absolutely depraved. An unbiblical view of man leads one to
unbiblical solutions with unexpected results."

"So you *are* saying that we are naive!" Dr. Ballard insisted.

"No, that's not what I'm saying. Let me illustrate. A
chemist takes a beaker of clear liquid marked 'water' and
shakes it vigorously and it suddenly explodes in his hand.

What happened? Someone switched labels on him and he didn't realize he was handling nitroglycerin. He was not naive and he was not evil; he was simply mistaken. And he was also injured. Unfortunately, anyone standing nearby at that moment was also injured.

"I'm not accusing integrationists of being naive or of intentionally injuring others. I'm saying that they are mistaken."

The class erupted with complaints and hisses. Dr. Ballard stood to his feet and quieted the students. He walked to the lectern as John Kryer took his seat. With a tight smile he said, "Well, that was the most gentle presentation of arrogance I have ever witnessed." Many in the class laughed and clapped in agreement. "Perhaps now you can see, students, why we have warned you about the extreme positions of nouthetic counseling. Nonetheless, Dr. Kryer, we thank you for taking time to chasten us today."

Dr. Ballard then turned to the class and said, "Dr. Kryer has agreed to remain on campus for a while to interact with any of you who are interested."

Humanist Observer

Whether psychology has caught up to religion, infiltrated it, or been adopted by it, the most popular versions of both psychology and religion are becoming less and less distinguishable.

The Biblical Counselor

How ironic it is that a self-avowed secular humanist is able to see the effects of integration when many Christians cannot!

The Word of God

A little yeast works through the whole batch of dough.
—Galatians 5:9

9

Psychology and the Church

Psychology is displacing the role of the church in modern Christianity. I do not believe that this is the conscious purpose of most Christian psychotherapists, but nonetheless it is happening. One of the foremost tools accomplishing this is the integration of secular psychological concepts into Christian counseling.

An apologist for this concept defines integration as "a recognition of the ultimate authority of the Bible, a willingness to learn what God has allowed humans to discover through psychology and other fields of knowledge, and a desire to determine how both scriptural truths and psychological data can enable us better to understand and help people."[1]

He says that integration is not "the same as a merger" and that "integration makes no attempt to elevate psychology to the level of the Word of God."[2] The author quotes Kirk E. Farnsworth's statement from *Whole-Hearted Integration*: "[Integration refers to] the uniting, but not fusing, of psychology and theology. Integration is the process whereby both disciplines retain their own identity while benefiting from each other's perspective and communicating the same truth."[3]

Let's see why it is impossible to integrate psychology into biblical counseling without seriously displacing the ministry of the church.

Overlap of Psychology and Theology

One psychotherapist has suggested that psychology and theology are basically the same discipline:

> Some of us think that psychology and theology are . . . independent and uncorrelated. If this is true, there cannot be a Christian psychology any more than there can be a Christian geology or physics. Others of us assume that insofar as the subject matter and intention of the two disciplines overlap, psychology and theology can be thought of as essentially the same discipline. With this in mind, some people are hoping to develop a single, unified, conceptual-theoretical system combining data and ideas from both branches of knowledge.[4]

The main problem, according to this psychotherapist, is that "some theologians [see things] in terms of ultimate truths, [and] 'ultimate truths' are foreign to psychology and tend to 'put off' psychologists."[5] He has hit upon the main issue of the controversy: ultimate truth. Integrationists frequently refer to "psychological truths" which have been given to us by God through general revelation. What they fail to explain is *how* one determines what is "true" in the vacillating world of psychotherapy. Ultimately, each therapist becomes the final judge of truth and incorporates into his counseling system that which appeals to him personally.

Therapy Versus Truth

An article entitled "An Eclectic Psychotherapy" suggests how truth often suffers through integration:

It thus appears that some type of explanation offered by the therapist during psychotherapy has a positive impact on the patient. It seems that whether or not the explanation or interpretation given is "true" in the theoretical or scientific sense is really of little significance in the therapeutic situation.... [This statement] challenges the therapist's own professional-scientific belief system and appears also to denigrate his or her professional work. Nevertheless, the implications of comparable outcomes among the major forms of psychotherapy, particularly recently, should make us face this issue in a forthright manner.[6]

Did you catch that? "It seems that whether or not the explanation or interpretation given is *'true'* in the theoretical or scientific sense is really of *little significance* in the therapeutic situation" (emphasis added). Secular psychologists may not care whether their explanations are true or not, but biblical counselors are *vitally* concerned with propositional truth.

Determining What Is True

Integrationist counselors try to carefully evaluate the findings of secular research and believe that they are able to sift out whatever is unbiblical. The question is, How does one determine what is invalid? Perhaps the question becomes clearer if we ask, "What is the ultimate authority by which we determine what is valid?" Most integrationists will sincerely reply, "Our ultimate authority is the Scripture!"

I do not question that they genuinely believe this. When one says, however, "The Word of God never claims to have all the answers to all of life's problems,"[7] he immediately places psychology in the seat of authority. The psychologist must now decide whether or not the Bible provides a solution for a given problem. How does he do that? He analyzes the problem according to his training, theory, and methodology. One popular Christian psychologist makes this important statement:

> Psychology, in order to be relevant to the real concerns of people, had to move beyond strict empiricism and to deal with concepts which cannot be measured directly. *As soon as psychology began to do more than report observable data, its conclusions necessarily required a great deal of subjective interpretation.* What we gratuitously refer to as the truths or findings of psychology are really a mixture of data and personal interpretation. Now here is the point. Interpretation reflects presuppositions. It is impossible for the discipline of psychology to remain metaphysically neutral and purely descriptive when it deals with unobservables. We must therefore move with extreme caution in accepting the conclusions of secular psychology into our Christian thinking[8] (emphasis in original).

We must exercise great caution before accepting the conclusions of *Christian* psychology as well. The integrationist method of determining validity is this: "It helps to look at research evidence, logical deductions and pragmatic reports showing whether or not ideas are workable. But for the Christian, there is another criterion against which psychology must be evaluated: the teachings of Scripture."[9]

I believe the order must be reversed. The first question a Christian must ask is "What does God say?" not "What does the evidence show?" or "Is it logical?" or "Does it work?" God often works in ways that appear to conflict with evidence, logic, or pragmatism. He reminds us that "my thoughts are not your thoughts, neither are your ways my ways" (Isaiah 55:8). When psychology is the determiner of truth, theology comes out the loser. Doctrines end up redefined according to psychological dogma.

Undermining Biblical Doctrine

One integrationist assures his readers that "integration does not try to recast theology in psychological terms, water down or contradict the truths of Scripture, infiltrate the church and weaken the gospel message, or substitute methods of psychology for the work of the Holy Spirit."[10] I will grant him one part of his statement—integrationists may not *try* to accomplish those things. But those are in fact the results.

Wendy Kaminer, an author who describes herself as "a skeptical, secular humanist, Jewish, feminist, intellectual lawyer,"[11] notes that "whether psychology has caught up to religion, infiltrated it, or been adopted by it, the most popular versions of both psychology and religion are becoming less and less distinguishable."[12] How ironic it is that a self-avowed secular humanist is able to see the effects of integration when many Christians cannot!

Let us examine the integrationist position point by point and see whether it is defensible.

Redefining Theology

"Integration does not try to recast theology in psychological terms," they say. Psychologist William Kirk Kilpatrick disagrees, however. He writes:

> I know a priest in one Catholic church who tells his congregation, "The purpose of Christ's coming was to say, 'You're O.K., and I'm O.K.'" In other churches parents are told that their children are incapable of sinning because "that's what psychologists tell us." In many evangelical churches, positive thinking seems to have taken the place of faith. Almost everywhere, salvation is becoming equated with self-growth or feelings of O.K.-ness. In short, Christians have let their faith become tangled in a net of popular ideas about self-esteem and self-fulfillment that aren't Christian at all.[13]

Ray Jurjevich, a clinical psychologist, says that many Christian ministers have been so brainwashed, or "Freud-washed," that they react angrily when someone challenges psychological assumptions. That is true, he says, even if the challenger is a *secular* psychologist. He tells of a workshop he attended where a learning-theory psychologist was disputing Freud's doctrine that an overly strict conscience produces neurosis. "Some ministers, conditioned by Freudian concepts, and some psychologists, even though sympathetic to religious values, were angry with Mowrer for threatening their comfortable integration into the current professional scene by thus questioning the dominant Freudian views."[14] *Christian* ministers were upset at a *secular* psychologist for challenging *Freudian* theories!

One famous psycho-cleric has redefined his entire reformed theology around psychological terms. Sin now means "any act or thought that robs myself or another human being of his or her self-esteem."[15] Hell is redefined as "the loss of pride."[16] Theology is now to be man-centered rather than God-centered.[17] Indeed, integrationists *do* "recast theology in psychological terms."

Even non-Christian observers see this fact. "The therapeutic view of evil as sickness, not sin, is strong in co-dependency theory—it's not a fire and brimstone theology," Wendy Kaminer scoffs. She suggests a reason for the trend: "Sickness...is more marketable than sin."[18]

Integrationists contend that they do not "water down or contradict the truths of Scripture," but the evidence indicates that diluted theology is the *inevitable* result of integration. Schuller waters down the straightforward message of Christ that we "must be born again" by redefining new birth as changing our "negative to a positive self-image."[19] Schuller not only waters down the truths of Scripture, but he feels it is necessary to move our attention from Scripture altogether. He says, "Where the sixteenth-century Reformation returned our focus to sacred Scriptures...the new reformation will return our focus to the sacred right of every person to self-esteem."[20] Carl Rogers watered down and contradicted the Scriptures by teaching that humans are basically good by nature rather than depraved and in need of salvation, and many Christian psychologists and pastors have endorsed the doctrine.

Weakening the Gospel Message

Psychologists promise that integration does not "infiltrate the church and weaken the gospel message," but when psychology has redefined salvation in terms of psychic feelings of well-being and being born again in terms of self-esteem, the gospel message is not only weakened, it is terminally stricken.

Kilpatrick warns that psychology does not make a "frontal attack on Christianity—I'm sure I would have resisted that. It was not a case of a wolf at the door: the wolf was already in the fold, dressed in sheep's clothing. And from the way it was petted and fed by some of the shepherds, one would think it was the prize sheep."[21] The invasion of psychology into the church's territory is subtle, but pervasive.

Psychotherapists see the church as a ready market for their services. "The churches are a sleeping giant which has incalculable potential for delivering mental health services to almost every community, large or small, throughout the country."[22] The church is not seen as a sacred institution charged with faithfully preaching the eternal Word of God. It is seen as a tool to increase psychology's market share of the counseling industry.

Substituting for the Holy Spirit

Integrationists claim that they do not "substitute methods of psychology for the work of the Holy Spirit." Yet a respected Christian psychologist has argued that the fruit of the Spirit can be produced by psychological techniques alone. He believed that there was no need for the Holy Spirit to develop spiritual fruit, since they could all be duplicated by any competent psychologist.[23]

This illustration is not an isolated exception. Many Christian psychologists hold the same view, whether or not they are willing to openly state it. The substitution of human methods and philosophies for the Holy Spirit's sanctifying work is the explicit result of integration. Who needs the sanctifying power of the indwelling Holy Spirit if man's heart can be changed by psychological therapy?

An example of how integration dilutes the doctrine of the Holy Spirit is found in a statement made by a well-known Christian psychologist:

> Dealing with our insides can be frustrating. Disciplined Christian living fails to resolve all the problems in our soul. *Inviting the Holy Spirit to take over our life leaves part of our being untouched.* Looking honestly at our insides with the help of a counselor leads sometimes to confusion and morbid self-preoccupation. But still *our Lord requires us to clean the inside of our personalities* before we can ever experience legitimate cleanliness on the outside. We must take an inside look if real change is to occur[24] (emphasis added).

What part of one's being is left untouched when the Holy Spirit enters the heart? What of God's promise that "if anyone is in Christ, he is a new creation; the old has gone, the new has come" (2 Corinthians 5:17)? The psychologist insists that it is up to *us* to clean our insides through professional counseling, but Paul says, "All this is from God, who reconciled us to himself through Christ" (2 Corinthians 5:18).

A Dangerous Yeast

One integrationist admits that "integration is not always wise. It is well known that parts of psychology clearly contradict Scripture and could never be accepted by or integrated into the Christian's conclusions and work.... It is important, therefore that integration be done carefully, selectively, tentatively and by individuals who seek to be led by the Holy Spirit."[25] But Paul warns, "A little yeast works through the whole batch of dough" (Galatians 5:9). What was Paul discussing in the context? A relatively compatible point of view, from an integrationist perspective—Judaism.

"No!" the integrationist might retort, "Paul was railing against legalism and a return to the Mosaic rules."

How true. And why? Because it was a "different gospel." Paul wrote, "I am astonished that you are so quickly deserting the one who called you by the grace of Christ and are turning to a different gospel—which is really no gospel at all. Evidently some people are throwing you into confusion and are trying to pervert the gospel of Christ (Galatians 1:6,7).

To connect this passage with the integrationist philosophy of counseling will win me few friends, I realize. But Paul's indictment was not popular either. He wrote, "Am I now trying to win the approval of men, or of God? Or am I trying to please men? If I were still trying to please men, I would not be a servant of Christ" (Galatians 1:10).

Confusing the Ultimate Issues

Integrationists contend that every Christian counselor borrows from the secular perspective, whether he knows it or not. They list methods and qualities which are shared by theologians and psychologists, such as therapeutic conversation, confession of failure, acceptance of others, rational thought and logic, caring, the giving of hope, encouragement, and other skills needed to move people toward mental health.

We must understand, however, that integration is not the sharing of methods and qualities, but the mixing of opposing *assumptions* and *conclusions* about the very nature of God, man, sin, rebellion, suffering, and salvation. The debate is not whether biblical counselors and integrationists both take notes with pen and paper and use similar tones of voice. The issue is over ultimate *truth* and *authority*.

Since integrationists feel that the Bible is silent on so many issues involving the mind, they turn to psychology to define human nature. Carefully read the following statement:

> Psychology is a science attempting to use precisely defined scientific terms. The Bible, on the other hand, is not a scientific volume and uses terms which are much more difficult to define with precision. Words like "ego," "emotion," and "depression" are psychological terms which do not have clear parallels in scriptural language. On the other hand, words like "mind," "soul," or "spirit" are Biblical terms which are psychologically meaningless.[26]

To declare that psychology uses "precisely defined scientific terms" is grossly inaccurate, and to use "ego" as an example of a precisely defined scientific term is sheer nonsense, for the ego cannot be observed, tested, or quantified scientifically. Furthermore, for integrationists to state that the word "mind" is a biblical term which is "psychologically meaningless" is an astounding admission, but one with which I fully concur. Psychology *is* inadequate to understand or define the entity known as the mind, for it is impossible to clearly differentiate the concepts of mind, soul, and spirit in scientific terms. Yet psychologists claim to be superior in treating "disorders" of the mind, the very thing that they admit is "psychologically meaningless."

Integrationists insist that if a Christian counselor is submissive to God, is active in his local church, is aware of the person and influence of Satan, and is consistent in his devotional life, then he can safely use secular techniques. In some cases that may be true, but if one's presuppositions about the nature of man and the necessary cures for his problems are based upon the theoretical foundations of godless men such as Freud, Jung, Adler, Maslow, or Fromm, those secular techniques may not be value-neutral. When one begins with secular assumptions, his counseling techniques will conform to worldly psychology rather than the Scriptures. As Adams writes:

> Throughout the Western world the concept of neutrality of system and method has

been preached almost as a sacred doctrine. The modern man thinks that he can hold his Christianity in one hand and a pagan system in the other. He sees no need to compare and contrast what he holds in his hands.... The Scriptures present an entirely different view. All of life is sacred; none is secular. All life is God-related; none is neutral. Systems, methods, actions, values, attitudes, concepts are either God-oriented or sinful. None are *neutral*[27] (emphasis in original).

Where Should Christians Go for Counsel?

Integrationists confuse the issues when they say that nouthetic counselors "criticize all psychological methods because they are 'secular and manmade' but then use many of these same methods, proclaiming that they are uniquely biblical."[28] The issue is not whether both systems "involve teaching, correcting, training, accepting, building up, advising, showing patience, comforting, strengthening, giving hope and being objective without losing compassion."[29] The issues are 1) *to whom* should Christians go for counseling that involves the changing of attitudes, values, and beliefs, and 2) *from what source* should their solutions come—humanistic philosophies and theories, or the inspired Word of God.

I commend integrationists who admit that "some methods must be rejected because they are clearly immoral and nonbiblical."[30] But counselors who have been so deeply saturated by the psychological theories of the world will have great difficulty in discerning and rejecting those methods which are questionable.

Christians should understand that psychology does not provide any *essential* techniques not already revealed in Scripture. Just as modern technology has not produced anything essential to evangelism, neither has psychology produced any essential counseling technique. Does this mean that because a technique or technological development is not essential it is wrong to use it? Of course not. The printing press greatly helped in making the Scriptures available to the general public. Computers help churches track their membership. Word processors greatly speed the production of correspondence and literature. But none of these are *essential*.

One defender of integration says that the claims that secular therapists have not discovered any essential techniques for counseling "have not been demonstrated and probably are not valid."[31] The burden of proof, however, does not lie with the biblical counselor, but with the integrationist. What purely psychological counseling technique has been discovered that is *essential* to the healing of souls and is not already portrayed in the Scriptures? I know of none.

Misrepresenting Genuine Biblical Counseling

Integrationists often misrepresent nouthetic (genuine biblical) counseling and imply that it is "done in an insensitive way that ignores the counselee's values, condemns his or her beliefs before any kind of rapport has been built, or applies some kind of memorized counseling formula."[32] While it may be true that some who describe themselves as nouthetic counselors are guilty of that sort of behavior, to characterize the entire system as insensitive, condemning, and lacking in rapport is simply inaccurate.

One Christian psychologist calls nouthetic counseling a "nothing buttery" system. "Their basic tenet is Nothing But Grace, Nothing But Christ, Nothing But Faith, Nothing But the Word."[33] He says he takes "issue with my Nothing Butterist colleagues primarily on two grounds: 1) their insistence that psychology has nothing to offer and 2) what counseling in their model so easily reduces to—identify sin and command change."[34] He calls nouthetic theory a "simplistic model of counseling" and characterizes it as merely "listening until you detect a sinful pattern of behavior and then pouncing on it authoritatively, instructing people to conform to biblical patterns."[35]

As in all counseling systems, there are nouthetic counselors who apply the concepts in unloving and insensitive ways, but such an inaccurate generalization lowers the debate to name-calling. Nouthetic theorists insist on the need for compassion in counseling. Adams states:

> The counselor must love people. That is one reason why he counsels. Because he does, he will be deeply distressed whenever he discovers that a counselee has lost hope. But even that distress must be balanced by enthusiastic hope. It is his task always to sound the note of biblical optimism that is warranted by the promises of God.[36]

Nouthetic counselors are characterized as being insensitive to human problems and emotions. Adams replies:

> It is not because Christian counselors are unconcerned about human pain and suffering... that they insist upon obedience to God's commandments rather than submission to one's feelings. Rather they do so, first, because God requires this and, secondly, because they know that it is only in this manner that the proper feelings of peace and joy can be achieved.[37]

The Ultimate Result

If one accepts the logical conclusions of psychology, sin must be reduced to medical dysfunctions and a person can no longer be held responsible for his behavior, his ethical conduct, his thought life, or his morality. Since man is ill rather than disobedient to God, he does not need salvation, but improved self-esteem.

If psychology is necessary to transform the human soul, Jesus Christ becomes a quaint relic of religious antiquity and the church must be recognized as an obsolete cultural vestige that man has outgrown. If psychologists can duplicate the fruit of the Spirit, sanctification is unnecessary and the Holy Spirit is irrelevant. If psychological counsel is necessary for solving the problems of life, the Bible must give way to *The New Harvard Guide to Psychiatry*. Pastors should sneak away quietly and find an honest job.

■ ■ ■

John Kryer stood to his feet as the students filed past him. One young man, Thomas Oser, brought him leftover copies of his notes. "Thank you for coming, Dr. Kryer. I know it wasn't easy for you to state your position. I can't say that you convinced me, but I do thank you for the way you presented your convictions. I never felt like you were attacking me personally."

Terri Cummins came up just then. "The first time I read your material I got pretty mad too, Dr. Kryer. Don't be upset that some took offense at your lecture."

"Oh, I'm not really upset, Mrs. Cummins," John replied. "A bit sad, perhaps."

"Don't be too discouraged," Thomas said. "You've made a lot of us realize we have to think this through again. Would you like to go with us to the coffee shop? We have a free hour. I'd like to ask you some questions."

"Sure," John said. Thomas and Terri walked John over to the campus coffee shop, where they found a table.

"Do you want coffee, tea, a soft drink, or what? I'm buying," Thomas offered.

"A diet Coke sounds good," John said.

Terri got herself some tea and sat down across from John. Thomas returned with his coffee and John's Coke. "Now I want to ask you something."

"Go ahead."

"I want to know why integration is such a big thing to you. Why are you so concerned about it?"

"Because I have seen the devastation that psychological counseling produces," John said. "I have seen happy marriages destroyed when people are taught to return to their past. I have seen believers recaptured by sin. I have seen the peace of God replaced by anxiety and sorrow."

"But doesn't that happen with biblical counseling too?" Terri asked.

"I'm not claiming that biblical counseling always succeeds. No counseling system can force a person to change if he doesn't want to. But I can honestly tell you this: I have never seen anyone who faithfully obeyed the truths of the Scripture disappointed by Christ. I have never seen a marriage destroyed when both husband and wife were committed to obeying the Scriptures."

"But it seems to me that we Christians should use whatever tools God gives us to minister to others," Thomas said. "I'm sure you don't oppose the use of modern technology in church ministry, do you?"

"Of course not," John smiled, knowing where the conversation was headed.

"Then why do you oppose a modern tool to aid in the healing of souls? That's what psychology really is, don't you think?"

"If it were, I would enthusiastically embrace it," John said. "But psychology is not a new resource such as computers and video. It's a belief system. Let me ask you something, Thomas."

"Okay."

"Can you honestly say there has been a substantial improvement in the mental health of America that even roughly corresponds to the growth of psychotherapy? I mean, are people happier now than they were before psychology was invented? Are Christians living fuller, more satisfying, more spiritual lives since psychology has flooded our churches?"

Thomas gave a half-smile and shook his head slowly. "No, I don't think so."

"Let me ask you another question. Are conservative Bible seminary students graduating with greater confidence in the Scriptures now than graduates a generation ago?"

"I don't know. I think we still have a lot of confidence in the Bible," Thomas said.

Terri tilted her head to one side as she looked Thomas in the eye. "Come on, Thomas. There are professors here who openly question the accuracy of Genesis and openly deny that Jonah is a historical person. And a lot of the students question the passages about homosexuality and submission of women to their husbands. Tolerance and egalitarianism are almost sacred doctrines here."

"Let me ask you one last question, Thomas," John said. "If psychology is a necessary tool for our complex modern times, as one of your deans has stated, how did believers cope for 19 centuries before psychology was formulated?"

"I see what you're driving at," Thomas said. "But what would you recommend in the place of psychological training at seminary?"

"I would recommend that seminaries return to teaching theology, biblical languages, hermeneutics, prayer, holiness, and principles of biblical counseling. Seminaries should be graduating pastors—not psychologists."

The Psychological Counselor

[If a person] wants to be a professionally qualified counselor, she'll have to spend a lot more time in school. Even so, there is no solid evidence to guarantee that this training will make her a better counselor.

The Biblical Counselor

After years of training, such a student, therefore, might be "professionally qualified" and licensed by the state to practice psychotherapy, but still functionally incompetent.

The Word of God

Do your best to present yourself to God as one approved, a workman who does not need to be ashamed and who correctly handles the word of truth.
—2 Timothy 2:15

10

Psychology and the Christian Counselor

The secular counseling establishment does not recognize biblical counseling as a legitimate discipline. Unfortunately, the *Christian* psychological counseling establishment holds a similar view. "To counsel in a church," integrationists say, "there are few requirements at all. Most pastoral counselors have only a course or two in counseling."[1] This may be true for some, but most pastors have spent years in the formal study of the Scriptures. In addition, they have lived with and among their people, sharing their hurts, comforting them in loss, confronting them with sin, and exhorting them to conform to the principles of God's Word.

The American church can be thankful indeed that pastors are protected from state regulation by the constitutional "separation of church and state." If it were possible, the psychological establishment would impose counseling regulations upon the clergy, and in some ways it already has. Insurance will not cover pastoral counseling, though it will pay for bizarre treatments such as nude therapy, masturbation therapy, and primal-scream therapy. While it has been repeatedly demonstrated from a secular perspective that no one therapy obtains better results than another, pastoral counseling is looked upon with condescension and sometimes outright hostility.

To obtain secular licensing, a pastor must go through psychological training. That is why seminaries now offer counseling degrees that are heavily weighted in favor of psychology rather than theology. Obviously, nouthetic counseling would never be approved by the state because it relies upon the Scriptures alone for its philosophy and framework.

Yet, as we noted before, studies have shown that there is no necessary correlation between training and counselor effectiveness. In fact, laypeople are often more effective than professional counselors, though they have never undergone formal psychological training.

Part of the reason for this is that traditional psychological theories and training deal with bizarre behavior and esoteric theories rather than the common personal problems that people actually encounter. Psychologist Ray Jurjevich describes his psychological training at the University of Denver: "What I got into during my graduate studies was only distantly related to my primary interests. Instead of human problems we had to study behaviors of animals, physiological reactions, statistical operations, theories of psychological testing, and what the atheist and anti-Christian Freud had to say."[2]

Jurjevich says the philosophy which dominated his training was "dominated by atheists, i.e., Freudians and behaviorists.... Religious people were at that time totally subservient to atheistic academicians and did not dare talk back to reputed experts in the 'human sciences.'"[3]

One of the subtle dangers of studying secular psychology is that there is just enough truth to confuse a student. Jurjevich comments: "My main problem was, as I later realized, that these teachings were not wholly false. They were rather partial truths about living human beings.... However, having been developed outside of God's grace, they missed the most important aspect of man—his immortal soul and its constant interaction with God's Spirit."[4]

There is great pressure in colleges and universities to parrot currently accepted theories. A professor is often discouraged from voicing an opinion contrary to the accepted dogma of the day. Szasz reports that he nearly lost his job when he dared to question the reality of mental illness: "Within a year of its publication, the Commissioner of the New York State Department of Mental Hygiene demanded, in a letter citing specifically *The Myth of Mental Illness*, that I be dismissed from my university position because I did not 'believe' in mental illness."[5]

Masson reports similar reactions to his criticisms of psychotherapies: "I learned that people who criticize establishment dogmas are not accorded a serious hearing."[6]

I believe that the same pressure exists in Christian colleges and seminaries. Those who follow the integrationist line are unlikely to allow a nouthetic point of view to be presented in a serious manner. I met a Christian psychiatrist from the Chicago area who once served on the board of a major Christian college. Because of his strong objections to the psychological indoctrination of the students, he has been ostracized and ridiculed by the administration and he no longer serves on the board. He is viewed as a radical because he believes that the Bible alone is sufficient to meet the needs of believers. He also believes that psychology is eroding the faith of believers.

Whether in a secular university or a Bible seminary, a student is in great danger of having his faith damaged when studying psychology. Jurjevich contends, "By human or demonic design, modern psychology is one of the best tools Satan has to separate souls from God and dull them to spiritual awakening."[7]

Secular Training for Christian Counselors

It is ironic that research has shown that professional training is not required for successful counseling. One explanation for the success of "untrained counselors" is that God has uniquely gifted some of His children with the ability to see through the smoke and haze of "dysfunctional behavior" and to get at the root causes by focusing on patterns of thinking, talking, and acting which differ from scriptural standards.

The primary qualifications of effective biblical counselors are biblical knowledge, godly wisdom, common sense, compassion, the courage to confront, and the willingness to hold a counselee accountable. One psychologist has said, "I know people who have never been to seminary and yet possess this gift. I wouldn't be afraid to trust these people with my mother or even the worst 'incurable' psychotic. These are the most competent counselors in the world."[8] What an admission!

Yet a Christian psychologist remarks that if a person "wants to be a professionally qualified counselor, she'll have to spend a lot more time in school. Even so, there is no solid evidence to guarantee that this training will make her a better counselor."[9] After years of training, such a student, therefore, might be "professionally qualified" and licensed by the state to practice psychotherapy, but still be functionally incompetent.

The Christian community would be better served if we would return the counseling of our people to the local church, where they can receive biblical instruction and be held accountable for their attitudes and behavior. There is no scientific justification for insisting that a person submit to years of training under systems diametrically opposed to all that the church of Jesus Christ stands for in order to counsel hurting people.

The Dangers of Psychological Training

Many Christian young people who go to college to become professional counselors have their faith severely damaged by the seeming sophistication of psychological theories. That this takes place in secular institutions is no surprise, but the fact that it also happens in *Christian* universities, Bible schools, and seminaries is truly disheartening.

Dr. James Dobson interviewed Dr. Gary Collins on a radio broadcast. They discussed Collins's book *Can You Trust Psychology?* "There are some writers," Dobson said to

Collins, "who are going around the country telling them that there is no such thing as Christian psychology, which puts you and me in a strange spot. I thought the Lord called me to do this work.

"Obviously, there are some reasons to be concerned about psychology, aren't there?" Dobson continued. "There's a lot of bad stuff going on under the name of psychology. Let's admit that." Collins agreed and gave examples of dangerous errors in psychology.

"But there are Christians, on the other side," Collins said, "and they look at psychology, and they hear people like Freud, they hear of people who are not sympathetic to anything Christian, people who may be some counselors, some—not all—but some counselors who will try to lure people away from their Christian faith, and so there are dangers out there."

Dobson mentioned a book that Collins wrote in 1977 called *The Rebuilding of Psychology*. He said:

> In it you talked about the five presuppositions of psychology, the foundational concepts on which the profession is based and they are all atheistic. They are all anti-Christ. Let me see if I can remember them.... One was determinism (that all behavior is caused, we have no free will, we don't bring anything to the decision making process, we're a product of experience)—that's crazy. God wouldn't hold us accountable for our behavior if it was deterministic. The second is experimentalism (if it can't be produced in a laboratory, if you can't prove it, it doesn't exist. God can't be proved, therefore He doesn't exist). The third is reductionism (you can reduce behavior down to smaller and smaller units so you can study it).... I'm not sure how that contradicts the faith, but I know that it does. The fourth was naturalism (there is no God, natural forces control the universe).... I can't remember the fifth.
>
> Collins: I think the fifth one was relativism (we don't have any standards of right and wrong, it all depends upon the circumstances)....

Dobson: Now if those are foundational concepts in psychology, Christians have good reason to say, "Hey, wait a minute, don't feed me that stuff because that's dangerous." And I must admit that there's a chunk of this understanding, this approach to man's behavior called psychology, that I just have to pick up and set aside. And anyone going into the field has that obligation if they want to follow Christ.

Collins: That's right. And I tried to say in that book . . . that we need to rebuild our psychology on a biblical foundation. We need to look at some of those principles, some of those foundation beliefs in psychology and modify them. . . . There are some absolutes. . . . There are some principles of right and wrong, and we need to be concerned about those, to bring some of those into our counseling positions.

Dobson: My greatest criticism of the field of counseling and psychology and my greatest concern about it is that an individual who is knee-deep in sin—I mean real old-fashioned sin, they have infidelity in their lives, or who knows what kind of dishonesty or deception or sin in all of its manifestations—might be tempted to go to a psychologist or a counselor and talk away his guilt instead of getting on his face before God and asking for forgiveness. And no amount of talk with a counselor will rid us of guilt—it's still there. . . . I've been concerned that even Christian counselors would help a person deal with the emotional fallout from sin without getting to the core of it.

Collins: I think that some of our professional colleagues who are Christians believe that, but then they get into their counseling rooms and they forget some of their theology.[10]

In their discussion regarding the dangers of secular psychological training, Collins said, "In psychology we're talking about human issues, and about how we pick . . . values, standards and ways of behaving, marriage and the stability of marriage, and I think that we have to recognize that there are a lot of values in the secular schools—secular graduate schools—that are inconsistent with Scripture."

Collins went on to describe his training in psychology and his experience at Purdue. "There were several people in that program that I was in that were Christians when we started, but by the end they certainly were not going to church and didn't make any claims to be Christians. So there is danger. And I have often wondered, how did the Lord preserve me?"

Dobson replied:

> Speaking for myself, I would not recommend that [Christian students go through secular psychological training] unless I knew and they knew that the major professor was at least tolerant of the Christian perspective and hopefully would be a believer himself or herself. I've just seen people get twisted and warped. I mean, why would you voluntarily go to Sodom and Gomorrah if you didn't have to? And many of the secular universities in this field are just about that.

As a further warning to potential students of secular psychology, Dobson said:

> If you are weak and if you get into those training programs and you begin to drift, and you start accepting some of the humanistic nonsense that is taught in the name of psychology or counseling, especially in the secular schools, and you come out and begin selling that garbage to people who are in a state of need, you will damage God's people and you will damage His kingdom the rest of your life.

Dobson and Collins continued to warn about the spiritual dangers of secular psychological training and the need for the church to support psychology students in prayer. They also said that these students need to maintain their walk with the Lord by being involved in a local church.

Toward the end of the program, Dobson said, "Those well-meaning Christian authors who are writing and saying that there is no such thing as Christian psychology and condemning the entire profession are really saying that the people of the future will have only secular individuals to turn to when they face those kinds of crises."[11]

I appreciate James Dobson for his strong stand on family values. I do not for a moment question his love for the Lord. But critics of psychology are *not* saying that Christians can only turn to *secular* counselors in times of crisis. The options are not merely *Christian* psychologists or *secular* psychologists. The critics of psychological counseling are saying that Christians should turn to their *pastors* and *elders* and other biblical counselors within their churches for guidance from the Scriptures rather than seeking psychological therapy.

The overall content of the conversation between Dobson and Collins and their many books reveal two sincere Christian gentlemen who love Christ and the Scriptures and who have a genuine desire to help people. They have recognized, however, that there is built-in danger for a Christian who studies psychology in the secular environment. I would take their concern one step further: There is also grave danger for students who study psychology in a *Christian* environment when the assumptions of the teachers are largely based upon the same humanistic foundations found in secular schools.

If professional Christian psychologists who have studied theology can be confused by the teachings of psychology, as one Christian psychologist confesses, how is the average Christian student equipped to "discriminate between what is harmful and what can be helpful"?[12]

Ultimately each student will have to face the question, Is God's Word sufficient for life and godliness, or isn't it?

Teaching Psychology to Seminary Students

Integrationists believe that psychology is a requirement for successfully ministering to humans. "As a study of human behavior, psychology prepares a person not only to counsel but also to mediate disputes, motivate volunteers, communicate effectively, lead group discussions, empathize with the hurting and serve spiritual meat in an appealing fashion."[13] The question begs to be answered: How did ministers ever serve the Lord before Freud, Jung, Adler, Fromm, Crabb, Minirth, and Collins came along to teach us these important ministry skills?

The integrationist view is held by many, if not most, seminary leaders. One of the administrative professors at Denver Seminary proudly told me that their counseling program was heavily integrated with psychology. He emphasized the view that psychological training is essential if a pastoral counselor is to avoid misdiagnosing the problems of counselees. Medical doctors are needed to deal with physical illnesses, he said, and psychological truths are necessary to treat psychological ailments.

The library at Denver Seminary is impressive from a psychological perspective. Hundreds upon hundreds of volumes of secular psychology pack the shelves. In order to enroll in Denver Seminary's Master of Divinity program in counseling, a candidate must have completed the Taylor-Johnson Temperament Analysis test, the Myers-Brigg Type Indicator, the Minnesota Multiphasic Personality Inventory, and Enrich (if married).

Neuhaus comments on psychological testing:

> In seminary teaching and administration, in pastoral counseling, and in dicta on sexuality, tattered ideas of psychological health are embraced with the enthusiasm of fresh discovery. It is doubtful whether Paul, Augustine, Francis, Luther, Wesley, or Dietrich Bonhoeffer could get past the battery of psychological tests employed by most Protestant seminaries today.[14]

Psychiatrist Lee Coleman writes a scathing indictment against psychological tests in his book *The Reign of Error*:

Whereas psychiatrists make their opinions appear scientific through the use of medical language, psychologists make their opinions appear scientific through the use of charts and statistics. But regardless of the mode of presenting the results, the psychologists, just as much as psychiatrists, must interpret the patient's test responses, and this act of interpretation is inherently subjective.[15]

In reference to the Minnesota Multiphasic Personality Inventory, Coleman says:

One of the clearest examples of subjectivity masquerading as science in the field of psychological testing is the widespread use of computers to score the answers to a personality questionnaire such as the Minnesota Multiphasic Personality Inventory (MMPI). The patient takes a true-false examination and the answers are fed into a computer that has been programmed to interpret the choices. The answers are graphed and appear to give objective measures of personality. But these graphs hide the fact that someone has previously decided what is a normal response and what is an abnormal response to each question. The computer sorts and catalogs the answers and prints out predigested conclusions, but the conclusions are only worth as much as the initial judgments fed into the computer.[16]

Coleman says that such tests are "pseudoscience" and that "since the designer's interpretation of possible responses rested on his personal views rather than empirical tests, the scoring of all later patients' responses must also be subjective."[17] Yet Christian seminaries use these tests to determine psychological fitness for counseling programs!

Psychology's Superiority Complex

Psychologists truly believe that they know more about the human heart than pastors do. They characterize pastors as unwitting and confused pathogenic agents who shape sick churches with sick theologies.[18] Critics of psychology are airily dismissed as having received little "in-depth training in psychology and therefore do not adequately understand the concepts involved."[19] Curiously, psychologists do not apply this same line of reasoning to themselves when they intrude into theological realms.

Yet centuries before psychology ever raised its head, pastors were successfully ministering to hurting people. Counseling Christians has been a part of the job description of the pastor since the beginning of the church. Adams states:

> The work of counseling as a special calling is assigned particularly to the pastor. Biblically, there is no warrant for acknowledging the existence of a separate and distinct discipline called psychiatry. There are, in the Scriptures, only three specified sources of personal problems in living: demonic activity (principally possession), personal sin, and organic illness. These three are interrelated. All options are covered under these heads, leaving no room for a fourth: non-organic mental illness. There is, therefore, no place in a biblical scheme for the psychiatrist as a separate practitioner. This self-appointed caste came into existence with the broadening of the medical umbrella to include inorganic illness (whatever that means). A new practitioner, part physician (a very small part) and a part secular priest (a very large part), came into being to serve the host of persons who previously were counseled by ministers but now had been snatched away from them and placed beneath the broad umbrella of "mental illness."[20]

A Biblical Role Model for Future Counselors

The reason Paul, Augustine, Luther, Knox, Wesley, Spurgeon, Moody, and other preachers were successful in ministering to the needs of generations since the time of Christ is that they had the Word of God, which is the best source of truths about human behavior.

Do integrationists actually believe that only psychologists are students of human behavior? Do we need psychotherapists to instruct ministers how to "mediate disputes," as they suggest? The book of Proverbs; Matthew 18; Acts 6; Philippians 2:3; 2 Timothy 2:14,24; and a host of other Bible passages give us specific guidelines.

A study of Moses, Joshua, David, and Nehemiah will provide far greater insights on how to "motivate volunteers" than psychological manuals such as Harold J. Leavitt's *Managerial Psychology*. He has added nothing to our knowledge of human nature when he writes, "While people are alike, they are also different.... They are subject to different kinds of stimulation ... they vary in kinds and degrees of motivation ... they behave in many different ways to achieve many different goals."[21] How deep. Does his book give essential insights into human motivation that David and Solomon did not share in their inspired writings?

Do we need to study Adler's pyramid (security, significance, and satisfaction) or Maslow's hierarchy of needs (physiological comfort, security, belongingness, self-esteem, and self-actualization) to learn how to move people to serve the Lord? Regarding Maslow, I doubt the wisdom of a man who encouraged nude therapy as a method of causing people to open up to one another. Call me old-fashioned.

Have psychologists taught us new ways of leading group discussions that were not known before recent "findings"? Psychology's encounter groups are subject to legitimate criticism, yet many religious leaders claim them as innovative ministry techniques. The fact is that the church has met in small groups for centuries to meet believers' needs.

Had the church failed to empathize with hurting people through the years until we received the revelations of Carl

Rogers? Are integrationists suggesting that the meat of the Word had not been served "in an appealing fashion" until psychologists taught the church communication skills?

While it is true that there are many ministers who do not deal with people effectively and who need to learn how to empathize, settle disputes, motivate people, and preach with greater power and interest, it is debatable that psychologists are in a unique position to dispense those skills.

The Desire for Psychological Validation

Churches, seminaries, denominations, and Christian leaders seem to have a deep longing for the approval of the psychological establishment. Note the next major Christian convention you are invited to attend. Of the major speakers, how many are psychologists? Look at the book tables and see how many titles deal with recovery and self-help. The spiritual authorities for our generation are psychologists—not theologians.

One reason so many Christian leaders seek psychological validation is that seminaries and churches have accepted the idea that psychologists are the final experts on the human condition. One psychologist asks:

> In view of all this contradictory evidence, why do people, and especially Christians, exhibit such confidence in psychotherapy? Why is it that when Christians experience problems in their lives they turn to this craze? Why do Christian schools and colleges offer these theories as facts? Why do priests and ministers so readily refer their people with problems to licensed professional psychotherapists? . . . Is it because principles of psychotherapy and psychology have sometimes been so carefully interwoven with biblical principles that the Christian cannot separate the two?
>
> However, the main reason why Christians have placed such inordinate confidence in psychotherapy may be that they have lost their

confidence in spiritual solutions for mental-emotional disorders.[22]

Martin Gross says that psychologists claim to have the final word on all human behavior: "As the Protestant ethic has weakened in Western society, the confused citizen has turned to the only alternative he knows: the psychological expert who claims there is a *new scientific standard of behavior* to replace fading traditions. . . . Mouthing the holy name of *science*, the psychological expert claims to know all"[23] (emphasis in original).

Why is psychology taught in seminaries and Bible colleges? Because the modern church has abandoned the Scriptures as the final authority for faith and life. How ironic that even *secular* critics of psychology are being ignored by seminaries even though "there is a growing band of psychologists and psychiatrists warning the churches that they have bought tainted goods, and urging them to reappropriate a peculiarly Biblical wisdom about mental and spiritual health."[24]

Rather than heeding the warnings about psychological infiltration, seminary leaders react with defensive hostility. They have not only allowed the camel's nose to sneak under the tent, but they have welcomed the entire double-humped beast into their dwelling with open arms and a warm kiss.

What the church needs at the end of this second millennium are leaders, pastors, seminaries, and Bible schools that will regain their confidence in the sufficiency of the Word of God. Perhaps then the members of Christ's body will reclaim their spiritual birthright of glorifying God with the wholeness and joy found in simple obedience to His Word.

■ ■ ■

This is Roger Patrick, your host on 'Today's Christian.' Today on KWFL we are interviewing Dr. John Kryer, a Denver-area pastor whose views on Christian counseling are creating a lot of controversy," the radio announcer said. "Tell me, Dr. Kryer, is it true that you have called Christian psychologists heretics?"

"No, Roger, that's not altogether true. I have said that I believe most Christian psychologists to be sincere believers in Jesus Christ. I have said, however, that many psychological teachings border on heresy and make some of the same serious errors that cults make."

"Such as?"

"To support certain psychological doctrines, Scripture is quoted out of context, thereby making it teach what it never intended to say. In other cases, Scripture is distorted, and sometimes it is denied altogether. As a result, God and man are redefined and man becomes the center of attention rather than God."

"I have seen a copy of your lecture notes, Dr. Kryer, and it does indeed seem as though you equate the integration of psychology and biblical counseling as a heresy."

"Well, I'll let you decide," Dr. Kryer said. "Would you approve of the use of Mormon literature or New Age doctrines in your church?"

"Of course not. But surely you don't—"

"Just a minute," John interrupted. "There is a lot of truth in Mormon literature. You can find good values, respect for authority, hope for the future, personal motivation—"

"But it is also full of half-truths and outright lies," the interviewer replied.

"I agree. But why wouldn't you just use the parts that are acceptable? A biblically literate person would certainly be able to discern between false teachings and truth, wouldn't he?"

There was a long pause as the radio host tried to think of an answer to John's argument. "The problem is, Dr. Kryer, that the average Christian doesn't know his Bible well enough to recognize false teaching when it is presented."

"You're so right. Yet we are told to trust Christian psychologists to sort out the false from the true in psychological teachings that are just as deceptive and just as deadly as cultic teachings."

"All right," Roger said in surrender. "Then give us some examples of these deadly psychological doctrines that contradict the Scriptures."

"We only have time for a few," John said, "but I'll try to hit upon some of the most important. First is the psychological view of the very nature of man. Even under some Christian therapies, man is viewed as a basically good being who is just dysfunctional. We are told to avoid calling humans sinners because it damages their self-esteem. The Bible, on the other hand, says that all have sinned and have willfully put God out of mind.

"A second major psychological doctrine is the belief that to heal the damaged psyche of those who suffered abuse, people must return to their past under the guidance of a therapist and embrace their pain. Nowhere is this doctrine taught in the Scriptures. In fact, the opposite is true. The Bible says to forget what lies behind and press on toward the goal.

"A third major error in psychological teaching is that we should follow our hearts—that is, trust our inner urgings and motivations—even when they clearly contradict biblical precepts. The Bible says that the human heart is desperately wicked and that we should not trust ourselves. Instead, we are told to trust the infallible Word of God and obey it even when our heart tells us otherwise."

"And you still insist that you are not calling integrationist psychologists 'heretics'?" the radio host asked.

"Well, Roger, there is no question that some of the teachings are heretical. There is, however, room in Christianity for differences of opinion on doctrinal issues. I would not, for instance, label my Nazarene brethren heretics because I disagree with much of the Arminian doctrinal system.

"I hesitate to label certain individuals as heretics because I think their error is unintentional. I believe they have been brainwashed, so to speak, and that they truly believe they have successfully integrated psychological theories with biblical truths. Some, however, have gone so far with their teachings on self-love that they have even labeled their doctrines as a 'new reformation.' They have redefined salvation in terms absolutely foreign to biblical theology."

"Do you feel that the psychologist who is associated with our university is a heretic?" Roger asked.

"No, I can't say that he is a heretic. I can say, however, that I believe many of his doctrines are not biblically based. In fact, some have come more from the theories of Freud than the doctrines of Paul."

"Well, folks," the host said, "you have heard Dr. John Kryer's accusations. Right after the news we'll be taking calls and you can talk to Dr. Kryer yourself." He gave the number for people to call, and went to the news. The phone lines were full in seconds. John adjusted the large earphones and cleared his throat while his mike was off.

"We're back with Dr. John Kryer, a Denver-area pastor who has made some pretty strong accusations against Christian psychologists. Our first caller is from Lakewood. Peter, you're on the air."

"Yes, thank you. Dr. Kryer, who in the world do you think you are to accuse some of the finest Christian leaders in history? What gives you the right to say these people are wrong and you are right?"

"That's a fair question, Peter," John replied. "First of all, I am just a pastor and who I am has nothing to do with it. Spiritual authority should not be based on scholastic credentials, though I have those. We could compare credentials and counseling experience all day and not arrive at any conclusion. The question should not be 'Who does this guy think he is?' but 'What does the Scripture say?'"

"All right," Roger said, "let's move on to the next line. Harold, in Aurora."

"Dr. Kryer, you said that it is wrong to go back into the past to solve our inner pains, right?"

"Unless you have sin that you have never confessed and made right," John agreed. "Or unless there is someone you have not forgiven."

"But how can you deny the fact of repressed memories that psychologists help to bring out so a person can deal with them?"

"The problem with repressed memories is knowing whether the person is remembering actual events or whether the memories are being created by the therapist. In many cases, there is evidence that the therapeutically induced memories are absolutely false. I suggest that a better course is to follow the scriptural command to forget what lies behind and to press on. I would emphasize forgiveness rather than revenge, as some wounded-heart therapists are preaching."

Roger passed John a note: "Keep your answers shorter, please!" John shrugged his shoulders in apology.

"Okay, our next caller is Rachel from Broomfield. Go ahead, Rachel."

"Hello?" a woman's voice said in slurred tones. Her radio squealed with feedback.

"Rachel," Roger said as he rolled his eyes toward the ceiling, "turn your radio off. You're causing feedback."

"Hello?"

"Turn your radio off!"

"Okay. Sorry. Can you hear me now?"

"Yes, Rachel. Go ahead."

"Dr. Kryer, I'd like to know why you think biblical counseling would be any more effective than psychotherapy. I've been under psychiatric care off and on since I was in my early twenties."

"Have you been on strong tranquilizers?" John asked.

"Yes."

"Have you had trouble with alcohol?"

"Yes," she said sleepily.

"Have you been told that you are an alcoholic?"

"Yes. And a schizophrenic."

"What kind of hope have the psychiatrists given you for full recovery?"

"None, really," Rachel replied. "They say I'll always have to be on this medication."

Roger slid his finger across his throat to tell John to cut the conversation short.

"We have to go to the next call in just a moment, Rachel," John said, "but let me tell you something. Jesus can give you hope for the present and the future. God's power is so great that when we fill our hearts with His Word, miracles begin to happen. I'd like you to call me at my office later on today, okay?"

"Okay. Thanks, Dr. Kryer."

"We have time for one final call. Vance, in Westminster, you're on the air. Oh, I see that you are a psychiatrist. Are you a Christian?"

"I certainly am," Vance said, "and it is this sort of simplistic drivel we have just heard that we professional counselors have been trying for years to correct. Now KWFL is giving air time publicizing an unqualified counselor who has the audacity to question the doctrinal purity of highly trained professionals. I am offended!"

"Well, Dr. Kryer?" Roger said with a smile.

"Vance? Dr. Vance McCall?" John asked.

"That's right, Reverend Kryer. I resent the aspersions you have cast on my profession."

"I understand your defensiveness, Dr. McCall. Denial of the obvious is a condition common to psychological therapy. I suggest rather than arguing back and forth, we examine each question by the Scriptures. I'd be glad to do that on any date convenient to you."

"Are you challenging Dr. McCall to a radio debate?" Roger asked eagerly.

"Certainly!" John replied. "I would be happy to examine our respective positions by the Bible alone."

"What do you say, Dr. McCall?"

There was silence on the line.

"Dr. McCall, are you still there?"

Finally there was a reply, "Yes, Roger, I'm still here."

"Will you debate Dr. Kryer?"

"I'm not sure," the psychiatrist said hesitantly. "It's easy to prove something by quoting a verse here or there out of context."

"You're right about that, Dr. McCall," John said.

"I'll have to think about it," Dr. McCall said.

"Well, folks, we have a challenge on the table. Dr. John Kryer has challenged psychiatrist Dr. Vance McCall to a debate on these issues. We'll get back to you with the details as soon as it's arranged. Now, here's some music."

Pulling his large earphones off, Roger looked over the table at John and said, "You've hit quite a nerve, Dr. Kryer!

You aren't going to be very popular in this town suggesting that psychologists are teaching heresy."

"Paul wasn't very popular either when he warned the Galatians of the very same problem," John replied.

The Psychological Counselor

I propose to demonstrate that not selfishness but absence of self is the root of most of our evils, that selflessness is our greatest personal, interpersonal, and social danger and has been so throughout most of our history.

The Biblical Counselor

Those who emphasize self-esteem fail to recognize that contentment with oneself, like happiness, is a by-product of obedient living.

The Word of God

Then Jesus said to his disciples, "If anyone would come after me, he must deny himself and take up his cross and follow me."
—Matthew 16:24

11

Psychology and the Bible

The problem with much of the teaching in Christian psychology is that it sounds so close to the truth. Integrationists frequently use Bible verses and Christian jargon to give seemingly biblical support for their psychological counsel. Indeed, I am sure many of these counselors have sincere intentions as they attempt to interweave biblical instruction with psychological concepts. Yet a careful examination of the books written by these counselors shows that the Scriptures, in many cases, are being handled quite carelessly. And because few Christians today know their Bibles well enough to detect teaching that stands in subtle or even blatant opposition to God's truth, many have actually been led further away from God rather than closer to Him.

How does this happen? There are at least nine ways that Christians are deceived by the unbiblical teachings of Christian psychology: 1) Scripture is quoted out of context; 2) Scripture is distorted by poor methods of interpretation; 3) Scripture is denied; 4) statements are added to or deleted from the Scriptures; 5) God is redefined; 6) man is redefined; 7) theological terms are redefined;

8) claims of new revelations are made; and 9) the leadership claims unquestionable authority.

Let's examine each one of those problems more closely.

Quoting Scripture Out of Context

As you read their books, note how integrationist writers often pull proof texts out of their biblical setting. An example is how John 3:17 is used in the book *Self-Esteem, The New Reformation*. The author writes:

> Surely Christ never puts down a human being, "For God sent the Son into the world, not to condemn..." (John 3:17). He builds up, redeems, and sanctifies persons and personalities. We might even conclude—at least have reason to suspect—that the level of the Lordship of Christ in a life can be measured by the rising level of Christian self-worth.[1]

The context of the verse shows that God is not pushing Christian self-worth, but rather is warning that humans are already condemned in their sin and that they desperately need Christ as their Savior. Read the follow-up verses:

> For God did not send his Son into the world to condemn the world, but to save the world through him. Whoever believes in him is not condemned, but whoever does not believe stands condemned already because he has not believed in the name of God's one and only Son (John 3:17,18).

Jesus was not declaring man's basic righteousness and the need of healthy self-esteem. On the contrary, He clearly stated in the next verse that "men loved darkness instead of light because their deeds were evil" (John 3:19). Pulling John 3:17 out of context makes it say something never intended in the passage. This sort of biblical quackery is rampant in psychological writings.

Distorting Scripture

To *distort* means "to twist out of natural shape" or "to misrepresent." It is a subtle thing and difficult to detect. Peter referred to this problem in his second epistle: "[Paul]'s letters contain some things that are hard to understand, which ignorant and unstable people distort, as they do the other Scriptures, to their own destruction" (2 Peter 3:16).

When a writer quotes the Scripture to support his position, he can make it sound very biblical. Satan is a master of this. When he was tempting Jesus to prove His deity, the devil quoted from Psalm 91. "If you are the Son of God," he said, "throw yourself down. For it is written: 'He will command his angels concerning you, and they will lift you up in their hands, so that you will not strike your foot against a stone'" (Matthew 4:6). The context of the passage that Satan quotes, Psalm 91:11,12, is that God comes to the aid of those who love and obey Him. Nowhere is there a hint that we have the right to deliberately place ourselves in danger to force God to act. That's why Jesus replied, "It is also written: 'Do not put the Lord your God to the test'" (Matthew 4:7).

Integrationists use the passages that talk about loving your neighbor as yourself (Mark 12:33; Luke 10:27; Romans 13:9,10; Galatians 5:14; James 2:8) to teach that until we learn to love ourselves we can't love others. Therefore, their doctrine goes, we really need to concentrate on loving ourselves. Then, in time, we will be able to love others too. The Bible says, however, that we *already* love ourselves. "After all, no one ever hated his own body, but he feeds and cares for it, just as Christ does the church" (Ephesians 5:29). Paul reproved the church because "everyone looks out for his own interests, not those of Jesus Christ" (Philippians 2:21). He wrote to Timothy predicting that in the last days "people will be lovers of themselves, lovers of money, boastful, proud, abusive, disobedient to their parents, ungrateful, unholy" (2 Timothy 3:2). In direct contrast, Jesus said, "If anyone would come after me, he must deny himself and take up his cross and follow me" (Matthew 16:24).

Paul says that distortion of the Word should have no place in the ministry. "Rather, we have renounced secret and shameful ways; we do not use deception, nor do we distort the word of God. On the contrary, by setting forth the truth plainly we commend ourselves to every man's conscience in the sight of God" (2 Corinthians 4:2).

Denying Scripture

When cults disagree with a biblical doctrine, they simply deny it. The founder of Christian Science, Mary Baker Eddy, didn't like Genesis 2:7: "The LORD God formed the man from the dust of the ground and breathed into his nostrils the breath of life, and the man became a living being." So she wrote, "Is this addition to His creation real or unreal? Is it the truth, or is it a lie concerning man and God? It must be a lie, for God presently curses the ground."[2]

Incredible as it sounds, one sincere integrationist has written that the Bible does not make a clear statement about man![3] The truth is that the Bible makes many statements about the nature of man, which, though not particularly complimentary, are clear. We are told that man is a direct creation of God, made in His image (Genesis 1:26). Man is ignorant intellectually and spiritually (Job 8:9; Ecclesiastes 8:7; Micah 4:12). Because of man's decision to sin, the world is under a curse of suffering (Genesis 3:16-19; Romans 8:20-22). Every individual person is a sinner by nature and by choice (Romans 3:10-18; 5:12). Man willfully rebels against God (Romans 1:18-32), and as a result, his understanding is darkened (Romans 1:21; Ephesians 4:18).

Obviously, the Bible *does* give a clear statement about man, why he is here, why he is so full of suffering, where he is headed, and how he will get there.

Adding to or Deleting from the Scriptures

Joseph Smith found it necessary to "discover" a whole new set of writings to support his unbiblical doctrines that God is a highly developed human, that humans can become gods with their own planets, that salvation must be earned by one's own efforts, and that the current leaders of the Mormon church are apostles giving new revelations from God.

In fairness, I cannot accuse integrationist writers of adding to the Scriptures overtly. They do, however, border on deleting from the Scriptures by ignoring the passages they don't like or which do not fit their psychological theories. In their emphasis upon man's innate goodness they gloss over the passages that clearly teach the depravity of man—passages such as "They are corrupt, their deeds are vile; there is no one who does good" (Psalm 14:1).

Redefining God

Though cults use Christian terminology, by twisting the Scriptures they redefine God as less than He is. They deny His sovereignty and power. In Mormonism, for example, God is defined as an exalted man who has merely evolved to a higher level. He is one god among many.

Though few integrationists deliberately attempt to redefine God, their doctrines have that very result. Under psychological dogma, God is not seen as the omnipotent Creator who fully understands the heart of man and reveals in His Word how to solve the deepest problems of living. Instead, we are told that Christians need the deep insights of secular psychology to truly cure complex inner hurts.

Redefining Man

In integrationist writings, man is redefined as basically good, but containing a dysfunctional inner child who longs to be loved and accepted. He is not a sinner in need of salvation, but a wonderful being who is OK and just needs to realize it.

Redefining Theological Terms

Theological terms are redefined so that they no longer mean what they did under historical orthodox Christianity.

Sin, selfishness, and salvation are given new meanings when connected to the integrationist theology of self-love. Walter Martin has observed:

> The revolutions in culture which have taken place in the vocabularies of technology, psychology, medicine and politics have not left untouched the religions of the world in general, and the theology of Christianity in particular.... It is therefore possible for the modern theologians to use the terminology of the Bible and historic theology, but in an entirely different sense from that intended by the writers of Scripture.[4]

Claiming New Revelations

Mormons have their new revelations: *The Book of Mormon, The Pearl of Great Price, Doctrines and Covenants,* and the ongoing prophecies of their presidents who are alive at the time. Christian Science has Mary Baker Eddy's *Science and Health, With Key to the Scriptures.* Seventh-Day Adventists have the writings of Ellen G. White. Scientology has *Dianetics,* written by L. Ron Hubbard. Jehovah's Witnesses have their own version of the Bible, which is called the *New World Translation.*

The new psychological faiths do not present a single new writing called scripture. Their source of new revelations comes from within. "You've got to learn to follow your heart," they say. A professor of psychology at a major university recently appeared on a talk show in Denver and told people how to interpret their dreams so they could find guidance for their lives. "Listen to your dreams," he said. "They can be a lot of help!"

One Christian woman I know has decided that she must disobey her husband and the elders of her church because she knows God spoke to her and told her to "follow my heart." She is being actively supported in her rebellion by Christian psychologists who warn against pastors and elders who oppress their churches with toxic faith and "beat people up with the Bible."

It seems to me that whenever a psychologized Christian is confronted with the convicting words of the Bible, he might claim that he is being bullied by the church. Though conviction isn't pleasant, God has said, "My son, do not make light of the Lord's discipline, and do not lose heart when he rebukes you, because the Lord disciplines those he loves, and he punishes everyone he accepts as a son" (Hebrews 12:5,6). Under today's revised rules for Christians, however, God Himself would be charged with abusing believers!

Claiming Unquestionable Authority

When all else fails, cult leaders claim that they are beyond question. Since they have received special knowledge and revelation, they scorn the ordinary humans who have the insolence to doubt their authoritative statements. Intimidation of their followers is a major tool that cult leaders use to keep their people in line.

In psychology, the intimidation factor is just as real. "Who are *you* to question *me*?" psychologists seem to say. (No matter that psychologists regularly contradict one another's observations, conclusions, and therapies.) It is this intimidation factor that has silenced so many pastors and kept them from questioning the statements that psychologists deliver as though they received them from God Himself. Psychologists are quoted from the pulpit as though their observations and theories are proven truth—truth as trustworthy as the Bible.

If an ordinary pastor dares to dispute the opinions of famous Christian "authorities" on marriage, sexual abuse, dysfunctionality, or a host of other psychological ailments, people are shocked and then a bit amused that a psychologically untrained clergyman is taking issue with his superiors. Condescendingly, they shake their heads and whisper, "Fanatic!"

Isn't it amazing that pastors are called fanatics for having the audacity to suggest that the Bible really is God's Word, that it really means what it says about mankind, and that it is sufficient to solve all our problems of living?

Why Psychology and the Bible Are Incompatible

At this point integrationists might want to ask, "What if somehow we *are* able to integrate psychological theory and biblical truth without undermining the Scriptures? Would *that* not become a truly biblical psychology?"

I contend that integrating the two is simply not possible because psychology is rooted in humanism, it opens the door to satanic influence, and it offers a faulty view of self that ultimately depreciates the value of Christ's completed work on the cross.

Psychology Is Rooted in Humanism

It is disturbing that so few people see the absolute impossibility of merging humanism with Christian doctrine. Those committed to humanism have no difficulty seeing the gulf that is fixed between the two systems. Corliss Lamont, who wrote *The Philosophy of Humanism*, has stated that "there is no place in the Humanist world view for either immortality or God in the valid meanings of those terms."[5] Atheist Paul Kurtz has said that "Christian humanism would be possible only for those who are willing to admit that they are atheistic Humanists. It surely does not apply to God-intoxicated believers."[6] Harold Rafton has said that humanism is "a rationalistic religion based on science, centered in man, rejecting supernaturalism but retaining our cherished moral values."[7] Doesn't that sound hauntingly similar to psychology?

David Noebel writes that "Humanist theology, start to finish, is based on the denial of God and the supernatural. This denial, however, leads the Humanist to another necessary theological conclusion: man is the Supreme Authority."[8] Since psychology is firmly rooted in the soil of humanism, it is obvious that psychology and the Bible approach the issue of solving human problems from two opposite and mutually exclusive poles.

The major theorists of psychology have been humanists with declared atheistic beliefs. Erich Fromm declared openly, "I am not a theist."[9] Abraham Maslow makes it plain that humanism and psychology go hand in hand: "Humanists for thousands of years have attempted to construct a naturalistic, psychological value system that could be derived from man's own nature, without the necessity of recourse to authority outside the human being himself."[10]

Psychology Opens the Door to Satanic Influence

"Claiming to be neutral scientists with no interest in the supernatural and no reason to study the demonic, most psychologists tend to assume that devils are nonexistent," an integrationist writes.[11] In contrast, the same writer says that some theological critics of psychology believe that "psychological methods, concepts and conclusions are channels through which Satanic, occult and Eastern mystical influences enter Western society."[12] He admits that *"there is evidence that occult practices have been accepted by a large and perhaps growing number of psychological professionals"*[13] (emphasis in original). He states that clinical psychologist Ralph Metzner "observed that I Ching, Tantra, Tarot, alchemy, astrology and other occult practices could be useful for producing mental health and giving meaning to life."[14] He points out that Carl Rogers is accused of introducing occult concepts into psychology.

Some Christian psychologists see no incompatibility between yoga, hypnotism, chanting, and Christianity. Having accepted the idea that psychology is a value-neutral science, integrationists often include unbiblical theories and methods in their own counseling practices.

Psychologists call meditation, guided imagery, and visualization forms of altered states of consciousness. Bill Zika writes, "During the past decade, a great deal of attention has been focused on the application of meditation, hypnosis, and other consciousness-altering techniques to psychotherapeutic outcomes."[15]

What are we talking about when we discuss altered states of consciousness, visualization, and guided imagery? According to E.L. Hillstrom, Associate Professor of Psychology at Wheaton College, many of these concepts are doctrines of Eastern religions:

Many have also adopted a modified theory of evolution which proposes that men are evolving mentally and even now are on the threshold of a revolutionary change. These changes would include new (or newly discovered) mental powers such as telepathy, psychokinesis (the ability to move objects by mental powers alone), the ability to enter into altered states of consciousness, to heal physical disorders in others by mental means, the ability to experience other "spiritual realities" (i.e., to contact spiritual beings), or even the ability to separate at will from one's body.[16]

Hillstrom says that mystical experiences can cause a variety of phenomena, and that "the varied altered states may also provide mystical and transcendent experiences in which supernatural forces or beings may be sensed, seen, or even communicated with."[17] Hillstrom believes that these supernatural beings are demonic in nature:

From a Christian perspective these developments within the consciousness movement are unsettling because the "spirit guides" sound hauntingly similar to demons, and the "spiritual evolution" they presumably promise seems to be no more than an elaborate scientific cover-up for one more diabolical attempt to deceive and destroy. The movement, whose stated goal is to unite science and religion, is apparently attracting fairly substantial numbers of educated men and women who may perceive it as a way to satisfy their spiritual longings without meeting the costly demands of Christianity. Christians should certainly be made aware of the potential implications and dangers of this new area of study.[18]

When our understanding of the very nature of man is derived from New Age psychologies rather than the Scriptures, confusion is inevitable. The Bible addresses such confusion when it says, "For the fool speaks folly, his mind is busy with evil: He practices ungodliness and spreads error concerning the LORD; the hungry he leaves empty and from the thirsty he withholds water" (Isaiah 32:6). When all they receive is psychological counsel, hurting people whose souls hunger and thirst for the healing truths of God's Word go away in greater pain. Peter puts it this way: "But there were also false prophets among the people, just as there will be false teachers among you. They will secretly introduce destructive heresies, even denying the sovereign Lord who bought them—bringing swift destruction on themselves" (2 Peter 2:1).

Blaming Everything on Demons

An equally destructive error takes place when a counselor attributes all dysfunctions to demonic possession. There are pastors and counselors—particularly in hyper-charismatic circles—who blame the devil for every problem of living. If a counselee is timid, they might attempt to exorcise the demon of fear. If a person yawns during a service, he might be diagnosed as having a demon of lethargy. If a man has trouble keeping his mind pure, he may be told he has a demon of lust.

At the request of a friend, I reluctantly attended a "signs and wonders" conference where people were being taught how to heal people and exorcise demons. I watched as groups of people formed circles around individuals, holding their hands out and shaking them at their targets as they yelled loudly in tongues.

One troubled man I had known for some time ran up to me, excited and wild-eyed. "Pastor Ed!" he exclaimed, "I've just been freed from the demon of lust!"

I asked him, "Do you mean that you'll never be tempted by lust again?"

"Never!" he replied. "I've been totally delivered!"

"Then, my friend," I said sadly, "don't look at any billboards on your way home. Don't open any magazines, or read any papers. Don't watch any television. Because you will find that lust quickly returns. It's something we have to fight every day as we submit to God."

He was grieved at my unbelief and insisted that he was permanently delivered. He walked away in disgust, convinced that his problems were over. He was attending a large charismatic church at the time, but was not taught the simple truths of God's cleansing forgiveness (1 John 1:9) and the believer's power to resist sin as he humbly submits to God, resists the devil (1 Corinthians 10:13; James 4:6,7; 1 Peter 5:5-9), and fills his heart with the Word of God in order to keep his ways pure (Psalm 119:9,11).

Within a year this man was arrested for sexually abusing his two little girls. If his was truly a case of demon possession, his counselors failed miserably to give him relief. The cure was not to perform sacred witchcraft, waving hands and chanting unintelligible syllables. What he needed was clear instruction from the Word of God about repentance and cleansing, godly counsel in renewing the mind, and a system of strict accountability within the local church.

Attributing every "dysfunction" to demons is an error as devastating as psychological theories of victimization; it removes personal responsibility for attitudes, actions, and reactions. It places the blame on others (in this case, demons), and prevents a counselee from honestly examining his heart in the light of the Scriptures.

This is not to discount the fact of genuine demonic possession or oppression. Much of what is diagnosed as insanity—schizophrenia, paranoia, manic-depression, multiple personalities, and the like—may indeed be demonic in origin. But most ordinary problems of living, such as lethargy, procrastination, anger, lust, and jealousy, should be seen as the result of sinful thinking or behavior. James asks, "What causes fights and quarrels among you? Don't they come from your desires that battle within you?" (James 4:1). Rather than blaming demons for sin, James says we are driven by our own selfish desires (verse 2), wrong motives (verse 3), worldliness (verse 4), and pride (verse 6). In James 1:14 he says, "Each one is tempted when, by his own evil desire [literally, "desire of the soul"], he is dragged away and enticed."

Psychology Offers a Faulty View of Self

Another major error that places psychology at complete odds with the Bible is the psychological concept of the self. Psychology advocates self-gratification, while the Bible teaches self-denial.

A sincere integrationist asks, "Is the building of self-esteem, the search for self-fulfillment or the actualizing of self-potential really as dangerous as some claim?"[19] He admits that "self-acceptance, self-esteem, self-gratification, self-fulfillment, self-assertion, self-confidence...have become widely accepted values in contemporary society."[20]

In his book entitled *Me, Myself & I*, the dean of the Graduate School of Psychology at Fuller Theological Seminary attempts to "more properly relate Christian theology to secular psychology."[21] He believes that we "desperately need the *insights* of psychology to help us *diagnose* our problems, coupled with the insights and *power* of Christianity to *solve* them"[22] (emphasis in original).

This Christian psychologist believes that a major cause of a twisted view of the self is pastors with faulty theology. "Personal harm is often perpetuated by well-meaning but unwitting preachers of the gospel," he writes. "*Sick pastors produce a sick theology that shapes a sick church to yield sick selves*" (emphasis in original). He goes on to say, "I call such ministers 'pathogenic agents' because they create pathology wherever they go."[23]

Does this psychologist understand the self better than the pastors he criticizes? He defines the self as "the essence of what it means to be a human being....The self is the totality of the person."[24] Later he says that "deep within each of us is a place we call the self. It is a secluded place at the very center of our being."[25] So are we now to conclude that deep within the self is another self? Evidently not, because a few pages later he writes, "The self is *not* a thing, a place, or a person."[26] To make it even clearer, he expounds, "The 'self' does not exist as such. It is not a person with a person. The self *is* the person. I am, you are, that person. There is no other entity within us."[27] But wait! He sheds further light on the question when he points out that "we can observe ourselves from without.... Self-awareness gives me the capacity to stand outside myself and *observe* what it is I am doing and feeling."[28] He describes this idea as "a self within myself."[29]

Am I missing something here? This is a man who criticizes *pastors* for not having an adequate understanding of or appreciation for the self, yet there seem to be some contradictions in his own explanation.

In his attempt to "more properly relate Christian theology to secular psychology" he rarely turns to the Scriptures, but hands down his psychological theories as though they were proven truths. As I read the book I found myself asking again and again, "Where is *that* taught in the Word?"

I agree that there is a great deal of pastoral confusion about the self, but it is not because *pastors* are the "pathogenic agents." The reason there is so much confusion is that seminaries and pastors have turned to psychology for insights about the human condition instead of the eternal truths of God's Word.

Why has the evangelical church been seduced by secular psychology's emphasis on the self? Pastor Don Matzat writes:

> Those who promote the integration of psychology with biblical theology have *failed to grasp the basic essence of the Christian faith*. I know that is a very serious accusation, but nonetheless, when you examine the writings of Christian psychologists, it is very evident. They speak of Christianity as a specific, limited body of religious truth addressing the subject of human behavior. For example, a popular book defining the principles involved in the integration of psychology and theology states: "Many individual Christians look to psychology for new insights that will relieve personal discomfort or despair. They hope that psychology will provide answers to *questions not specifically*

addressed in Christianity"[30] (emphasis in original).

Matzat makes an excellent point, and his book deserves careful consideration in this debate. He continues:

> According to this way of thinking, the integration of psychology with theology poses no problems. Both disciplines deal with the same subject matter of human behavior and are both dedicated to helping people live more meaningful lives. Since it is philosophically correct to say that all truth ultimately comes from God, it is therefore reasonable to suggest that psychology is able to fill up that which is lacking in the body of Christian truth. This understanding is based upon a wrong definition of the very essence of Christianity.[31]

According to Matzat, integrationists have redefined the purpose of Christianity and have lost sight of the person and work of Christ. The heresy is not merely in substituting psychological principles of counseling for biblical principles of counseling. The heresy is substituting *anything* for the completed and sufficient work of Christ. Matzat writes, "Since the essence of Christianity is found in the person and work of Jesus Christ, any claim that the Christian faith falls short in providing answers for the needs of hurting people is in fact a criticism of the sufficiency of Jesus Christ."[32]

A Biblical View of Self

What does the Bible teach about the self? The Scriptures deal with the self as desperately needing reformation. Little, if anything, is mentioned which would support the modern psychological and sociological confidence that man is basically good.

In stark contrast to the prevailing view, the Bible paints an accurate picture of the self. It speaks of self-appraisal (Romans 2:1), the need for self-control (Galatians 5:23), man's propensity for self-deception (Jeremiah 17:9; Galatians 6:3), the desperate need for self-denial (Matthew 16:24), man's continual striving for self-exaltation (Ezekiel 31:10,11; Obadiah 3; Luke 14:11), man's need for self-examination (Psalm 139:23,24; 1 Corinthians 11:28; 2 Corinthians 13:5; Galatians 6:4), man's inherent selfishness (Proverbs 11:26; 21:13; Malachi 3:8-10; Luke 12:15; 1 Corinthians 13:5), man's belief in his own self-righteousness (Luke 18:9; 1 Corinthians 10:12), and man's inclination toward whining self-pity (Proverbs 19:3; Lamentations 3:39; Philippians 2:14; 4:11-13; 1 Timothy 6:6; Hebrews 13:5).

Sin and Self

The genesis and taproot of sin is self. Satan's rebellion began with the desire to exalt him*self* to the position of God. In Isaiah 14 Satan is represented by the "king of Babylon." God accused him of saying in his heart, "*I* will ascend to heaven" (verse 13); "*I* will raise my throne above the stars of God" (verse 13); "*I* will sit enthroned... on the utmost heights" (verse 13); "*I* will ascend above the tops of the clouds" (verse 14); "*I* will make my*self* like the Most High" (verse 14). His was the ultimate attempt of becoming the self-made man.

The apostle John confronts this concept and breaks self-sin into three categories: the lust of the flesh, the lust of the eyes, and the boastful pride of life (1 John 2:16). A perfect case history is found in Genesis 3:6. Eve "saw that the fruit of the tree was good for food [the lust of the flesh], and pleasing to the eye [the lust of the eyes], and also desirable for gaining wisdom [the boastful pride of life]." Adam voluntarily joined her in the rebellion and sin entered our race.

When God confronted them with their sin, Adam and Eve resorted to the psychological behaviors of self-excuse, victimization, and the blaming of others. "The woman *you* put here with me—she gave me some of the fruit," Adam said, no doubt pointing at Eve. In effect he said, "Look, God, I'm a victim of circumstances. *You're* the One who put the woman here! Not only that, but *she* gave me the fruit. Don't blame me."

When God turned to Eve, she said, "The serpent deceived me, and I ate." She might as well have said, "Hey, it's not *my* fault. Don't blame *me*. I'm as much a victim as Adam!" But God didn't buy their excuses. He banished them from the Garden and the curse of sin came upon the whole earth.

God will not accept our excuses either. We can claim to be innocent victims, but the Scriptures teach that we willfully choose our rebellious ways (Romans 1:18-32). God says that we are without excuse (verse 20). Psychology, however, says that mankind is basically good but dysfunctional because of what others have done to us. If we only learn to love ourselves, the theory goes, we will naturally love others and do what is kind.

The main scriptural passage that self-love advocates use to support their doctrine is Matthew 22:36-40, and the phrase they lift from this passage is "You shall love your neighbor as yourself." Note, however, that this passage does not in any sense *command* self-love. Instead, it *assumes* the fact of self-love—that man *already* loves himself. I stress this point because self-love is such a foundation of psychological doctrine.

Paul points out the fact of self-love in Ephesians 5:28,29, where he commands husbands to love their wives as they already love their own bodies, for "no one ever hated his own body, but he feeds and cares for it, just as Christ does the church." Understand that Paul is not calling for self-love. Rather, his emphasis is upon loving the Lord and loving one's mate in an unselfish manner.

The Bible's Call to Self-Denial

Paul deals with the issue of self-denial in Philippians chapter 2. He warns believers against doing anything "out of selfish ambition or vain conceit, but in humility consider others better than yourselves" (verse 3). He reminds us that we should be unselfish, as was Christ, who gave up the glories and pleasures of heaven to become a man willing to serve others rather than Himself (verses 5-11). Paul further commands us to "do everything without complaining or arguing" (verse 14) in order to be a pure and shining testimony to our depraved generation.

Jesus clearly taught that we must deny ourselves if we are His disciples. In Matthew 16:24 He said, "If anyone would come after me, he must deny himself and take up his cross and follow me." This is the very opposite of the psychological doctrine of self-love. Self-denial can mean leaving home, friends, and cherished possessions (Luke 18:29,30). It can mean giving up one's livelihood (Luke 5:27,28).

Self-denial involves restraining one's appetites (Proverbs 23:1,2,20), controlling the natural impulse to worry about food and clothing (Luke 12:22), and keeping a spiritual perspective on the natural anxieties which come from the daily pressure of living (Luke 21:34). Self-denial demands that Christ's disciples exercise self-discipline for the sake of eternal priorities (1 Corinthians 9:27).

How can a person become less self-consumed and more centered upon the needs of others? Jesus makes reference to the process in Matthew 16:24 when He says we must take up our own individual crosses. Paul picks up this theme frequently and teaches that we must put the self to death, so to speak. He tells us in Romans 6:6 that "our old self was crucified with him." In Romans 8:13 Paul writes that we must "put to death the misdeeds of the body." He commands that we "put to death . . . whatever belongs to your earthly nature: sexual immorality, impurity, lust, evil desires and greed" (Colossians 3:5).

Peter supports the concept of self-denial when he writes that the believer "does not live the rest of his earthly life for evil human desires, but rather for the will of God" (1 Peter 4:2).

Does all of this mean that the Christian is to lose his individuality, that he is to blend into "the Force" in a manner similar to what Hindus teach? Is there some metaphysical act that one must perform in which he literally kills the self? Of course not. What Jesus, Paul, and Peter are dealing with is *selfish motivation*.

Paul understands that man's greatest slavery is to self,

and that the chains of sin are composed of the links of selfishness. The cause of most "mental problems"—marital and family dysfunctions, or personal anxiety—are connected to an unhealthy preoccupation with one's self.

Achieving Freedom from Self

Galatians 5 is an essential passage for understanding the biblical concept of the self. Paul writes in verses 1-6 about genuine freedom and how it can be achieved only through faith in God and loving behavior. Knowing that man is innately selfish, Paul warns against using freedom to indulge one's sinful nature (verse 13). Instead, we are to "serve one another in love" (verse 14).

The purpose of God's law was to instruct mankind in character and behavior. If the key element in successful social development is self-love, we would expect to find the concept taught as a central truth. However, Paul says that successful interaction is based upon this summary of the law: "Love your neighbor as yourself" (Galatians 5:14). Note again that he does not say that one must first love himself so that he can love his neighbor properly, for people already love themselves.

How can we love others as we are commanded? Paul tells us in Galatians 5:16,25, "Live by the Spirit, and you will not gratify the desires of the sinful nature.... Keep in step with the Spirit."

The contrast is obvious: We will live for self or for God. If we live for self, there will be mental and social distress. If we live for God, we will find mental, social, and spiritual harmony in our lives.

There you have it. We can attempt to change people's lives by giving psychological counsel that is rooted in humanism and that points to self, or we can give biblical counsel that is rooted in divine wisdom and points to God.

There is no middle road.

■ ■ ■

The phone rang at the offices of Faith Evangelical

Church. "It's for you, Pastor," Sarah said over the intercom. John Kryer sighed wearily and turned from his computer. Mondays were ordinarily reserved for catching up on paperwork and writing a book on pastoral counseling.

"Who is it, Sarah?" he asked as he picked up the phone.

"It's Elsie Mapps on line one. She wants to set up another counseling session."

John pushed the lighted button and said, "Hello, Elsie."

"Hello, Pastor. I need to set up another counseling session with you."

Elsie had been struggling with alcohol for most of her adult life. Since coming to Faith Church, she had maintained sobriety for over a year. But pressures in her marriage had become so intense that she had once again sought comfort in liquid form.

"Did you do what I asked at the last session?" John inquired.

"Yes. I've already been to the doctor and he prescribed Antabuse for me. I'm taking it daily and I'm back in church every week."

"I've seen you there, Elsie," John said with a smile in his voice. He took his appointment book out of his pocket and flipped through the pages. "The first opening I have is a week from Wednesday, at 3:00."

"That's fine, Pastor," she agreed.

"I've got you down, Elsie," he said as he wrote the appointment in his book.

He had barely turned back to the computer when Sarah buzzed the intercom again.

"Yes, Sarah?"

"You have a call from Larry Alexander of Mountain View Community Church," she answered.

"Thanks, Sarah." He punched line one and said, "Hi, Larry! What can I do for you?"

"Hi, John. Do you have a minute to talk?"

"Of course. What's up?"

"I have a couple of counseling cases I'd like to run by you." Larry was a young pastor in a nearby church and attended the same local pastors association with John. "They're both pretty strange."

"Tell me about them," John encouraged.

"The first is an exhibitionist. He's been arrested twice already for exposing himself. He's a member of our church, and was being considered for a leadership role. If we hadn't been alerted by a policeman in our church who was aware of the pending charges against this man, our church could have been severely damaged."

"What have you done about it so far?" John asked.

"Well, I've confronted him with the accusations, and he has admitted everything. But I don't know where to go from here."

"One thing you'll need to do is to set up a strict system of accountability for him. Is he married?"

"Yes. He's got the sweetest little wife, and of course she's heartbroken about it. It's really made her question her own femininity."

"Bless her heart. She deserves better than that. I'm assuming that pornography has been involved at some point."

"That's true. In fact, before each time he exposed himself, he had stopped by an adult bookstore and flipped through the magazines."

"Right!" John said with disgust. "*Adult* bookstore! Isn't it amazing that one of the most juvenile acts a man can take part in—pornographic stimulation—is called 'adult'? It's a perfect example of Isaiah 5:20, 'Woe to those who call evil good and good evil.'"

"It sure is," Larry agreed. "What kind of accountability do you suggest we place him under?"

"Do you think he will submit to the church's authority in this matter?" John asked.

"He'll *have* to if he's going to remain in our church. Plus, his wife has told him that unless he gets help, she's going to leave him."

"Mm-hmm. How did he respond to that?"

"It seemed to shake him up pretty good. I think he really loves her and the kids, but he says he has this sexual addiction that he has no control over," Larry continued.

"And what is your opinion of the term 'sexual addiction'?" John probed.

"I don't really know, John. I mean, I've read some of the counseling books and they seem to support the concept that some people are actually addicted to illicit sex—that there's nothing they can do about it."

"What does the Bible say, Larry?"

"Well, it seems to me that the Bible takes a fairly firm position about sexual purity and that God holds every human accountable for his behavior."

"A *fairly* firm position'?" John questioned.

"Well, actually, the Bible is rigid at that point, isn't it?" Larry replied. "It's just that our entire culture is so relativistic nowadays. When we pastors take a firm stand on moral issues, people think we're being fundamentalist hypocrites."

"And are we so afraid of the names the world calls us that we're willing to risk our integrity with the Lord? It's easy for all of us to fall into the John 12:43 trap: 'They loved praise from men more than praise from God.' I'm not aiming that at you, Larry. I'm admitting that I often feel the same pressure to compromise."

"I hear you. Well, back to the accountability issue. What do you suggest?" Larry asked.

"You need to set up a closely monitored schedule so that he has to account to his wife and to you for every minute of the day, from the time he gets up until the time he goes to bed. That way he knows he can't stop at the porn shop for 30 minutes on his way home from work.

"Second, I suggest you place him on a thorough program of discipleship, including Bible memorization. Explain to him that he is not suffering from an addiction, but from sinful choices that he has allowed to dominate his thinking and his actions."

"How can I make that hard of a statement, John, when there are so many psychological findings supporting the addiction concept?"

"I know that addiction is the accepted psychological doctrine, Larry, but more and more secular researchers are coming to the position that much of what is now passing for addiction is the result of volitional choices, not uncontrollable urges.

"So much of current psychological theory is dictated by political considerations rather than hard science. So help your counselee to remove the excuse of addiction from his sinful behavior.

"If he is truly a believer, you can teach him how to rely on a moment-by-moment relationship with the Holy Spirit. Show him how to saturate his mind with the Scriptures so that when he is tempted with lustful thoughts he can draw on the truths and power of the Word. Show him from Ephesians 6 that he is in a spiritual battle, not merely a physical one. Have him list for you the television programs he is watching—every one of them, specifically. You'll have to help him evaluate whether or not he should even keep a television in his house."

"Wow, John!" Larry exclaimed. "This is more work for *me* than it is for *him!*"

"Not really," John laughed, "but counseling and shepherding your flock is not easy work. It's time-consuming and exhausting. But that is the work God has called His pastors to do."

"Man! I think I'd rather refer people to a Christian counselor, John. I don't have time to deal with every troubled person in my congregation."

"I know just how you feel, Larry. But how can you in good conscience send your people to psychologists and counselors who rarely deal with Christians' problems from a truly biblical perspective? Far too often they merely take secular psychological concepts and hang a Bible verse or two on them to make them sound biblical."

Larry coughed uncomfortably. "Well, I just assumed that a Christian counselor would counsel from a biblical point of view."

"I understand that," John said. "I used to do the same. I referred my people to Christian psychologists believing I could trust them to guide believers. But the more I read Christian counseling books, the more I began to see that a large percentage of their underlying philosophy is based on humanistic ideas that are in direct contradiction to biblical truths."

"But, John, I just don't have time to counsel a lot of people and still tend to all my other work."

"I know, brother! And the more you counsel, the more people will start coming to you. Eventually you'll find that you have to train a corps of lay counselors so they can help carry the burden. But I still don't see how we can turn God's people over to the godless philosophies of the world," John insisted. "Now, what was the second case?"

"Oh, it's even worse, John! The man also has a sexual obsession, but his case seems far more serious."

"How so?"

"Well, first of all, he's a former pastor. He got so deeply involved in pornography and lust that his wife left him. He seems to have a deep-seated anger toward women in general. He's told me that he has posters of women on his wall that he shoots red-dye pellets at. He has gone up to the university campus at Boulder with a knife and actually stalked some of the young women. I think he could actually be violent," Larry said worriedly.

"There's every likelihood that he will indeed hurt or kill someone soon if he doesn't get control of his lust and fantasies of violence. Have you considered the possibility of demonic involvement?"

"The thought crossed my mind. Do you think that's what it is?"

"I don't know, but it seems possible. And he has certainly opened himself up to the attacks of the enemy by feeding on pornography. How is he involved in your church?"

"In no official way, thank the Lord," Larry answered. "But he now claims that he has been suddenly delivered from his lust and wants to be involved in our home Bible studies. It isn't that I doubt God's power to change a person, but I'm nervous about allowing him to be in a small group situation where there are women present."

"I don't blame you," John agreed. "Has he shown any evidence of genuine repentance for his sin? Have you seen him express deep sorrow?"

"Well, he seems to be heartbroken over the fact that his wife has left him, but I can't say that he has really shown much remorse for his sinful fantasies," Larry answered. "What do you think I should do?"

"Well, Larry, I agree that he should not be allowed in a small group situation where women attend. I would insist that he come under the direct supervision of the elders and establish the same sort of accountability we discussed with your first case."

"I hate to admit it, John, but I really don't even want him in my church!"

"I can understand how you must feel, but I can't endorse that unless he refuses to accept strict discipline and close supervision by godly men in the church. If he is sincere in his desire to change, he will be grateful for the personal care this will entail."

"Well, I'll give it some thought," Larry said uncertainly. "Thanks, John, for helping me think these things through. I think I have a better idea now of how I'm going to proceed."

"You're welcome, my friend," John replied. "God bless." He hung up the phone and turned back to his manuscript and tried to concentrate once again. A few moments later Sarah interrupted his thoughts. "Pastor, Cliff Chase is on line one."

John dropped his head in frustration, then smiled and chuckled to himself, "I may as well accept the fact that I'm not to write today." He turned to his desk and lifted the receiver to his ear. "Hello, Cliff. What can I do for you?"

"John! I heard you on KWFL. I'm convinced! The Lord has convicted me that I need to counsel my own people. How do I learn what to do? Where do I start?"

"You've already started, Cliff," John replied. "You've been studying the counseling manual for years! You have a strong biblical foundation. Now you just need to know a few basics on how to apply the Scriptures to individual problems."

"Would you be willing to teach me?"

"Of course, Cliff. I would suggest that we work together with Walt and Ellen Harrison. They have agreed to begin counseling. Were you aware of that?"

"I wasn't sure, John. I haven't seen them at church since I referred them to you. I assumed they were attending your church."

"They have been, Cliff, but my goal is to see them pull their marriage together and return to your congregation. I think if you become involved in the counseling, they will do just that.

"Let me tell you what I want you to do to get ready," John continued. "I want you to get your most reliable theology text and your Bible to refresh your heart and mind on the basic doctrines."

"Which ones, John?"

"All of them. I want you to review the doctrines on the existence of God, His character, the Trinity, their respective roles as they relate to human beings, the depravity of man, the plan of salvation in Christ, and the inerrancy and infallibility of the Scriptures. Go over them again. Review your doctrinal statement and look up the verses so that you know what you believe, why you believe it, and where you can find the doctrines taught in the Word. Will you do that?"

"I said I was ready, John," Cliff replied with determination, "and I meant it!"

PART FOUR

A Biblical Alternative to Psychology

The Psychological Counselor

We are not questioning the sufficiency of Christ. We are merely saying that the Bible does not address many of the problems facing contemporary human beings, and that we need the valid findings and insights available from psychology to help hurting souls.

The Biblical Counselor

There are no truly unique problems that modern man experiences. Sexual, verbal and physical abuse have been with us since the days of Cain. Marriage problems, poor self-esteem, addictions of every sort, Attention Deficit Disorder, jealousy, violent rage, depression, and virtually every other psychological dysfunction are recorded in biblical case histories.

The Word of God

His divine power has given us everything we need for life and godliness through our knowledge of him who called us by his own glory and goodness.
—2 Peter 1:3

12

A Biblical Foundation for Counseling

We are about to embark on the most exciting part of this book. It isn't enough merely to condemn integrated counseling systems; hurting people need to know that there is a more powerful alternative—a counseling philosophy based on the eternal Word of God. For in the Bible God has in fact provided for our every need. Joy, freedom, and recovery from damaged lives are all available to us! Christians don't have to go through years of intensive therapy to experience genuine inner peace. Breathe deeply, relax in the Lord, and take time to read these final chapters to confirm in your heart and mind that God has provided everything—yes, *everything!*—we need for our physical, mental, social, and spiritual well-being.

Presuppositions

All philosophies start with presuppositions. Science itself rests upon presuppositions which cannot be tested empirically. Materialistic theories postulate the eternal existence of energy and matter, but cannot *prove* it. Evolutionary theory believes by faith that the cosmos organized itself without divine intervention, but cannot *prove* it.

Psychology is a humanistic religion which assumes that man is essentially good and that he contains the power to heal himself, but cannot *prove* it. Freudian psychological theory presupposes the existence of unconscious drives that produce conflicts between the id, ego, and superego, but cannot *prove* it. Behavioral psychology presupposes that humans are merely highly developed animal forms whose behavior can be modified by external stimuli, but cannot *prove* it. Integrationist psychology presupposes the general validity of secular psychological theory and believes that when it is added to biblical concepts, the result is a superior therapy, but cannot *prove* it.

It is therefore not irrational or unfair for biblical counseling to be based on presuppositions about God, man, salvation, and the sufficiency of the Scriptures.

The Existence of God

The Christian worldview begins by assuming the existence of God (Genesis 1:1; John 1:1; Hebrews 11:6), and continues with the belief that God can and has revealed Himself to man through the general revelation of creation (Romans 1:20), conscience (Romans 2:15), the special revelation of His written Word, the Bible (2 Timothy 3:16,17; 2 Peter 1:21), and the personal and final revelation of His Son, Jesus Christ (Hebrews 1:1-3). These presuppositions are not based on blind faith alone, however. There is a vast amount of empirical evidence—in geology (the study of the physical structure of the earth), paleontology (the study of fossils), astronomy, biology, genetics, and the other scientific disciplines—to support the concept of a Creator who designed, formed, and sustains the cosmos.

Christian acceptance of the authority of the Scriptures rests upon the presupposition of biblical inerrancy and infallibility. In contrast to the continually changing findings of psychology, the Word of God claims absolute dependability. Psalm 111:7 says, "All [God's] precepts are trustworthy." The statements and principles of the Scriptures endure the test of time, while psychological theories change from day to day. The psalmist writes, "Your word, O LORD, is eternal; it stands firm in the heavens" (Psalm 119:89).

Though the assumptions of biblical dependability receive support from archaeological, historical, and scientific evidences, such confirmations do not constitute "scientific proof," for they are not repeatable, as scientific method demands. The same is true, however, for evolutionary theories. Apologetics (defense of the Scriptures) provide rational assurance which can satisfy man's intellect, but there still remains the choice of faith which each person must apply to his ultimate source of authoritative truth.

God's Character

Christian counseling moves beyond the existence of God to the presupposition of God's benevolent and righteous character. It is essential to understand this balance between God's compassion and His absolute holiness. He is loving and just. Merciful and stern. Tender, yet demanding. To describe Him only in terms of compassion and love mistakenly depicts God as a cosmic Santa Claus—a benign and slightly senile grandfather figure. On the other hand, to picture God only in terms of righteousness and judgment wrongly portrays Him as a vengeful Thor who furiously casts lightning bolts of wrath upon a helpless creation.

A comprehensive biblical theology is essential, therefore, for successful Christian counseling. If we want to understand ourselves, we must first learn about God. He must be accurately portrayed and perceived in His fullness. He must be seen as omniscient (all-knowing), omnipresent (everywhere), and omnipotent (all-powerful). His omniscience guarantees that He understands our deepest sufferings and needs. His omnipresence assures us that God is not a distant deity who does not care, but is ever present to aid His children. His omnipotence guarantees that God can deliver on His promises of healing, peace, and joy.

To ignore any facet of God distorts one's worldview. It assures a faulty interpretation of reality that will lead to an inaccurate diagnosis of a counselee's problem and cure. That is precisely why a biblical counselor needs a solid theological foundation rather than psychological indoctrination. What a tragedy it is that more and more seminary students are enrolling in psychologically driven counseling programs rather than traditional biblical and theological curricula! How sad it is that pastors often have more confidence in the writings of modern-day psychologists than the prophets who penned the holy Word of God!

God's Person—The Trinity

A crucial assumption of biblical counseling is the reality of the Trinity. For some people the biblical teaching about the Trinity seems esoteric and abstractly theological, but it provides some vital and practical implications for counseling. It is a revealed truth, not a psychological insight or finding. Though the word *trinity* does not appear in the Bible, the teaching that the one eternal God exists in three eternal Persons—Father, Son, and Holy Spirit—is clearly presented (Matthew 28:19; John 14:26; 15:26; 2 Corinthians 13:14; 1 Peter 1:2). Each Person of the triune God has the full attributes of deity; they are eternally equal, and though their functions within the Godhead overlap, there appear to be distinctions in their respective roles.

The Role of the Father in Counseling

The titles used to describe the Persons of the Godhead are helpful in understanding their functions, especially as they relate to man's needs. Let's look first at some of the names of the Father. He is described as "Almighty" in Genesis 17:1. It is this attribute of omnipotence that guarantees God's ability to intervene and to heal, in the counseling sense. He provides solutions to the deepest psychological problems that humans experience.

In Deuteronomy 33:27 He is called the "Eternal God." God has always existed. Since He has seen and understands every condition that man is subject to, He is never at a loss for the perfect solution. It is in direct contrast to God's divine nature that the psalmist wrote about our human beginnings: "Your eyes saw my unformed body. All the days ordained for me were written in your book before one of them came to be" (Psalm 139:16).

Perhaps we need to be reminded that "[God] knows how we are formed, he remembers that we are dust. As for man, his days are like grass, he flourishes like a flower of the field; the wind blows over it and it is gone, and its place remembers it no more" (Psalm 103:14-16). Man is subject to aging, suffering and death. Through Christ, however, God has promised His children immortality: "For the trumpet will sound, the dead will be raised imperishable, and we will be changed. For the perishable must clothe itself with the imperishable, and the mortal with immortality. When the perishable has been clothed with the imperishable, and the mortal with immortality, then the saying that is written will come true: 'Death has been swallowed up in victory'" (1 Corinthians 15:52-54). These truths have tremendous implications for counseling the depressed, the ill, and the grieving.

God the Father is described by James as the "Father of lights." This title indicates God's perfect knowledge and wisdom. He understands and reveals truth, and His truth does not change with every new fad. "Every good and perfect gift is from above, coming down from the Father of the heavenly lights, who does not change like shifting shadows" (James 1:17). God's light is explained throughout the Scripture. The applications to counseling are obvious. Look at the following verses and see how God's wisdom applies to our deepest needs.

• Psalm 27:1—"The LORD is my light and my salvation—whom shall I fear? The LORD is the stronghold of my life—of whom shall I be afraid?" Our knowledge of God has a practical benefit for believers. We get our ultimate truth, or light, from God, and as a result of this intimate knowledge we do not have to fear. A proper understanding of the Father can help overcome irrational worries.

A man came to me one Sunday after the morning service and said, "Pastor, God has done such a work in my life! When I began attending church here, I was being treated for anxiety disorder. I was having panic attacks and the doctors were giving me Valium and other drugs. Now that I'm learning about God, I am completely drug-free. My heart rate is normal." His face glowed with joy and peace because of the truths of God's Word.

• Psalm 36:9—"For with you is the fountain of life; in your light we see light." The light of God gives the believer an understanding of life itself. That is what so many counselees are seeking—meaning and purpose for their very existence.

• Isaiah 60:20—"Your sun will never set again, and your moon will wane no more; the LORD will be your everlasting light, and your days of sorrow will end." This promise to Israel certainly applies individually to every believer as well, for as we learn to walk in God's light, He removes our sorrow and replaces it with joy.

• 1 John 1:5—"This is the message we have heard from him and declare to you: God is light; in him there is no darkness at all." God fully understands man. His Word shines a bright spotlight into the darkest regions of our hearts to reveal sin and to point the way to the Savior and to genuine inner healing.

• 2 Samuel 22:2—God is described as our Fortress, Deliverer, Rock, Shield, Horn of Salvation, Stronghold, Refuge, and Savior. These titles reflect the protection and security which God offers to His people. What blessed truths these are when counseling a person who is full of fear and desperately in need of comfort!

• Matthew 6:26—God is called our "heavenly Father." Carefully studying His character can help a person to understand what an earthly father ought to be. This is especially important if a counselee had an abusive childhood or if he did not have a good father model to imitate. Paul picks up this image in Ephesians 5:1, where he implores us to "be imitators of God, therefore, as dearly loved children."

Other titles of God the Father are equally helpful in developing a biblical counseling system. He is called the "Holy One of Israel" in Psalm 71:22; the self-existent "I

Am" in Exodus 3:14; the "Judge" in Genesis 18:25; the "living God" in Joshua 3:10; and "my strength" in Exodus 15:2. These few examples can be developed by a counselor or counselee to gain a more complete understanding of the nature and character of God the Father.

The Role of the Son
in Counseling

It is just as important to develop an accurate Christology in biblical counseling, for we are told in Hebrews 1:2 that "in these last days [God] has spoken to us by his Son, whom he appointed heir of all things, and through whom he made the universe." If we want to more fully understand the Father, we must study the Son.

Nothing could be more practical in the arena of personal counseling than the coming of God the Son to earth. His coming fulfilled the promises God made through the ages that He would provide a remedy for sin and separation from the Father. The Son is the best explanation of the Father, for "the Son is the radiance of God's glory and the exact representation of his being" (Hebrews 1:3).

He is our merciful and faithful High Priest, who makes atonement for our sins (Hebrews 2:17). What a glorious comfort it is to know that "we do not have a high priest who is unable to sympathize with our weaknesses, but we have one who has been tempted in every way, just as we are—yet was without sin" (Hebrews 4:15)! This is an important truth for hurting people because "such a high priest meets our need—one who is holy, blameless, pure, set apart from sinners, exalted above the heavens" (Hebrews 7:26). This truth is meant to have an impact upon our mind and emotions: "Therefore," the writer of Hebrews says, "... fix your thoughts on Jesus, the apostle and high priest whom we confess" (Hebrews 3:1).

In one way or another, sin is the ultimate cause of mental and emotional problems. The incarnation—the coming of Christ to earth in human form—is God's ultimate solution. God the Son "appeared once for all at the end of the ages to do away with sin by the sacrifice of himself" (Hebrews 9:26). His purpose in coming was to minister to the needs of mankind: "The Son of Man did not come to be served, but to serve, and to give his life as a ransom for many" (Mark 10:45).

How did Jesus' coming actually affect human dysfunctions? The apostle John explained, "The reason the Son of God appeared was to destroy the devil's work" (1 John 3:8). This is not just a theological overcoming of evil, for it has a practical bearing on the believer's day-to-day lifestyle. Jesus, having experienced the human condition, knows our desperate need to be delivered from the clutches of evil and the fear that sin produces. As Hebrews puts it, "Since the children have flesh and blood, he too shared in their humanity so that by his death he might destroy him who holds the power of death—that is, the devil" (Hebrews 2:14). It is literally through Christ's death on the cross that Satan is overcome and the believer can experience deliverance. How does Christ do this? By giving us a new worldview, a new perspective on life's meaning, and by assuring us that our 70 or 80 years on earth are just the beginning. As a result, Christ is able to "free those who all their lives were held in slavery by their fear of death" (Hebrews 2:15).

Furthermore, Christ's coming has given us an example of real mental and emotional well-being. He encourages us to examine His life and "learn from me, for I am gentle and humble in heart, and you will find rest for your souls [*psuché*]" (Matthew 11:29). In this context, it is interesting to note that the Lord offers us rest for our *psyche*. He is the ultimate psychologist. We are told that "Christ suffered for you, leaving you an example, that you should follow in his steps" (1 Peter 2:21). For the suffering Christian who is seeking peace of heart and mind, no other study is more significant than the life, character, and teachings of Jesus Christ.

The Role of the Holy Spirit in Counseling

The third Person of the Trinity, the Holy Spirit, is equally critical for true healing of the heart and mind. He is described by several names that help us see His role in counseling. Jesus calls the Holy Spirit "the Counselor" in John 14:16 and then tells us that the Holy Spirit is always available (He abides forever), that He will help us to remember Christ's teachings (John 14:26), that He will testify about Christ (John 15:26), that He will convict mankind of sin (John 16:7,8), and that He will guide us into all truth (John 16:13).

The Holy Spirit is the One who actually applies the truths of God's Word to the believer's life. He makes theology come alive. He does this in several ways.

One, as He dwells within believers, He motivates us toward compliance with God's will. God describes this process in Ezekiel 36:27: "I will put my Spirit in you and move you to follow my decrees and be careful to keep my laws."

Two, we are told that the indwelling of the Holy Spirit can actually change our very nature, for "if anyone is in Christ, he is a new creation; the old has gone, the new has come!" (2 Corinthians 5:17). Though Paul confesses the struggle between the old nature and the new (Romans 7), he assures us that "you, however, are controlled not by the sinful nature but by the Spirit, if the Spirit of God lives in you" (Romans 8:9). This is a life-changing and liberating truth that must be emphasized in biblical counseling. We are no longer slaves to the past. We are not what we once were. We are changed. We are new in Christ!

And three, the Holy Spirit's work in our lives is continuous and complete: "As for you, the anointing you received from him remains in you, and you do not need anyone to teach you" (1 John 2:27). This does not mean that we never need instruction, but that there is no new teaching apart from the Word that is *essential* for the believer's sanctification. John emphasizes this point in the next phrase: "his anointing teaches you about all things." John even anticipates the secular skepticism that questions the reality of the Holy Spirit's work by saying that the "anointing is real, not counterfeit"; therefore, he pleads with believers to "remain in him" (1 John 2:27).

When we seek psychic healing from the secular precepts of worldly counseling, we are, in effect, denying the sufficiency of God. I am convinced that this is not the intention of my integrationist colleagues. I believe that many of them love the Lord Jesus deeply and want to serve Him faithfully. But I think they are convinced that the Bible does not deal with many, if not most, of the problems of modern living, and that we must therefore seek solutions in scientific research and psychological findings. They do not seem to understand that to insist the Bible lacks essential truths necessary for man's inner health is to deny the sufficiency of the Scriptures.

God's Provision for Counseling

A necessary presupposition of biblical counseling is that God has indeed provided *every* essential truth the believer needs for a happy, fulfilling life in Christ Jesus. It is the belief that God has not left us lacking in *any* sense. The apostle Peter states it emphatically in his second epistle: "His divine power has given us everything we need for life and godliness through our knowledge of him who called us by his own glory and goodness" (2 Peter 1:3).

Note the word *everything*. God has provided absolutely *everything* man needs for physical and spiritual life. This is a primary consideration. If Peter is correct, then God has given us all the information we need to function successfully in this life. *Every* essential truth, *every* essential principle, *every* essential technique for solving human problems has been delivered in God's Word. Peter underlines this fact when he writes, "[God] has given us his very great and precious promises, so that through them you may participate in the divine nature and escape the corruption in the world caused by evil desires" (2 Peter 1:4).

This is to be the goal of biblical counseling—escaping the corruption of the world. We are not told merely to cope or to survive as victims. We are not told just to do the best we can; we are told we can escape the corruption of the world through obedience to the truths of God's Word.

Some reply, "Yes, but God *could* provide for our inner healing through psychological means, couldn't He?"

Of course He *could*, but there is no biblical evidence that He *does*. Instead, the Scriptures demand that we accept personal responsibility for our inner health. Peter insists that we "make every effort to add to your faith goodness; and to goodness, knowledge; and to knowledge, self-control; and to self-control, perseverance; and to perseverance, godliness; and to godliness, brotherly kindness; and to brotherly kindness, love" (2 Peter 1:5-7). Note that we must "make every effort." God does not produce sanctification in His children as we sit passively waiting. We are to cooperate fully with the Holy Spirit as He develops His fruit within us.

Paul refers to this cooperative submission in Galatians 5:16: "So I say, live by the Spirit, and you will not gratify the desires of the sinful nature." He amplifies it further: "Those who belong to Christ Jesus have crucified the sinful nature with its passions and desires. Since we live by the Spirit, let us keep in step with the Spirit" (verses 24,25). These are active choices that Paul commands us to make.

The result, according to Peter, is that "if you possess these qualities in increasing measure, they will keep you from being ineffective and unproductive in your knowledge of our Lord Jesus Christ" (2 Peter 1:8). Life does not have to be empty, pointless, and confusing for God's children.

"But," Peter warns, "if anyone does not have [these qualities], he is nearsighted and blind, and has forgotten that he has been cleansed from his past sins" (2 Peter 1:9). I am saddened when I see a believer dragged back into the putrid muck of former years by a counselor who is convinced that a person can only be healed in the present by returning to his past. The counselee is made to forget "that he has been cleansed from his past sins," and the pain and depth of guilt he feels is even greater than before he knew Christ.

Peter condemns teachers who "secretly introduce destructive heresies, even denying the sovereign Lord who bought them—bringing swift destruction on themselves" (2 Peter 2:1). Now I repeat that I do *not* believe most integrationists intentionally deny the Lord, but when they destroy believers' confidence in the sufficiency of Christ's work on the cross, that is the net effect.

They claim that their innovative therapies will solve inner problems and that people respond because it seems so sophisticated to accept psychological findings and so simplistic to follow the Word of God. Peter says that teachers who deny the Scriptures "mouth empty, boastful words and, by appealing to the lustful desires of sinful human nature, they entice people who are just escaping from those who live in error" (2 Peter 2:18).

He describes the devastating results:

> They promise them freedom, while they themselves are slaves of depravity—for a man is a slave to whatever has mastered him. If they have escaped the corruption of the world by knowing our Lord and Savior Jesus Christ and are again entangled in it and overcome, they are worse off at the end than they were at the beginning. It would have been better for them not to have known the way of righteousness, than to have known it and then to turn their backs on the sacred command that was passed on to them. Of them the proverbs are true: "A dog returns to its vomit," and, "A sow that is washed goes back to her wallowing in the mud" (2 Peter 2:19-22).

Once again, I must pause to emphasize that I am not accusing my integrationist brethren of intentionally enslaving their counselees. I truly believe that they are sincerely trying to help the hurting. I love them and respect them. But I grieve that they dispense psychological remedies that are doomed to failure rather than the truths of God's Word—truths that are the "power of God for the salvation of everyone who believes" (Romans 1:16). It is *God's* power that transforms the human heart.

Man's Fallen Condition

Biblical counseling accepts the unpleasant doctrine of the depravity of man. The Bible paints a bleak picture of the condition of man's heart:

Genesis 6:5—The LORD saw how great man's wickedness on the earth had become, and that every inclination of the thoughts of his heart was only evil all the time.

1 Kings 8:46—There is no one who does not sin.

Psalm 14:3—All have turned aside, they have together become corrupt; there is no one who does good, not even one.

Proverbs 20:9—Who can say, "I have kept my heart pure; I am clean and without sin"?

Ecclesiastes 7:20—There is not a righteous man on earth who does what is right and never sins.

Isaiah 53:6—We all, like sheep, have gone astray, each of us has turned to his own way; and the LORD has laid on him the iniquity of us all.

Isaiah 64:6—All of us have become like one who is unclean, and all our righteous acts are like filthy rags; we all shrivel up like a leaf; and like the wind our sins sweep us away.

Romans 3:23—For all have sinned and fall short of the glory of God.

Galatians 3:22—But the Scripture declares that the whole world is a prisoner of sin.

1 John 1:8—If we claim to be without sin, we deceive ourselves and the truth is not in us.

1 John 5:19—The whole world is under the control of the evil one.

In direct contradiction of Scripture, a foundational precept of psychology is the inherent goodness of the human heart. It is sometimes described as "the innocent child within." Man is seen as a victim, not a sinner, and as long as he perceives himself as an innocent casualty rather than a willful rebel, he will remain in his sins. Yet man's only hope for change is to acknowledge his fallen condition and helplessness before God and to cry out in faith for God's transforming power to be applied.

Man's Confusion

One result of the fall of man into sin is confusion. On his own, man is unable to discern how desperate his condition actually is. That is why counselees are so frequently in "denial." The alcoholic says, "I don't really have a problem. I can stop drinking anytime I want." The man who is inflamed with lust says, "It isn't wrong to read *Playboy*. Erotic stimulation is perfectly normal and I should not feel guilty." The couple who have tired of each other reason in their minds, "God wouldn't want us to remain unhappy all our lives. Surely He would approve of our divorce."

Jeremiah explains why humans are so confused: "The heart is deceitful above all things and beyond cure [or "desperately wicked"]. Who can understand it?" (Jeremiah 17:9). By nature, we are so deceitful it seems we can't even tell ourselves the truth. We lie to ourselves and say "I'm not really bad" or "It isn't my fault" or "I'm justified in how I feel or what I did."

Not only are we unable to fully understand our own hearts without the light of God's Word, but other humans are also unable to analyze our inner motivations. Even the psychological experts are at a loss to accurately explain why a person does what he does. That is why psychiatrists fail so miserably in predicting whether a felon will repeat his crime upon release from prison.

God asks, "Who can understand man's heart?" Then He answers the question: "I the LORD search the heart and examine the mind, to reward a man according to his conduct, according to what his deeds deserve" (Jeremiah 17:9,10). God alone is capable of discerning a person's true inner condition, and He reveals that condition through His Word: "For the word of God is living and active. Sharper than any double-edged sword, it penetrates even to dividing soul and spirit, joints and marrow; it judges the thoughts and attitudes of the heart" (Hebrews 4:12).

No psychological text can do that. No temperament analysis test can reveal a person's real nature or problem. Depending on such unreliable tools only increases the confusion which a troubled person suffers.

Man's Rebellion

The root of original sin was selfism, and the essence was rebellion. Satan rebelled against God with the intent of setting himself up as the Most High. Rebellion always affects one's judgment, and Satan must have believed he could actually pull off the first palace coup. Since that initial act of anarchy, Satan has led mankind into a perpetual series of rebellions and the result has been chaos, destruction, and misery.

God warns us that rebellion is not a harmless and natural part of growing up, but that it is desperately wicked. In fact, He says that "rebellion is like the sin of divination, and arrogance like the evil of idolatry" (1 Samuel 15:23). Divination (consulting evil spirits) and idolatry are two of the most serious offenses against God, for they reflect man's "in-your-face" attitude toward God.

There are terrifying consequences for rebellion. Samuel warned Israel, "If you do not obey the LORD, and if you rebel against his commands, his hand will be against you, as it was against your fathers" (1 Samuel 12:15). Perhaps the most frightening consequence of rebellion is that God allows us to destroy ourselves: "Why do you persist in rebellion? Your whole head is injured, your whole heart afflicted" (Isaiah 1:5).

Rebellion is the desire to control one's own life rather than to submit to God. It is described in Psalm 2:1-3: "Why do the nations conspire and the peoples plot in vain? The kings of the earth take their stand and the rulers gather together against the LORD and against his Anointed One. 'Let us break their chains,' they say, 'and throw off their fetters.'"

What was true of ancient man is still true today. We are all rebels at heart. We don't want to listen to God. We have "rebelled against the words of God and despised the counsel of the Most High" (Psalm 107:11).

Why do we choose to rebel? Because it is part of our very nature to do so. Paul writes, "The sinful mind is hostile to God. It does not submit to God's law, nor can it do so" (Romans 8:7). Since people have dismissed the concept of God, "'there is no fear of God before their eyes'" (Romans 3:18). Spiritual things are simply ridiculous to the natural man: "The man without the Spirit does not accept the things that come from the Spirit of God, for they are foolishness to him, and he cannot understand them, because they are spiritually discerned" (1 Corinthians 2:14).

Modern man has dismissed the concept of God as an archaic relic of our superstitious past. As a result, he has decided to rely upon his own experience, reason, and feelings to guide his beliefs, attitudes, and behavior. Fallen, confused, and rebellious, man is dysfunctional in every sense of the word. He is left in a state of darkness, groping for meaning and direction. Jesus described it this way: "If your eyes are bad, your whole body will be full of darkness. If then the light within you is darkness, how great is that darkness!" (Matthew 6:23).

Man's Hopelessness

Another assumption of biblical counseling is that, left to himself and without God's help, man is hopeless and powerless to change his true inner nature and his ultimate destiny. Biblical counselors recognize the fact that individuals are able to alter their thinking patterns, attitudes, and behavior to a limited extent, and that the results of those changes can provide a temporary measure of psychological relief. The assumption of man's hopelessness is not an argument or justification for fatalism—the passive acceptance of one's lot in life—but a recognition of reality.

Think this presupposition through carefully. It is based upon the biblical doctrine of man's desperate need for God. Unregenerate man is "separate from Christ... without hope and without God in the world" (Ephesians 2:12). Unless he has been redeemed through Christ, a person's ultimate destiny is eternal separation from God, and his fear of death is natural and rational. As life draws toward its end, a person may feel like Job: "My days are swifter than a weaver's shuttle, and they come to an end without hope" (Job 7:6). In contrast, Paul says that when believers in Jesus Christ come face to face with death, they do not have "to grieve like the rest of men, who have no hope" (1 Thessalonians 4:13).

A primary goal, therefore, in biblical counseling is sharing the "blessed hope," Jesus Christ (Titus 2:13). What a contrast this is to integrated counseling systems that try to provide hope for clients through innovative techniques of psychotherapies! While psychology points abuse victims to their past, biblical counseling points them to present and future victory in Christ. In contrast to "inner child" theories, biblical counseling seeks to move counselees toward maturity in Christ. Instead of leading people through 12 steps of recovery, biblical counseling teaches how to follow in Christ's steps. The central truth, the primary focus, the philosophical foundation, the reality of hope, the power for change, and the goals of biblical counseling are *all found in Jesus Christ.*

The Sufficiency of Christ

It all boils down to this: No matter how it is worded, regardless of how cleverly it is packaged, whether or not the motive is sincere, *counseling that is merged with psychological theory does* not *believe that Christ is sufficient to heal the troubled heart.*

Some would reply, "We are not questioning the sufficiency of *Christ.* We are merely saying that the *Bible* does not address many of the problems facing contemporary human beings and that we need the valid findings and insights available from psychology to help hurting souls."

That's exactly my point! When you say the Scriptures are not enough, you are in fact saying that *Christ* is not enough, for the Bible is about Christ from cover to cover. Its purpose is to reveal His coming, His life, His mission, His teachings, His death, His resurrection victory, His return to heaven, His current advocacy, His preparation of our heavenly dwelling places, His imminent return, His future reign, and the eternity He has planned for all believers.

Every spiritual/mental/emotional human need is met in Christ. Jesus claimed as much when He said, "I am the way and the truth and the life" (John 14:6). In Him we can find meaning and direction—the Way. We discover the answer to the deepest of all philosophical questions, "What is truth?" In Him we encounter life at its deepest, fullest, and richest. He removes the mystery of origins and destinies. When we walk close beside Him, He removes all fear, and He heals the wounded heart.

Paul writes, "God is able to make *all* grace abound to you, so that in *all* things at *all* times, having *all* that you need, you will abound in *every* good work" (2 Corinthians 9:8, emphasis added). He amplifies this promise in Philippians: "And my God will meet *all* your needs according to his glorious riches in Christ Jesus" (Philippians 4:19, emphasis added). Sounds *all*-inclusive, doesn't it? All of these things He does *with and through the written Word* as the Holy Spirit applies it to our hearts.

The solution to our deepest problems of living is not psychotherapy, but *Christotherapy*. Rather than analyzing our painful dysfunctions, "let us fix our eyes on Jesus, the author and perfecter of our faith, who for the joy set before him endured the cross, scorning its shame, and sat down at the right hand of the throne of God" (Hebrews 12:2).

The Sufficiency of God's Word

To claim the belief that Christ is sufficient while saying that the Bible is deficient simply will not work, for the two are inseparable foundations: It is through the written Word of God that we come to understand the living Word of God.

Jesus is called the Word of God (John 1:1,14; 1 John 1:1; Revelation 19:13), and the Scriptures are also called the Word of God (Psalm 119; Ephesians 6:17) because they both are supernatural revelations about God.

Peter explained the connection this way:

> Grace and peace be yours in abundance through the knowledge of God and of Jesus our Lord. His divine power has given us everything we need for life and godliness through

our knowledge of him who called us by his own glory and goodness. Through these he has given us his very great and precious promises, so that through them you may participate in the divine nature and escape the corruption in the world caused by evil desires (2 Peter 1:2-4).

God's provision for our needs—His grace—and the peace we so desperately seek are available, Peter says, through "the knowledge of God and of Jesus our Lord." Furthermore, God's power has already given us *everything* we need for life and godliness" (emphasis added). That is all-inclusive. No essential need has been left unattended by our gracious God. How did He provide for every need? "Through our knowledge of him." And how do we obtain knowledge about Christ? Through the written Word.

As earnestly as I know how, I plead with you to understand this vital truth: God has provided answers in His Scriptures for *every* possible spiritual/mental/emotional problem that mankind *has ever* and *could ever* experience. There are no truly unique problems that modern man experiences. Sexual, verbal, and physical abuse have been with us since the days of Cain. Marriage problems, poor self-esteem, addictions of every sort, Attention Deficit Disorder, jealousy, violent rage, depression, and virtually every other psychological dysfunction are recorded in biblical case histories.

It is astonishing that *Christian* psychologists are claiming that psychology has something to offer that the Bible does not provide. Pastor John MacArthur, whose church was sued for biblically counseling a young man who went on to commit suicide (although he was also under psychiatric care), writes about the trial:

> Most surprising to me were the so-called Christian psychologists and psychiatrists who testified that the Bible alone does not contain sufficient help to meet people's deepest personal and emotional needs. These men were

actually arguing before a secular court that God's Word is not an adequate resource for counseling people about their spiritual problems! What is truly appalling is the number of evangelicals who are willing to take such "professionals'" word for it.[1]

This debate is not as complex as many would have us believe. Either the Bible is adequate or it isn't. It's that simple.

■ ■ ■

I'm glad to see you again, Ellen, Walt," John said cordially as the Harrisons walked into his office for their appointment. Cliff Chase sat off to John's left and stood as they came in. "You remember that I asked your permission for Cliff to join us in these sessions, don't you?"

"Yes," Walt said, a little uncomfortably, feeling that Cliff might have been hurt by their attendance at Faith Evangelical instead of Cliff's church. "Hi, Cliff. How are you doing?"

"Really well, Walt, thanks!" Cliff said. "I've missed you and Ellen. Thanks for letting me sit in on your sessions. John has agreed to tutor me in counseling, and I can't think of anyone I'd rather learn with than you two," he said sincerely, with a warm smile.

Ellen couldn't help but smile back and Walt positively beamed with relief.

"Are you ready to sign the counseling contract?" John asked Ellen.

"Yes, I guess I am," she said with a resigned attitude. He slid the form over to her and she read it again. Shaking her head slightly, she signed her name and handed the form back to John.

"From the counseling form and from the first session, I understand that you are a believer in Jesus Christ. Is that correct?"

"Absolutely," she affirmed without hesitation.

"And, as a Christian, do you believe that the Bible is actually God's Word to us?"

"Of course I do."

"All of it or just part of it?"

"Every last word," Ellen replied with genuine conviction.

"That's encouraging," John said as he reached over and picked up his Bible. "Let me show you a passage in the Word, Ellen." He quickly flipped to the book of Second Peter. He turned his Bible around so Ellen could read it. "Would you please read the passage out loud for me? Start there about verse 3 and go on down to about verse 9 or 10."

Ellen took John's Bible and began to read, "His divine power has given us everything we need for life and godliness through our knowledge of him who called us by his own glory and goodness. Through these he has given us his very great and precious promises, so that through them you may participate in the divine nature and escape the corruption in the world caused by evil desires."

John stopped her and asked, "Ellen, tell me in your own words what those verses mean."

She silently read verses 3 and 4 again, and her forehead wrinkled as she sat thinking deeply. "I . . . I don't know," she finally stammered.

"Let's take the verses thought by thought," John led her gently. "Whose power is Peter talking about?"

"God's?" she ventured.

"Right. And what has He given us through His power?"

"Everything we need for life and godliness."

"*How* much of what we need?" John prompted.

"It says *every*thing."

"And what does God give us everything for?"

"For life and godliness," Ellen answered as she pointed to the verse with her finger.

"Does that include every part of a believer's existence?" John asked.

"What do you mean?" Ellen asked sincerely.

"Is there *any* area of a person's life that God has not provided for?"

"It doesn't look like it, from these verses," Ellen admitted. "I see where you're going with this, Pastor Kryer. But isn't it possible that God has provided for our inner hurts, our psychological problems, by the psychological truths discovered in our own day?"

"Of course it's *possible*. With God anything is possible. But there are at least two weaknesses with that argument. The first is the question of *how* one determines whether a psychological finding is *truth*. How does one prove a psychological theory using empirical scientific method?" Seeing from her expression that he was stretching Ellen's understanding, John slowed down. "Take, for instance, Freud's concepts of the *id*, *ego*, and *superego*. How does one prove they even *exist*, let alone define their effect on people's lives? They cannot be seen with any scientific instrument, they do not react with chemical precision, and they cannot be quantified."

Walt held up his hand and said, "Excuse me? What do you mean they can't be 'quantified'?"

"I mean there is no way for a scientist to measure or weigh the *id* or the *ego*. No one can scientifically observe the 'inner child' that psychologists are so fond of talking about. For that matter, they can't even define the *mind*, let alone examine it."

"Wait a minute!" Ellen interrupted. "Of *course* scientists can examine the mind. They do it all the time!"

"Really? Tell me how they do it," John said.

"Well," Ellen moistened her lips and looked around the room, thinking quickly, "when brain surgeons apply an electrode to a person's brain, they can cause a person to lift his hand involuntarily or stimulate a memory, or change the expression on his face. I read about it in a magazine."

"True enough," John agreed, "but all they are doing is examining the *brain* and moving the physical body. The brain and the mind are not the same, any more than the body and the soul are the same. One is merely the vehicle for the other. Though they affect each other, they must not be confused with one another. Since scientific method cannot be used to prove psychological theory, it is an error to put the words *psychological* and *science* together. And since truth itself is a philosophical and religious concept, the words *psychological* and *truth* cannot logically be connected."

Ellen held her hands up. "I surrender!" she said with a weak smile. "You said there were two problems with the argument that God could use psychological truths—okay! psychological *theories!*—to apply His healing power to our modern needs. What's the second?"

"The second error in that philosophy," John replied, "is the belief that modern living is categorically different from life in previous eras."

"Come now, Pastor Kryer," Ellen scolded. "Even you must admit that modern life is much more complex and pressured than it was in ancient times."

"Let's discuss it," John returned with a smile. "In what ways is life more complex and pressured?"

"In *every* way! Our schedules are more hectic! There's so much more information to absorb. We're always hurried just to keep up with all the activities we're expected to be involved in! There are more depressions and dysfunctions than in times past. We live in crowded cities, move about on congested highways, and breathe polluted air. They are discovering new mental illnesses every day. That's why there is such an overwhelming need for psychologists and psychiatrists and why mental health clinics and hospitals seem to be springing up everywhere."

"You're confusing the results of psychological thinking with the cause, Ellen," John corrected.

"What do you mean?"

"There is good reason to question whether there are more psychiatrists today because there are more 'mental illnesses'—as you call them—or whether there are more 'mental illnesses' because there are more psychiatrists."

Walt laughed out loud, then looked at Ellen's glare and stifled himself.

John continued. "Let's look at your premise for a moment, that 'modern life is more complex and pressured than in the past.' Other than our modes of transportation, communication, and technology, what has *really* changed in human life? Obviously, we can travel more quickly from city to city because of flight and we can communicate by way of telephones and satellites, and mass production has allowed us to manufacture material goods more efficiently and cheaply, but has *man* actually changed in his essential nature?"

"I don't know," Ellen said hesitantly.

"I contend, Ellen, that our modern advances have actually made our lives *less* complex than our ancestors' because we do not each have to master as many skills as they did. Past generations had to build their own homes and furniture, spin their own wool, make their own clothing, haul their own water, process and preserve their own food, defend their homes against the elements and enemies, and so forth from the first light of day until sunset. What they couldn't do for themselves they had to find a way to barter for. We, on the other hand, have so much leisure time that we waste countless hours watching television and trying to think of things to do."

"Exactly!" Ellen said, emphasizing the point with her finger. "Modern society is dysfunctional because of the breakdown of the social fabric that held families and friends together. Isolation is one cause for the deep depressions and psychic distress that we see all around us. Our hearts are wounded by the cruelty inflicted on us by others."

"I agree that modern man has allowed the family to fall apart. Little wonder, with the emphasis on personal gratification rather than responsibility. But Ellen, do you really believe that family breakdown is a *modern* phenomenon? Do you think that man has experienced deep depressions only in the twentieth century? Don't you realize that the ancients experienced intense emotional pressure when their enemies stood outside their city walls threatening them with horrible torture and slow death? Hasn't man struggled with the abuse of alcohol since the beginning of time? Sexual abuse is recorded again and again in the Bible. I doubt that you can point to a single psychic ailment of modern times that has not been evident throughout history."

He waited, letting the point sink in. Ellen didn't answer.

"One further point," John said, "and we'll move on. If psychology is the absolute necessity that many Christian leaders would have you believe, we must feel sorry for all the saints who lived in the days of Abraham, Moses, David, Ezekiel, Jesus, Paul, and the early church."

"I don't follow you," Ellen said glumly.

"Well, if psychology is essential to the healing of souls, how in the world did the ancients ever deal with persecution, suffering, and death without the invaluable insights of Freud, Maslow, Minirth, or Crabb? How were Martin Luther, the Puritans, Charles Spurgeon, D.L. Moody, and a host of other preachers able to minister to millions of people with just the simplistic statements of the Word of God?"

Walt nodded and said, "Good point, Pastor Kryer." Cliff was writing on his notepad as fast as his hand could move.

"Ellen," John said gently, "Let's finish the passage you began to read earlier."

Ellen looked down at the Bible that lay in her lap and read, "For this very reason, make every effort to add to your faith goodness; and to goodness, knowledge; and to knowledge, self-control; and to self-control, perseverance; and to perseverance, godliness; and to godliness, brotherly kindness; and to brotherly kindness, love. For if you possess these qualities in increasing measure, they will keep you from being ineffective and unproductive in your knowledge of our Lord Jesus Christ."

She stopped and looked up at John. "Why, those are the very character traits—or qualities, as it says here—that psychologists try to produce in their clients!"

"Now you're starting to see it, Ellen," John smiled with relief. "Read that next verse and we'll finish up for today."

Ellen read softly, "But if anyone does not have them, he is nearsighted and blind, and..." she stopped, suddenly choking with emotion. Tears began to well up in her eyes and ran down her face as she whispered brokenly, "...and has forgotten that he has been cleansed from his past sins."

She looked up through the mist in her eyes. "I was forgiven when I came to Christ! I didn't have to go back and dredge up the past! How could I have been such a fool?"

She turned to Walt, who was also crying, and whispered because that was all the voice she could muster, "Oh, Honey! I'm so very sorry! Can you ever forgive me?"

Walt reached over and grabbed her soft fingers in his large calloused hands and whispered back, "Oh, Ellen, of course I forgive you! Forgive me for being so harsh!"

They stood, forgetting that John and Cliff were in the room. They embraced as they cried together with tears of sorrow, repentance, and joy. "I love you, Walter!" Ellen said and kissed him.

"I love you more than I can say, Darling," Walt answered softly and hugged her tightly to his chest.

John swallowed hard, pulled a handkerchief out of his pocket, wiped his eyes, and blew his nose. Walt and Ellen suddenly remembered John was there, turned to see him, and began to laugh. Cliff stood behind him, his face glowing with joy.

"Don't mind my tears," John said. "I'm well-named. I'm a real crier!"

They all laughed again. "Sorry, preachers!" Walt said, wiping the tears from his face. "I forgot you guys were here!"

"I'm glad you did, Walt," John answered. Turning to Ellen he said, "Is there anyone else you should ask forgiveness from?"

She looked blankly at him. "I don't know. Unless you mean . . . God."

John smiled and nodded. "Why don't you tell Him you're sorry for doubting His forgiveness and His Word."

Walt and Ellen sat back down, this time holding hands. They all bowed their heads as Ellen prayed, "O Father, I am so very sorry for turning my back on You. How could I have believed that I needed to work through the very things You forgave and cleansed years ago? Please forgive me for listening to the fallible theories of men rather than finding answers in Your Word. Cleanse my heart again, and fill it with the joy I once knew. Forgive me for not being the wife I should have been for Walt. Thank You that He stayed with me through all of this. Make our marriage stronger than ever as we learn to trust You daily. In Jesus' glorious name I pray this. Amen."

Walt squeezed her hand and prayed, "Dear Lord, my heart is so full of gratitude right now for giving us answers today. Thank You for Pastor Kryer, who knew how to open Your Word to us. Bless him and his ministry. Thank You for Cliff caring enough to be here with us. Thank You for bringing my wife back to me, and forgive me for doubting Your power to do it. We love You, Jesus. Amen!"

"Amen!" John agreed. Looking up, he asked Ellen, "What are you going to tell your psychologist?"

"I'm going to cancel all further appointments! I've got the Word of God to guide me!"

"Don't be surprised if he doesn't receive your news enthusiastically," John warned. "When you talk with him don't be harsh, accusing, or sarcastic. Be gentle, sincere, and loving, as Jesus would have you be with everyone. Be firm when he tries to convince you to return. Share with him that, as a Christian, you have found that you have all the resources you need for solving the problems of living in the Word of God."

Ellen nodded, "I will, Pastor Kryer."

"There's one other thing," Walt said. "I haven't talked this over with Ellen yet, but I think we should return to our own church family."

"I couldn't agree with you more!" John said with a smile. "What do you think, Cliff?"

"Nothing would make me happier, Walt, Ellen! Welcome back home!"

The Biblical Counselor

Who among us would deny that many, if not most, pastors are currently incompetent to counsel their people effectively? But the challenge before us is this: If we will not take the time to become competent, to whom will our people turn? The evidence is that they will turn to psychiatrists, psychologists, and social workers.

The Word of God

Preach the Word; be prepared in season and out of season; correct, rebuke and encourage—with great patience and careful instruction. For the time will come when men will not put up with sound doctrine.
—2 Timothy 4:2,3

13

A Biblical Place for Counseling

Christ has given a unique call, mission, and authority to the church to counsel God's people. The ultimate purpose of counseling is to sanctify—set apart, reserve specially for God, make holy—God's people, positionally and experientially. In other words, biblical counseling is concerned with leading a person into salvation, whereby God considers that person holy due to his position in Christ (positionally sanctified), and into a personal daily walk with God, whereby one actually experiences a holy lifestyle (experientially sanctified). God has not authorized any other organization to carry out that responsibility.

Paul describes these two forms of sanctification in 1 Thessalonians, where he connects sanctification with peace and freedom from guilt. Note that Paul views sanctification as affecting every portion of a person's being: "May God himself, the God of peace, sanctify you through and through. May your whole spirit, soul and body be kept blameless at the coming of our Lord Jesus Christ" (1 Thessalonians 5:23).

This is where theology and real life come together. It is where theory is put into practice. This is what separates a professing Christian from the genuine article. This is what changes the desperately wicked heart into a heart that desires to please the Father.

Don't be put off by the terms *sanctification* and *holiness*. For many people these words conjure up a negative image of a monk cloistered away from real life in a forbidding and silent monastery, never having to face the day-to-day pressures of living. That concept of sanctification, however, is not the kind Jesus presented. His gentle and joyful holiness was lived out in the dusty streets of Nazareth, Capernaum, and Jerusalem as He walked and talked with real people. Remember, He was criticized by the self-righteous Pharisees for His friendship with "sinners."

Holiness and Love

God's call for us to live holy lives is based on His love for us, His children. The motivation for holiness that pleases God the most is our love for Him. Let me explain.

My wife, Marlowe, and I have four children and we are incurably proud of them. Our two oldest daughters are enjoying their studies at Moody Bible Institute, preparing to serve the Lord. Our third daughter is a vibrant witness in high school, and our only son has given us perpetual joy since he came kicking and screaming into our lives in the maternity ward.

In our family devotions, we have sometimes discussed the fact that each of us has a responsibility to uphold our family's five-century-long heritage of faith in Christ and living for the Lord. My wife and I have no guarantee that all our children will continue in our spiritual heritage, but the bond of love that we all have for one another, our commitment to the Word, and our identity as a Christian family come as close to a guarantee as we can find. Because we love our children, we want them to love our Lord. And because they love us as parents, they want to please us, and have responded to the Lord as well.

In the same way, our desire to please our heavenly Father ought to stem naturally from love. It is the loving parent-child relationship that God refers to in 2 Corinthians 6:18: "I will be a Father to you, and you will be my sons and daughters." Paul then says, "Since we have these promises, dear friends, let us purify ourselves from everything that contaminates body and spirit, perfecting holiness out of reverence for God" (2 Corinthians 7:1). This reverence is not primarily motivated by fear, but love. Because we are God's children, we are "to put on the new self, created to be like God in true righteousness and holiness" (Ephesians 4:24). Peter reminds us that "it is written: 'Be holy, because I am holy'" (1 Peter 1:16).

Holiness and Fear

If love alone is not enough to motivate the believer to holiness, the writer of Hebrews warns us, "Without holiness no one will see the Lord" (Hebrews 12:14). Peter emphasizes this fact when he writes, "Since everything will be destroyed in this way, what kind of people ought you to be? You ought to live holy and godly lives" (2 Peter 3:11). I don't want to linger over fear as a primary motivator. Fear of God has its legitimate place, but love is infinitely more pleasing to God as our reason for holiness.

The Source of Holiness

We want holiness, but don't know where to find it. Some seek it in mystical experiences, good works, or acts of penance. According to Jesus, however, sanctification comes through the Word of God: "Sanctify them by the truth; your word is truth" (John 17:17).

Real change of character happens when the truths of God's Word are understood and applied in an individual's life. There is no shortcut to spiritual maturity. It does not come by a mystical experience or new revelation. It does not come through psychological findings or clinical research. Sanctification comes when our hearts and minds are saturated with the truths of God's Word and those truths are activated in our lives by the Holy Spirit when we consciously seek to obey Him.

Let's see how the Word of God and the church are connected in the issue of counseling believers.

God's Center for Biblical Counseling

God has specifically chosen the church to evangelize the world with Christ's Word (Matthew 28:19,20). He has appointed the church to edify believers by teaching doctrine and applying biblical truths to matters of daily living. Evangelism and edification—both of these belong to the church.

Someone may properly point out that these functions of the church are not necessarily limited to the local church, but belong to the universal church (all believers of all nations in all times). This would include believers ministering from and through parachurch organizations. I do not dispute that fact. Let me suggest, however, several reasons why I believe counseling should take place within the local church.

Church, Not Parachurch

The local church is able to invest time and care on individual believers as no parachurch organization can. The term *parachurch* is revealing. *Para* means "beside"; connected with the word "church," it stands for a group that comes alongside the church to help the church fulfill its function. The parachurch organization may include people who belong to the church, but it is not in and of itself the church.

There are groups, such as James Dobson's "Focus on the Family," formed to aid and support the family unit, but those organizations are not families *per se*. Groups that are organized to aid the church in its universal ministry are composed of members of the church, but they are not the church in its local sense. Independent counseling centers may be trying to help the church in the healing of souls, but they are not the church in the biblical sense.

Part of the problem may be due to an inaccurate perception of the church itself. Some think of it as an organization, but it is more accurate to think of the local church as an organism. It is a living body composed of many members, each of whom has a specific function: "In Christ we who are many form one body, and each member belongs to all the others" (Romans 12:5). "Now you are the body of Christ, and each one of you is a part of it" (1 Corinthians 12:27). As the body of Christ in its universal sense (Ephesians 1:22; Colossians 1:18) and in its local form (1 Corinthians 12:27), the church is a single unit with interdependent members whose Head is Christ.

Each local congregation is to be an intimate family of believers. The church is called God's family in Ephesians 3:15, "from whom his whole family in heaven and on earth derives its name." Believers are not just members of a human organization, they are also part of the household of God. "Consequently, you are no longer foreigners and aliens, but fellow citizens with God's people and members of God's household" (Ephesians 2:19). Believers are called a spiritual house and a holy priesthood: "You also, like living stones, are being built into a spiritual house to be a holy priesthood, offering spiritual sacrifices acceptable to God through Jesus Christ" (1 Peter 2:5). Individually and universally, members of His church "are God's temple and ... God's Spirit lives in you" (1 Corinthians 3:16). Only the church is pictured in these ways.

To qualify as a biblical church, a group must have some form of recognized leadership such as elders, deacons, and pastors (Ephesians 4:11; Titus 1:5), and it must have some structure by which corporate decisions are made (Acts 15:2). It must be a group of believers in Jesus Christ who gather regularly for worship, Bible study, administration of the ordinances of the church (baptism and the Lord's Supper), fellowship, personal care for one another, counsel, correction, discipline, and restoration. Paul is clear about the purpose of the church and the ministries of its leaders:

> It was he who gave some to be apostles, some to be prophets, some to be evangelists, and some to be pastors and teachers, to prepare God's people for works of service, so that the body of Christ may be built up until we all reach unity in the faith and in the knowledge of

the Son of God and become mature, attaining
to the whole measure of the fullness of Christ
(Ephesians 4:11-13).

God has chosen the church alone to bring His children
into "the whole measure of the fullness of Christ." A parachurch counseling clinic that is not under the direct supervision and authority of a local church simply cannot produce
that kind of result.

Personal Care for Fellow Members

In contrast to the disengaged clinical approach that
professional counseling often follows, church leaders are
able to care for their members and become emotionally involved with their people. Paul demonstrated this devotion
to the church when he wrote, "You have such a place in our
hearts that we would live or die with you" (2 Corinthians
7:3) and, "We loved you so much that we were delighted to
share with you not only the gospel of God but our lives as
well, because you had become so dear to us" (1 Thessalonians 2:8).

The psychotherapeutic relationship is very different
from what Paul describes. When the psychologist leaves his
office, he does not have to concern himself with the impact
his advice will have on the entire congregation. It is a rare
psychologist who encourages his clients to call him any
hour, day or night, if there is a family emergency. Nor is
he called upon to provide food, clothing, and aid in case of
a financial crisis. His is a professional relationship that
begins and ends at the office door. He is a "doctor," not a
shepherd.

Knowledge of the Counselee
by Pastor and Elders

The pastor and elders of a church are able to know their
people intimately. They live with their people and know
their problems, sins, and stubbornness as well as their victo-
ries, joys, spiritual growth, and relationship to the Lord.

Paul commanded the leaders of the church to "keep watch over yourselves and all the flock of which the Holy Spirit has made you overseers. Be shepherds of the church of God, which he bought with his own blood" (Acts 20:28). Peter said that church leaders are to "be shepherds of God's flock that is under your care, serving as overseers—not because you must, but because you are willing, as God wants you to be" (1 Peter 5:2). Note in the same verse that the motivation for ministry should not be because a person is "greedy for money, but eager to serve." What a contrast to the psychotherapy industry, where patients must pay high hourly fees and professionals may not have the time to help those who cannot pay! Paul said, "I will very gladly spend for you everything I have and expend myself as well" (2 Corinthians 12:15).

Shared Experiences

One of the key strengths of the local church is that members can share common experiences. A pastor who has spent years with his people has shared the trials and tribulations that his people have gone through. In order to understand the thinking of an individual, a counselor needs firsthand knowledge of that person's cultural background. In the church setting, a pastoral counselor can identify with and understand his people in a way that an outside clinical counselor cannot.

Paul connected cultural implications with ministry in 1 Corinthians 9:

> Though I am free and belong to no man, I make myself a slave to everyone, to win as many as possible. To the Jews I became like a Jew, to win the Jews. To those under the law I became like one under the law (though I myself am not under the law), so as to win those under the law. To those not having the law I became like one not having the law (though I am not free from God's law but am under Christ's law), so as to win those not having the law. To the weak I

became weak, to win the weak. I have become
all things to all men so that by all possible
means I might save some. I do all this for the
sake of the gospel (verses 19-23).

In genuine biblical counseling, there is an identifica-
tion with the people and a personal sharing of life. There is
no hint of uninvolved professionalism. Paul wrote the saints
of Thessalonica: "We were gentle among you, like a mother
caring for her little children. We loved you so much that we
were delighted to share with you not only the gospel of God
but our lives as well, because you had become so dear to us"
(1 Thessalonians 2:7-8). Professional counselors cannot
afford to invest such time and emotion in their clients. To
survive financially, they have to quickly move on to the next
"patient."

Accountability

Perhaps the single most important reason that Christian counseling belongs in the local church is that the
counselee can be held accountable for his beliefs, attitudes,
and actions by the church leadership. And it is for that same
reason that so many Christians look for counsel anywhere
but their own church. One of the first questions I ask a
counselee who does not attend our church is, "Why aren't
you getting counsel from your own pastor?" The most
common answer seems to be, "I don't want my pastor to
know about my problems."

A few years ago a couple came to my office on the brink
of divorce. When I asked why they were not seeing their
own pastor, they admitted that they had kept up a spiritual
charade for years at their church, pretending that their
marriage was fine. They didn't want their own church to
know of the sin in their lives. I agreed to meet with them for
a short time, but told them they would eventually have to
return to their own pastor for the conclusion of counseling
and for the purpose of ongoing accountability. After a few
sessions, it became apparent that both had no intention of
changing their hearts or their behavior. They were trying to

outwait each other, hoping the other would file for divorce. They weren't about to go back to their own pastor for counseling, either. They didn't want to be held accountable.

We live in the no-fault generation. No one wants to take responsibility for his own sinful actions. We have found excuses for every conceivable failure by relabeling sins as dysfunctions and illnesses. Many churches have bought into this unbiblical philosophy and have joined with the psychological establishment in declaring that humans are all victims and need support and understanding. The Bible, however, says, "I tell you that men will have to give account on the day of judgment for every careless word they have spoken" (Matthew 12:36) and, "each of us will give an account of himself to God" (Romans 14:12). Jesus reminds us, "Behold, I am coming soon! My reward is with me, and I will give to everyone according to what he has done" (Revelation 22:12).

The biblical church has a built-in system of accountability which the Lord has authorized: "Obey your leaders and submit to their authority. They keep watch over you as men who must give an account. Obey them so that their work will be a joy, not a burden, for that would be of no advantage to you" (Hebrews 13:17).

No psychologist or counselor in an independent clinic can claim this spiritual authority. They have no such mechanism for holding the counselee accountable to obey biblical principles.

Discipline

Since there is no effective system of accountability in parachurch counseling, there is no means of discipline in the case of disobedience. And since the counseling relationship is more clinical than personal, a psychologist would find it difficult to earnestly reprove a sinful client.

Paul got involved with his people: "Remember that for three years I never stopped warning each of you night and day with tears" (Acts 20:31). Because of his spiritual authority, he could say to the Corinthians, "I already gave you a warning when I was with you the second time. I now repeat it while absent: On my return I will not spare those who sinned earlier or any of the others" (2 Corinthians 13:2). In balance, Paul was careful to explain his benevolent intentions: "I write these things when I am absent, that when I come I may not have to be harsh in my use of authority—the authority the Lord gave me for building you up, not for tearing you down" (2 Corinthians 13:10).

Discipline is rarely used in the modern church. Perhaps the pastor fears a lawsuit or is concerned about his job security. Unfortunately, it is true that many pastors are viewed as expendable employees rather than shepherds of their flocks, and in such cases it is dangerous to confront rebellious members. Nonetheless, God has called pastors to rebuke and exhort with all authority: "Preach the Word; be prepared in season and out of season; correct, rebuke and encourage—with great patience and careful instruction" (2 Timothy 4:2). It is a blessed church that has a fearless but loving pastor who will courageously confront sin with the Scripture and discipline his people with the authority of the Word. If necessary, such a pastor will follow the procedure Jesus gave in Matthew 18:

> If your brother sins against you, go and show him his fault, just between the two of you. If he listens to you, you have won your brother over. But if he will not listen, take one or two others along, so that "every matter may be established by the testimony of two or three witnesses." If he refuses to listen to them, tell it to the church; and if he refuses to listen even to the church, treat him as you would a pagan or a tax collector (verses 15-17).

The psychologist or parachurch counselor has no comparable means of discipline other than discontinuation of counseling, and since the professional counselor's income is dependent upon prolonged therapy, there is little incentive to actively confront the counselee with his sin.

Follow-Up

When a person receives spiritual counsel from his church, it is important to follow up on the progress of the counselee. The interaction goes beyond the counseling office into the worship, training, and fellowship activities of the congregation. Other members of the church can be enlisted, with the counselee's knowledge, to help maintain the progress that is achieved. This is especially important in matters of substance abuse, lust, perversion, and other long-term habitual sins. The pastor, elders, and lay counselors can work as a team ministering for a sustained period.

Also, with a church there is no cutoff of service due to insurance running out. Termination of counseling is generally reserved for willful rebellion and disobedience, since biblical counselors are concerned about the long-term success of their counselees. With Paul they say, "Let us go back and visit the brothers in all the towns where we preached the word of the Lord and see how they are doing" (Acts 15:36).

Encouragement

Biblical counselors are especially equipped to encourage counselees because they truly believe that people can permanently change through the truths of the Scriptures as they submit to the inner work of the Holy Spirit. Christian counseling is able to give a realistic perspective to the inevitable suffering that people experience in daily living. Paul and Barnabas ministered from that perspective, "strengthening the disciples and encouraging them to remain true to the faith. 'We must go through many hardships to enter the kingdom of God'" (Acts 14:22).

When counselees have grown in the Lord, they in turn can encourage others. Those who have learned to solve their problems biblically can help others find the same freedom. "Now that you have purified yourselves by obeying the truth so that you have sincere love for your brothers, love one another deeply, from the heart" (1 Peter 1:22).

Biblical counseling is encouraging because it aims at sparing believers from unnecessary suffering. Counseling in the church should be more than remedial. It can be preventive when biblical principles of living are taught from the pulpit as well as in the counseling office. Paul says that the written Word is given to teach believers how to live: "I am writing you these instructions so that, if I am delayed, you will know how people ought to conduct themselves in God's household, which is the church of the living God, the pillar and foundation of the truth" (1 Timothy 3:14,15).

Moving people from a life of darkness into light is another part of the encouragement available in the church. Biblical counseling can do that because its truths are not based upon the ever-changing findings of psychology, but upon the eternal revelations from God Himself. Such knowledge can produce great confidence for change. That is why Jesus said, "Put your trust in the light while you have it, so that you may become sons of light" (John 12:36). Paul reminded former pagans at Ephesus that "you were once darkness, but now you are light in the Lord. Live as children of light" (Ephesians 5:8). He told the Thessalonians, "You are all sons of the light and sons of the day. We do not belong to the night or to the darkness" (1 Thessalonians 5:5).

Counselors in the Church

Since the church has a unique calling and mandate for the healing of souls, pastors need to reclaim their God-given role which has been usurped by the priesthood of psychologists. Many of today's Christians are wandering in spiritual darkness, much like the people of Jesus' day: "When he saw the crowds, he had compassion on them, because they were harassed and helpless, like sheep without a shepherd" (Matthew 9:36). What a tragedy it is that so many believers are seeking wisdom outside the church because their own shepherds are unwilling to feed their flocks!

God has given the standard for His undershepherds: "... shepherds after my own heart, who will lead you with knowledge and understanding" (Jeremiah 3:15). When pastors fulfill their calling and tend their flocks carefully, their people 'will no longer be afraid or terrified, nor will any be missing,' declares the LORD" (Jeremiah 23:4). Peter exhorts the leaders of the local churches, "Be shepherds of God's flock that is under your care" (1 Peter 5:2).

Insisting on Biblical Counseling

Local church members can encourage their pastors in the task of counseling by challenging them to do the work of counseling. They can support their pastors' study and growth. They can provide financially for tuition, books, and other training expenses. The lay leadership of a church can come alongside their pastor in the task of counseling by studying lay-counseling courses such as those provided in *How to Counsel from Scripture*[1] and *Ready to Restore*.[2] Pastors who may be hesitant in undertaking the ministry of counseling may need personal encouragement from their people.

Churches must express their concerns to seminaries and Bible colleges and urge that their counseling programs return to teaching Scripture rather than psychology. This is especially true of churches that support seminaries through their denominational contributions. Unless local churches clearly voice their distress about the slide toward humanistic philosophies, their seminaries will move ever further from the Word.

Elders and deacons must challenge the membership of their churches to seek counsel from their pastors, elders, and trained laity rather than from secular or psychological sources. Believers must be taught that personal problems should be brought to their own churches before seeking help elsewhere. Frequently, members are reluctant to divulge their problems to their own pastor, feeling that he might expose them to the congregation or that he might look down upon them because they are not perfect. The pastor, then, must assure his people of confidentiality and consistent love, and that his purpose is to minister to their deepest needs.

The Final Responsibility

Returning Christian counseling to the church is up to pastors and laity. If pastors refuse to prepare themselves for this important task, psychologists will gladly accept their members as clients. If churches fail to hold their pastors accountable to perform this ministry, many will allow psychologists to do their job. Counseling is hard work and it is time-consuming, but the rewards of dealing intimately with the needs of the parishioners are well worth the cost.

Let's return to the Scriptures for the solutions to our problems. God has provided *everything* we need for life and godliness. We must not allow anyone to convince us otherwise.

■ ■ ■

"This is KWFL, Christian radio for the Rockies, inviting you to stay tuned to one of the most interesting programs you have ever heard. This is Roger Patrick, your host for the next 90 minutes on 'Today's Christian.' Our guests today are Dr. Vance McCall, Christian psychiatrist and director of Greenway Counseling Services in Westminster and the chief psychiatrist at Mount Haven Psychiatric Hospital, near Broomfield, and Dr. John Kryer, pastor of Faith Evangelical Church and director of Faith Counseling Ministries."

Roger looked across the large oak table in the studio at his two guests. All three men wore large earphones and sat facing studio microphones. A large glass window separated them from the control room, which was filled to capacity with electronic instruments.

"Gentlemen, I have to tell you, we have never had so many calls as we did when you two had a verbal exchange recently when Dr. Kryer was a guest on this program. I was surprised how upset some of the callers were, Dr. Kryer. Pastors, therapists, and counselees seemed in fairly general agreement that you are way off base in your assessment of Christian counseling."

"That doesn't surprise me, Roger," John replied. "I am aware that I represent the minority opinion and that we face an uphill battle to convince the church that our faith in and commitment to the Scriptures is being subtly eroded."

"Well, let's get started, gentlemen," Roger said. "First, let's define your two views on counseling. Correct me if I'm wrong, Dr. McCall, but I understand that your approach is to integrate psychological truths with biblical truths to form a more complete system. Is that an accurate representation?"

"That's close, Roger. I need to emphasize that in Christian counseling we do not accept all psychological theories at face value. We recognize that there are many secular concepts that are in conflict with the Word of God, and we reject those concepts. We believe, however, that there is much to be gained from the research and insights of psychological studies and that much can be integrated into biblical counseling. The final test—and I must emphasize this—the final test of what is valid and acceptable for the Christian must be the Bible."

"All right," Roger said, "now for your position, Dr. Kryer. If I understand correctly, you believe that the Bible alone is sufficient to guide Christians in solving all their problems. Is that a fair summary of your approach?"

"Let me say it this way, Roger: I believe that the Scriptures contain all the *essential* information needed for a believer to handle every problem of living. Peter writes in his second epistle, chapter 1, that God's 'divine power has given us everything we need for life and godliness through our knowledge of him who called us by his own glory and goodness.' Either that statement is true or it isn't."

"But isn't it possible, John, that part of God's total provision is found in general revelation?" Vance McCall asked. "Paul wrote in Romans chapter 1 that God has revealed Himself through nature as well as the written Word. If something is true, it is true regardless whether it is recorded in the Bible or in a science text. All truth is God's truth."

"I agree that all truth ultimately reaches back to God, Vance, but the problem is in determining what is *actually* true or what is only *apparently* true. Certain 'facts' of science have to be revised on a fairly regular basis due to the discovery of new information. In psychology, many of the so-called 'truths' are nothing more than theories that have not, and cannot, be verified either scientifically or scripturally."

"Give us an example of that, Dr. Kryer," Roger asked.

"All right. The theory of repressed memories is representative. It is a widely taught concept in Christian psychological writings and therapy that a person needs to dredge up old memories of painful events in the past in order to deal with them. This concept goes back to some of the theories of Freud and Jung. It cannot be proven scientifically and there is absolutely no biblical support for such a practice."

"I think it is a bit arrogant, John, for a pastor to make such sweeping indictments about theories you are obviously ignorant about," Vance McCall said. "There are hundreds of studies that support the fact of memory repression and the debilitating effects of repression."

John turned in his chair to face McCall. "You must be aware, Vance, that those studies do not qualify as scientific. Merely formulating questionnaires and interviewing even thousands of people about their memories does not prove a single thing. There is no scientific way to ascertain whether a person's memory of an event—or the lack of an event—is an accurate reflection of what took place in time and space, or whether the memory was actually produced by therapist suggestion, a television program, a book, a conversation, or an upset stomach."

"So are you saying that it's better for a person to push his deepest feelings back into his subconscious? Or are you denying that his traumatic experiences ever happened?" McCall challenged.

"I am not suggesting that counselees push their memories away or that they deny that bad things happened to them. When I counsel someone who suffered sexual abuse, I do not encourage him or her to deny that the event took place. I do not minimize the trauma. But I am not willing to victimize him further by making him 'embrace his pain' again, as so many psychologists teach."

"How would you suggest they free themselves of those memories, then, John, if they don't go back and work through them?"

"I suggest they follow the scriptural model found in Philippians chapter 3. Paul, who also had some very painful memories, wrote, 'Forgetting what is behind and straining toward what is ahead, I press on toward the goal to win the prize for which God has called me heavenward in Christ Jesus.'"

"So they just muddle on through life, pretending nothing bad happened, right?"

"I never ask my counselees to pretend that what is false is true," John replied evenly. "I help them to see that healing takes place when we refocus our attention from ourselves to the Lord. Hebrews 12 verse 2 says, 'Let us fix our eyes on Jesus, the author and perfecter of our faith.' I want them to see that when they are born again in Christ, the old things pass away, as Paul says in 2 Corinthians chapter 5, verse 17. It is cruel to make a person return needlessly to his past. Peter likens that to a dog returning to his vomit."

The debate continued for nearly an hour-and-a-half as John Kryer and Vance McCall jousted back and forth on the goals of counseling and how lasting change is really accomplished. McCall expounded on psychodynamic theory and cognitive therapy. John explained four biblical steps for permanent change found in 2 Timothy.

"Change doesn't have to take years of therapy," John concluded. "It can begin the instant a person realizes his position in Christ."

"Oh, come now, John," Vance scolded. "Even you must realize that many problems take a long time to solve. There are some deep-seated dysfunctions that require expert analysis and therapy to heal."

"Well, Vance, psychologists and psychiatrists would love to have us all believe that, because the longer you can keep your patients in therapy, the more money you stand to make," John said, looking Vance McCall squarely in the eyes.

"Are you accusing Christian therapists of deliberately keeping patients in treatment in order to run up their bills?" McCall asked tightly.

"I wouldn't make a blanket statement that all Christian therapists are doing that, because I believe some are sincerely trying to help others. But if a person's total income is derived from counseling revenue there is little incentive to see clients released from therapy quickly, is there?"

"No reputable therapist would abuse counseling for financial purposes, Reverend Kryer!" McCall said hotly.

"Oh, really? Have you heard of some psychiatric hospitals that are offering kickbacks to high school counselors to funnel patients into their systems so they can collect insurance payments, Dr. McCall?" John said as he faced the psychiatrist.

Vance McCall turned white. "I . . . I . . . I can't believe that you would suggest that a Christian would do such a thing!"

"I can't speak for a person's salvation experience, Dr. McCall, but Christians are not immune to greed. I do know, however, that kickback schemes are unethical, deceitful, and highly illegal, and that those who engage in them are sure to get caught."

Roger noticed the tension level rising in the studio. "Are you personally aware of that sort of thing happening in this area, Dr. Kryer?"

"Yes, Roger, I do know of that sort of thing taking place in our area and I expect that such activity could lead to some prosecutions in the near future. But let me say this: The profit motive in counseling is one of the reasons I believe counseling should be returned to the local church. Pastors' incomes are not usually dependent upon counseling fees. Pastoral counselors are interested in the permanent transformation of their counselees and are willing to hold them accountable to the Word of God rather than to provide excuses for sinful behavior."

The program drew to a close and Roger thanked John and Vance for coming. McCall shook Roger's hand and hurried toward the exit. "I have an appointment across town, Roger," he said. "Thanks for letting me come."

Roger turned to John. "I don't think you made a friend there. I have to admit, you've raised some questions in my mind about psychological counseling, Dr. Kryer. I'm not convinced, but I'm open."

"Well, that's a start, Roger," John said with a smile. He gathered his notes, put them in his briefcase, and left the station. He walked toward his car and saw Vance McCall waiting for him.

"That was quite a performance, Reverend Kryer," he said. "But I don't think many will be persuaded. Psychology will be here long after you and your kind have faded into antiquity."

"That may be true, Vance, but that doesn't change the fact that God's Word is still the power of God unto salvation to all who believe. God is the only One who can really change a person from the inside out."

The Biblical Counselor

Actual permanent correction, therefore, can only be accomplished when a person has been born again and has experienced the regenerating work of the Holy Spirit. A counselor who does not understand this dynamic principle will try to help his client change outward behaviors by dealing with symptoms, but, ultimately, the counseling will fail unless the counselee makes a personal commitment of his inner being to Jesus Christ.

The Word of God

Therefore, if anyone is in Christ, he is a new creation; the old has gone, the new has come!
—2 Corinthians 5:17

14

A Biblical Method for Lasting Change

"Has God *really* said..." the serpent whispered, introducing doubt into the Garden so long ago. Throughout the centuries, the devil has prompted man to question God's warnings about the consequences of sin, His promises of redemption, and His healing power. The answer to all of these is found in 2 Corinthians 5:17: "Therefore, if anyone is in Christ, he is a new creation; the old has gone, the new has come!" Believers since the time of Christ have found God's promise to change man's inner character through the work of the Holy Spirit to be true. But in our own generation, Satan has once again created doubts in God's people that God really means what He said.

Christian psychologists have added to these doubts when they suggest that "inviting the Holy Spirit to take over our life leaves part of our being untouched."[1] To declare such a thing is to say that if anyone is in Christ, he really is *not* a new creation. The old things have *not* really passed away; all things have *not* become new. No, if the psychologists are right, the old things have to be dredged back up and fondled until a mystical healing takes place. The bottom line is this: If 2 Corinthians 5:17 is wrong, then the

Bible is false and Jesus is a liar. Paul would respond, "Not at all! Let God be true, and every man a liar" (Romans 3:4).

The Source of Total Transformation

Let's look at what God says about the changes He produces in people's lives. He promises, "I will give them an undivided heart and put a new spirit in them; I will remove from them their heart of stone and give them a heart of flesh" (Ezekiel 11:19). That is a description of a *total* transformation of the inner being. With that comes an entirely new lifestyle: "We were therefore buried with him through baptism into death in order that, just as Christ was raised from the dead through the glory of the Father, we too may live a new life" (Romans 6:4).

This is not a superficial change that lasts only a short time, "for you have been born again, not of perishable seed, but of imperishable, through the living and enduring word of God" (1 Peter 1:23). According to Ephesians 4:24, this is a "new self, created to be like God in true righteousness and holiness." Paul repeats this concept in Colossians 3:10, where he says the new self "is being renewed in knowledge in the image of its Creator."

This is a difficult concept for intellectuals to understand. Just as Nicodemus wondered how a grown man could be born again (John 3:3), modern scholars ask, "How can accepting Christ as Savior really transform a troubled mind? Surely it takes more than the Bible and the Holy Spirit to permanently heal the dysfunctional."

While some people insist that years of therapy are required to cleanse the troubled soul of painful memories, Paul recommends "the washing of rebirth and renewal by the Holy Spirit" (Titus 3:5). The Bible provides real hope: "Praise be to the God and Father of our Lord Jesus Christ! In his great mercy he has given us new birth into a living hope through the resurrection of Jesus Christ from the dead" (1 Peter 1:3). In view of psychological claims, is that "living hope" to be understood only as a warm theological sentiment? Does Jesus' resurrection mean nothing to our practical day-to-day experiences in this depraved world? If so, the world has the right to laugh at Christians for clinging to such a weak and powerless faith.

Biblical Case Histories of Change

Let's look at some case histories in the Bible that show the transforming power of God through Jesus Christ. Look first at the change that took place in Peter's life. In Matthew 26:74, he cursed and denied the Lord because of his fear of the Jewish leaders. Yet in Acts 2:22-24 we witness a dramatic change as he fearlessly accused the Jews of murdering Jesus:

> Men of Israel, listen to this: Jesus of Nazareth was a man accredited by God to you by miracles, wonders and signs, which God did among you through him, as you yourselves know. This man was handed over to you by God's set purpose and foreknowledge; and you, with the help of wicked men, put him to death by nailing him to the cross. But God raised him from the dead, freeing him from the agony of death, because it was impossible for death to keep its hold on him.

Peter's life was undeniably and forever changed by the resurrection power of Jesus Christ and the indwelling work of the Holy Spirit.

Look at the change in the demon-possessed man in Mark 5. He was described as violent and in agony of soul. "Night and day among the tombs and in the hills he would cry out and cut himself with stones" (verse 5). But after his personal encounter with Jesus, when his town's people came to see what was happening, "they saw the man who had been possessed by the legion of demons, sitting there, dressed and in his right mind; and they were afraid" (verse 15). He was "in his right mind" not after years of therapy, but after only a few minutes with the Savior.

A little further on it says that the man begged to go with Jesus. "Jesus did not let him, but said, 'Go home to your family and tell them how much the Lord has done for you, and how he has had mercy on you.' So the man went away and began to tell in the Decapolis how much Jesus had done for him. And all the people were amazed" (verses 18-20). Why do you suppose they were amazed? Because he had been hopelessly insane and now he was obviously healed. The Lord who cured dysfunctional minds centuries ago still heals hearts and minds in our own day.

Some integrationists might argue, "That may be true if the problem is demon possession, but for common problems of modern life we still need psychotherapy. For example, what about serious psychological problems like sexual addictions?"

Well, let's consider the woman of Samaria. Meeting her at the city well, Jesus asked her for water. "The Samaritan woman said to him, 'You are a Jew and I am a Samaritan woman. How can you ask me for a drink?'" Jesus sensed an opportunity to minister and turned the conversation to spiritual things: "If you knew the gift of God and who it is that asks you for a drink, you would have asked him and he would have given you living water" (John 4:9,10).

When the woman showed an interest, Jesus invited her to get her husband so he could join their conversation. "'I have no husband,' she replied. Jesus said to her, 'You are right when you say you have no husband. The fact is, you have had five husbands, and the man you now have is not your husband. What you have just said is quite true'" (John 4:17,18).

The woman was so amazed at Jesus' insight into her life that she recognized Him as a prophet. Jesus explained to her that He was the Messiah her people and the Jews had been expecting for so long. "Then, leaving her water jar, the woman went back to the town and said to the people, 'Come, see a man who told me everything I ever did. Could this be the Christ?' They came out of the town and made their way toward him" (John 4:28-30). John writes that many of the townspeople became believers because of her testimony, and "they urged him to stay with them, and he stayed two days. And because of his words many more became believers. They said to the woman, 'We no longer believe just because of what you said; now we have heard for ourselves, and we know that this man really is the Savior of the world" (verses 39-42). A woman who might be described as a nymphomaniac was totally changed and became a sincere evangelist through the power of God!

The apostle Paul's conversion was so intense that even his name was changed. Consider these contrasting descriptions of Paul's attitude toward the members of the early church: "Saul was still breathing out murderous threats against the Lord's disciples" (Acts 9:1) and "then Paul answered, 'Why are you weeping and breaking my heart? I am ready not only to be bound, but also to die in Jerusalem for the name of the Lord Jesus'" (Acts 21:13). Only Christ can produce such sweeping change of character!

Personal Case Histories of Change

Example after example could be given of Christ's transforming power not only from the Scriptures, but also from the testimonies of today's saints. Every Bible-preaching pastor could relate story after story of dysfunctional people who have been saved and are being sanctified by the gentle work of the Holy Spirit in their lives.

I could tell you of a woman who was on her way to commit suicide when she saw our church's banner on a movie-theater roof. She slipped into our service unnoticed and was gloriously saved by the grace of God. She had lived a life of sorrow, immorality, and abuse, but she became a beautiful witness of God's transforming grace.

Then there was a young man who timidly sat in the darkness at the back of the theater one Sunday. His shoulder-length hair and biker outfit masked the pain in his heart, and he was trapped by alcohol and drugs and deathly afraid of the future. Christ met him that morning and drew him into the family of God. He became a new creation in Christ and was freed from substance abuse. Now he and his wife and darling children work faithfully with us in our church. He serves as one of our elders.

A young lesbian began attending our church and listened intently to the promises of God. She found freedom in Christ and rejoices in what God has done for her. A young father struggled with deep anxiety and depression for years until he turned his life over to Christ and found relief. Now he is an example of patience and joy as he faithfully serves in our ministries. I could go on and on, but this is the point: Christ promises to change human lives if we will only follow His directions. And He keeps His Word!

Real Change for *Your* Life

Paul instructs believers to follow an entirely different therapy: "Do not conform any longer to the pattern of this world, but be transformed by the renewing of your mind. Then you will be able to test and approve what God's will is—his good, pleasing and perfect will" (Romans 12:2). Fortunately, the Lord does not merely tell us to be transformed; He tells us *how* it can actually be accomplished.

Four Biblical Steps
to Permanent Change

In the Scriptures, God has given us a clear four-step process of transformation. It is found in 2 Timothy 3:16,17: "All Scripture is God-breathed and is useful for teaching, rebuking, correcting and training in righteousness, so that the man of God may be thoroughly equipped for every good work."

Step One: Teaching Doctrine

Our belief system is the foundation of our every thought and action. Some have said, "You are what you eat." In the spiritual realm, we are what we *believe*. If we want to help people solve the problems of living, we must teach them solid doctrine.

Many Christians actually believe that the truths of the Bible are just too complicated for the average person to understand. Please don't make that common mistake. The Scriptures were given to be read, understood, and obeyed by *everyone*.

We need to know about God and His attributes, His role as Creator, man's sinful condition, and God's plan of salvation. We need to know about the practical working of the Holy Spirit in our personal lives. All of that is food for the soul. That's what Jesus meant when He said, "'Man does not live on bread alone, but on every word that comes from the mouth of God'" (Matthew 4:4).

New believers will not understand the deeper truths of God all at once, but if they are truly born again they will "like newborn babies, crave pure spiritual milk, so that by it [they] may grow up in [their] salvation" (1 Peter 2:2). God wants believers to feed on the meat of the Word, not just milk, as they mature. The writer of Hebrews makes this plain:

> We have much to say about this, but it is hard to explain because you are slow to learn. In fact, though by this time you ought to be teachers, you need someone to teach you the elementary truths of God's word all over again. You need milk, not solid food! Anyone who lives on milk, being still an infant, is not acquainted with the teaching about righteousness. But solid food is for the mature, who by constant use have trained themselves to distinguish good from evil (Hebrews 5:11-14).

Knowing how to distinguish good from evil is one of the purposes of doctrine. Because modern Christians have so little doctrinal training, they are easily led into false doctrines and empty philosophies. Not being familiar with the basic truths of the Word, they fall for psychological pabulum being advertised as deep wisdom. Their souls hunger for deeply satisfying truths, but they are given shallow and tainted solutions for their heartaches.

Jesus said that the reason people fall for error is that they "do not know the Scriptures or the power of God" (Matthew 22:29). The reason Christians are enticed into immorality, pornography, lust, unfaithfulness, and divorce is not just carnal weakness. The greater cause is that they do not know the truths of the Bible or God's power to deliver them from temptation. They believe the addictive lie that "I just couldn't help myself." Many Christians call themselves alcoholics because they believe the disease myth and the dogma that once an alcoholic, always an alcoholic. Yet the Scriptures clearly promise total cleansing and power over sin. The reason so many believers are being dragged back into their painful past is that they believe the theories of psychologists who act as though they know more about the wounded heart than God does.

Doctrine can be called another name: wisdom from God. Solomon exhorts us to make the pursuit of wisdom our top priority: "Wisdom is supreme; therefore get wisdom. Though it cost all you have, get understanding" (Proverbs 4:7). He insists that there is no better investment: "Blessed is the man who finds wisdom, the man who gains understanding, for she is more profitable than silver and yields better returns than gold" (Proverbs 3:13,14). Paul exhorts Timothy, "Watch your life and doctrine closely. Persevere in them, because if you do, you will save both yourself and your hearers" (1 Timothy 4:16).

Biblical counseling is deeply concerned with accurate doctrine. Paul told Titus that a minister "must hold firmly to the trustworthy message as it has been taught, so that he can encourage others by sound doctrine and refute those who oppose it" (Titus 1:9). In counseling, I am not nearly as concerned with the latest finding or newest therapy as I am with a counselee's beliefs. I want to know what the counselee believes about God, what he believes about man's need, what he believes about Jesus, and what he believes about the work of the Holy Spirit. I want to know whether he is committed to obeying all the commands of Scripture or he is inclined to submit only to the principles that please him.

I want the counselee to understand the character of Jesus so that he will have God's model against which to measure his own attitudes and actions. The goal in counseling is for believers to "reach unity in the faith and in the knowledge of the Son of God and become mature, attaining to the whole measure of the fullness of Christ. Then we will no longer be infants, tossed back and forth by the waves, and blown here and there by every wind of teaching and by the cunning and craftiness of men in their deceitful scheming" (Ephesians 4:13,14).

Spiritual growth—developing maturity in Christ—and permanent change require accurate doctrine.

Step Two: Rebuking

The second step in the process of permanent change is confronting sin. It may be called rebuke, reproof, admonition, or any appropriate expression of disapproval of wrong beliefs, attitudes, or actions. The Greek term in 2 Timothy 3:16 is *elegmos,* which means "an exposure of." It is pointing out sin for the purpose of helping our brothers. As James says, "Remember this: Whoever turns a sinner from the error of his way will save him from death and cover over a multitude of sins" (James 5:20).

Note that Jesus balances this responsibility by warning us to examine our own hearts before we dare to rebuke someone else: "You hypocrite, first take the plank out of your own eye, and then you will see clearly to remove the speck from your brother's eye" (Matthew 7:5). That is why a counselor's personal life is very relevant to the counseling situation.

Reproof is an uncomfortable procedure for the counselor and the counselee. I understand the reluctance with which pastors rebuke sinful behavior in their people. It is dangerous to tell a prominent member of the church board that he is sinning. It is risky to confront a strong-willed chairwoman of a music committee about divisive attitudes. The pastor's job may well be placed on the line. Nonetheless, God has called faithful preachers of the Word to the ministry of rebuking.

Think how Nathan the prophet must have trembled on his way to David's palace to confront him about his sin with Bathsheba. Yet with the authority of God he pointed at David and said, "Thou art the man!" Boldly he asked, "Why did you despise the word of the LORD by doing what is evil in his eyes? You struck down Uriah the Hittite with the sword and took his wife to be your own. You killed him with the sword of the Ammonites" (2 Samuel 12:7,9).

Fortunately for Nathan, David was tenderhearted toward the Lord and received the rebuke as from God and genuinely repented. Not all counselees react that way. Still, even if his life had been required, I believe Nathan would have fulfilled his calling. Pastors and counselors, we must do the same for our Lord and for our people. Failure to do so is a form of malpractice, and God will hold us accountable. "Rebuke your neighbor frankly so you will not share in his guilt" (Leviticus 19:17).

A person who truly wants to change will receive rebuke. He will repent if he has the attitude David had: "Let a righteous man strike me—it is a kindness; let him rebuke me—it is oil on my head. My head will not refuse it" (Psalm 141:5).

We need to remind our people that loving, biblical rebuke is from the Lord: "My son, do not despise the LORD's discipline and do not resent his rebuke" (Proverbs 3:11).

God does not enjoy rebuking His children, but He firmly says, "Know then in your heart that as a man disciplines his son, so the LORD your God disciplines you" (Deuteronomy 8:5). I am comforted to know that "the LORD disciplines those he loves, as a father the son he delights in" (Proverbs 3:12). Though reprimand is unpleasant, it is a necessary part of the process of change, and it is a proof of God's love and our relationship to Him.

A counselee who turns away from rebuke in pride and anger is not really interested in change. Until he humbles himself before the Lord and is ready to listen and obey, he will continue his destructive patterns. Though the rebuke may be received negatively, the biblical counselor is obligated to obey the Lord. Jesus commands believers to rebuke one another: "If your brother sins, rebuke him, and if he repents, forgive him" (Luke 17:3).

As a point of balance, Paul reminds us to have a right attitude when we rebuke another: "Do not rebuke an older man harshly, but exhort him as if he were your father. Treat younger men as brothers" (1 Timothy 5:1). Nonetheless, Paul insists that ministers fulfil their duty to "preach the Word; be prepared in season and out of season; correct, rebuke and encourage—with great patience and careful instruction" (2 Timothy 4:2). If there are those who resist, Paul says to "rebuke them sharply, so that they will be sound in the faith" (Titus 1:13). Because the biblical counselor is speaking from the platform of the Scriptures, he is to "encourage and rebuke with all authority. Do not let anyone despise you" (Titus 2:15).

If a counselor loves his counselees, he will rebuke them when necessary and will lovingly plead with them to respond, as God urges us: "Those whom I love I rebuke and discipline. So be earnest, and repent" (Revelation 3:19).

It is not enough for a counselor to point out sinful behavior and to tell a counselee to mend his ways. That's like a doctor with a patient who complains of pain in his shoulder. "When does it hurt?" the doctor asks. The patient lifts his arm over his head with great effort and misery, and says with a grimace, "When I raise my arm like this." The doctor takes his glasses off, leans back in his chair, and says, "Then don't raise your arm like that." The doctor didn't really help the patient. All he did was rebuke the action causing the pain.

Biblical rebuke gets down below the surface error to discover the real cause of sinful attitudes and behaviors. Almost without fail, the immediate cause of sin is wrong belief, wrong thinking patterns, selfishness, or some combination of the three. The young husband who is bitter toward his wife for resisting his too-frequent demands for sex may complain that she is "frigid" and unresponsive. But the truth is that he has a wrong understanding of God's purpose for sexual intimacy. He has allowed his mind to dwell on lustful thoughts, and is thinking only of his own physical urges rather than his wife's needs. An examination of the man's doctrinal (yes, *doctrinal!*) beliefs about sex, his pattern of dwelling on sexual thoughts, and his self-interest must be compared with biblical teaching on each of those issues in order to expose the sin behind the behavior.

Step Three: Correction

Let's review the process so far: "All Scripture is God-breathed and is useful for teaching, rebuking, correcting and training in righteousness, so that the man of God may be thoroughly equipped for every good work" (2 Timothy 3:16,17). The first step for change is teaching right belief, or doctrine. The second is rebuke, or the recognition and exposure of error in belief, thinking, or action.

The third step is correction of those errors. The Greek term *epanorthosis* (*epi*, "to"; *ana*, "up," or "again"; *orthoo*, "to make straight") is almost a picture of step three, for it literally means "to make upright again."

Paul explains this process in Ephesians 4 when he says, "You were taught, with regard to your former way of life, to put off your old self, which is being corrupted by its deceitful desires" (verse 22). There is an active choice required in correcting one's self: putting off the old self, or, as Paul calls it, the "sinful nature." He reminds us that we do not have to satisfy our old nature: "Therefore, brothers, we have an obligation—but it is not to the sinful nature, to live according to it" (Romans 8:12).

Paul readily admits that Christians have experienced all of the evil desires common to man: "All of us also lived among them at one time, gratifying the cravings of our sinful nature and following its desires and thoughts. Like the rest, we were by nature objects of wrath" (Ephesians 2:3). He is more explicit in 1 Corinthians 6:9-11:

> Do you not know that the wicked will not inherit the kingdom of God? Do not be deceived: Neither the sexually immoral nor idolaters nor adulterers nor male prostitutes nor homosexual offenders nor thieves nor the greedy nor drunkards nor slanderers nor swindlers will inherit the kingdom of God. And that is what some of you were.

This is one of the most important passages in biblical counseling. Note how Paul describes the Corinthians:

"That is what some of you *were*." He is saying to them, "You no longer *are* what you once were. God has totally transformed you! The old labels of your past life no longer apply."

Putting off the old nature requires an active choice of the one desiring change, but without the supernatural work of God, it is impossible. Paul completes the description of the process in 1 Corinthians 6:11: "But you were washed, you were sanctified, you were justified in the name of the Lord Jesus Christ and by the Spirit of our God." It is the work of the Holy Spirit to "wash" us clean—to correct us, to set us upright again. This is done in the name of Jesus as we identify with His crucifixion by considering our old desires as though they were dead. "For we know that our old self was crucified with him so that the body of sin might be done away with, that we should no longer be slaves to sin" (Romans 6:6).

Choosing to change is difficult, to be sure. We humans hate change because of our fear of the unknown. We grow comfortable with the familiar, even if it is harmful. On the one hand, we want things to remain the same, yet pain and guilt can become so oppressive that we are motivated to seek relief. That is why a sense of guilt is necessary and productive. Just as physical pain is a sign that something in our body is damaged and needs to be treated, so spiritual pain—conviction and guilt—are given to us to show us that something in our inner man is wrong and that we need to seek correction.

Correction begins when a person accepts Jesus as Savior and Lord. "But you were washed, you were sanctified, you were justified in the name of the Lord Jesus Christ and by the Spirit of our God" (1 Corinthians 6:11). And it continues as the believer endeavors to "live by the Spirit, [so that he]... will not gratify the desires of the sinful nature" (Galatians 5:16).

Actual permanent correction, therefore, can only be accomplished when a person has been born again and has experienced the regenerating work of the Holy Spirit. A counselor who does not understand this dynamic principle will try to help his client change outward behaviors by dealing with symptoms, but ultimately the counseling will fail unless the counselee makes a personal commitment of his inner being to Jesus Christ.

Step Four: Instruction in Righteousness

Correcting what is wrong in a person's life through faith in Jesus Christ enables a counselee to put off the old nature, at least for a time. The battle between the old nature and the new continues, however, as Paul confessed in Romans 7:15-19:

> I do not understand what I do. For what I want to do I do not do, but what I hate I do. And if I do what I do not want to do, I agree that the law is good. As it is, it is no longer I myself who do it, but it is sin living in me. I know that nothing good lives in me, that is, in my sinful nature. For I have the desire to do what is good, but I cannot carry it out. For what I do is not the good I want to do; no, the evil I do not want to do—this I keep on doing.

Correction is a choice. "What shall we say, then? Shall we go on sinning so that grace may increase? By no means! We died to sin; how can we live in it any longer?" (Romans 6:1,2). And just as correction is a choice of submission that each person must make, so maintaining one's walk with God is also a matter of choice. Paul calls this part of the change process putting "on the new self," and indicates that it happens when we are "made new in the attitude of your minds" (Ephesians 4:24). The characteristics of the new self are "true righteousness and holiness."

The Scriptures indicate that the focus of our mind largely determines the results. Paul writes about the enemies of Christ, that "their destiny is destruction, their god is their stomach, and their glory is in their shame. Their mind is on earthly things" (Philippians 3:19). Paul said that those who "oppose the truth—men of depraved minds...as far as the faith is concerned, are rejected" (2 Timothy 3:8). Writing to Titus, Paul says, "To the pure, all things are pure, but to those who are corrupted and do not believe, nothing is pure. In fact, both their minds and consciences are corrupted" (Titus 1:15).

In order to put on the new nature, Paul advises the child of God to "set your minds on things above, not on earthly things" (Colossians 3:2). Peter takes up this theme when he writes, "Prepare your minds for action; be self-controlled; set your hope fully on the grace to be given you when Jesus Christ is revealed" (1 Peter 1:13). When the believer commits himself to this process, the result is similar to what God promised Israel: "I will put my laws in their minds and write them on their hearts. I will be their God, and they will be my people" (Hebrews 8:10).

Paul clarifies this process in Romans 12:1,2 and declares that putting on the new nature involves every area of one's life—physical, spiritual, social, and mental: "I urge you, brothers, in view of God's mercy, to offer your bodies as living sacrifices [physical discipline], holy and pleasing to God—this is your spiritual act of worship [spiritual discipline]. Do not conform any longer to the pattern of this world [social, cultural discipline], but be transformed by the renewing of your mind [mental discipline]."

Each of these four areas needs to be explored in counseling. What is the counselee doing physically that is displeasing to the Lord? What spiritual principles is he violating that contribute to his problems? What social and cultural compromises is he making that prevent him from living a life that is pleasing to the Lord? What is the focus of his mind? Is he filling his thoughts with worldly values, goals, and solutions, or is he concentrating on Christ Himself and the glorious promises in His Word?

God offers His children incredible fringe benefits for following His blueprint for change. Not only has He provided a way for us to live eternally in the future, but He gives us the keys to joyful living in the present.

Characteristics of the Transformed Life

Psalm 119 is only one of many passages on the transforming power of God's Word. Consider some of the characteristics that can be manifest in believers' lives when they fill their inner beings with biblical principles.

- **Their lives are obedient to the Lord:** "Blessed are they who keep his statutes and seek him with all their heart. They do nothing wrong; they walk in his ways. You have laid down precepts that are to be fully obeyed" (verses 2-4).
- **Their lives are full of praise:** "I will praise you with an upright heart as I learn your righteous laws" (verse 7).
- **Their lives are characterized as pure:** "How can a young man keep his way pure? By living according to your word" (verse 9).
- **They have victory over sin:** "I have hidden your word in my heart that I might not sin against you" (verse 11).
- **They enjoy obeying the Lord:** "I delight in your decrees; I will not neglect your word" (verse 16).
- **They receive direct counsel from the Word:** "Your statutes are my delight; they are my counselors" (verse 24).
- **They are refreshed and strengthened by the Word:** "My soul is weary with sorrow; strengthen me according to your word" (verse 28).
- **They are people of integrity:** "I have chosen the way of truth; I have set my heart on your laws" (verse 30).
- **They experience inner freedom:** "I run in the path of your commands, for you have set my heart free" (verse 32); "I will walk about in freedom, for I have sought out your precepts" (verse 45).
- **They become unselfish:** "Turn my heart toward your statutes and not toward selfish gain" (verse 36).
- **They turn away from worthless and destructive practices and philosophies:** "Turn my eyes away

from worthless things; renew my life according to your word" (verse 37).

- **They have hope:** "Do not snatch the word of truth from my mouth, for I have put my hope in your laws" (verse 43); "remember your word to your servant, for you have given me hope" (verse 49).

- **They experience comfort in the midst of suffering:** "My comfort in my suffering is this: Your promise renews my life" (verse 50); "I remember your ancient laws, O LORD, and I find comfort in them" (verse 52).

- **They develop good judgment:** "Teach me knowledge and good judgment, for I believe in your commands" (verse 66).

- **Their hearts are sensitive:** "[Unbelievers'] hearts are callous and unfeeling, but I delight in your law" (verse 70).

- **They have eternal values:** "The law from your mouth is more precious to me than thousands of pieces of silver and gold" (verse 72).

- **They develop wisdom:** "Your commands make me wiser than my enemies, for they are ever with me" (verse 98); "I have more insight than all my teachers, for I meditate on your statutes" (verse 99); "I have more understanding than the elders, for I obey your precepts" (verse 100).

- **They find guidance:** "Your word is a lamp to my feet and a light for my path" (verse 105).

- **They have an aversion for evil:** "Because I consider all your precepts right, I hate every wrong path" (verse 128).

- **They understand deep truths:** "The unfolding of your words gives light; it gives understanding to the simple" (verse 130).

- **They sorrow over the sinfulness of the world:** "Streams of tears flow from my eyes, for your law is not obeyed" (verse 136).

- **They experience joy in the midst of trouble:** "Trouble and distress have come upon me, but your commands are my delight" (verse 143).

- **They become people of prayer:** "I rise before dawn and cry for help; I have put my hope in your word" (verse 147).
- **They remain true to God even through persecution:** "Many are the foes who persecute me, but I have not turned from your statutes" (verse 157).
- **They have peace and stability:** "Great peace have they who love your law, and nothing can make them stumble" (verse 165).
- **They receive help from God:** "May your hand be ready to help me, for I have chosen your precepts" (verse 173).

And these promises are from one psalm alone! They are promises for *every* child of God who will seek His truth, regardless of how serious our problems are. They are promises for me. They are promises for you.

Go back and note all the characteristics of mental health that are related to the Scriptures. How *dare* psychologists tell us that the Scriptures are deficient in ways that only modern psychology can supply! The Bible provides *all* the necessary information for "training in righteousness, so that the man of God may be thoroughly equipped for every good work" (2 Timothy 3:16,17). *Thoroughly* equipped.

Instruction in righteousness is the maintenance program for spiritual and mental health. Too many Christians mistakenly believe that they can experience "maintenance-free" spirituality; that it comes without choice, effort, or discipline. The truth is that it requires *daily* submission of our wills to the Lord by feeding on His Word to sustain the transformed life. There really is no mystery to this process; it just seems like too much work. We would rather depend upon a radio preacher or televangelist for our spiritual food. We would rather warm our hearts with contemporary music than the cleansing coals of God's Word. We would rather pick up the newspaper than the Bible. We would rather play than pray. We want excuses instead of exhortation. We want man's theories instead of God's truth. We want comfort rather than conviction. We want to be entertained more than we want holiness. We want self-esteem instead of self-denial. But instruction in righteousness requires us to turn back to God and His Word.

There you have it—four steps in a biblical method for permanent change: doctrinal teaching, acceptance of rebuke, correction of wrong patterns of thinking and acting by putting off the old nature, and building up the new nature through instruction in righteousness.

Summary of Contrasts

In summary, let us review the two systems that claim to effect change in people's lives. One comes from the heart of God, the other from the heart of man. You must decide which system you will follow.

Psychology has offered an alternative to Christianity with a fully developed system of faith. Christianity starts with the assumption "In the beginning, God . . ."—the existence of the Creator—while psychology starts with the assumption "In the beginning, bog . . ."—the evolutionary theory. Christianity sees man as a special creation of God, made in His moral image, while psychology views man as the end result of billions of years of random events.

Christianity believes that the Bible is the inerrant Word of God and the only absolute source of truth; psychology believes that truth is where you find it and that man's mind is the final judge. Christianity has a leadership of ministers who preach from the Scriptures; psychology has a priesthood of therapists who quote one another. Christianity is supported by the tithes and offerings of its disciples; psychology is supported by fee schedules and insurance payments.

The Bible claims to have explanations for man's deepest questions: Where did we come from? Why are we here? How are we to behave? How can we change? What is our future? Psychology claims to have even deeper answers for these ultimate questions, which can only be revealed by therapists who have had years of formal training.

The Bible claims to reveal the motives of the human heart, while psychology claims to explain the unconscious drives of the human mind. Christianity claims that humans can be transformed by the miraculous and mysterious power of God. Psychology claims that it can transform man by helping him to understand, accept, and love himself.

The Bible says that man is by nature a sinner, separated from the life of God. Psychology says that man is essentially good and needs to recognize his full potential. The Bible says that without Christ, man is hopeless; psychology says that man is limited only by his imagination. The Bible says that man is lost and that Christ is the only way; psychology says it can help man find his own way.

The Bible calls sin by name; psychology says that man suffers from disorders. The Bible says that God's people must not conform to the world; integrationists say that we must counsel the way the world does. The Bible says that each person is responsible for his own choices; psychology says that each person is a victim of his environment.

The Bible says that man can be forgiven, cleansed, and healed. Psychology says we must return to our past, embrace our pain, and explore our inner self. The Bible's answer for guilt is man's repentance and God's forgiveness; psychology's way is for the conscience to be desensitized. The Bible says that we must crucify self; psychology says that we must actualize self. The Bible says that our battle is spiritual; Freud says that the battle is sexual.

Down through the centuries, without the aid of psychotherapy or innovative techniques, Christianity has produced millions of permanently transformed lives by the liberating truths found in Jesus Christ. In barely one century, psychology has captured the minds of millions with a message that has enslaved mankind to vacillating theories which promote sinful behavior.

Psychology points man to self. The Bible points man to God.

■ ■ ■

Charles Duncan was in his counseling office at the high school when he heard his name paged over the intercom. "There's a phone call for you on line two, Mr. Duncan," a student assistant said.

"Thanks, Melanie," he said as he punched the flashing button on his phone. "Hello?"

"Charles Duncan?" a voice said.

"Yes."

"This is Vance McCall. I promised I'd get back to you on our conversation of a couple of weeks ago."

"Yes, Dr. McCall. I've been expecting to hear from you."

"Listen, Charles, I want to be sure you didn't misunderstand our conversation. I may have inadvertently given you the impression that we would actually pay you a 'finder's fee' for referring clients to us. That isn't what I intended to communicate to you. What we are actually looking for are consultants such as yourself who would work with us as counselors on a part-time basis and your pay would be set up as a straightforward salary. We don't want to give the impression that we are doing anything unethical or illegal. I hope you understand. I certainly apologize if there's been any confusion."

"As a matter of fact, I don't think I misunderstood you at all, Dr. McCall. You made yourself quite clear. You were talking of a 'finder's fee' and a kickback arrangement and I do believe it was unethical and illegal."

"Well, I'm sorry you feel that way, Mr. Duncan," McCall sniffed. "I won't bother you again." The phone clicked dead.

Charles called John Kryer and told him what had just happened. "Then he hung up on me," he finished.

"It seems as though Dr. McCall is covering himself, Charlie. Maybe he will think twice before trying to recruit another school counselor. After all, he must wonder whether we know the legal ramifications of his using school personnel as bounty hunters to secure new patients for his clinic."

■ ■ ■

During the next few months, John continued to tutor Cliff Chase in biblical counseling and Cliff grew in confidence as he learned how to apply the Scriptures to the individual problems that he encountered in his ministry.

He read books on counseling, medicine, and drugs and he enrolled in an off-campus doctoral program in biblical counseling. He delighted in the challenge of reading and writing as he wrestled with case histories and the practical application of the Scriptures.

He watched as Walt and Ellen Harrison continued to grow in their walk with the Lord and their commitment to each other, and he was amazed at the joy they projected and shared with the entire church. Ellen was especially vocal. One evening at church she stood and spoke to the congregation about the changes she had experienced in the past months. "Most of you know Walt and me. You know that we have had some serious problems in our marriage this last year. I want to tell you why and to warn you to avoid the pit I fell into.

"I was sexually abused by my father when I was a teenager," she said. "As a result, I felt dirty and worthless for much of my life. Walt and I were not believers when we got married, and we both drank a lot and got caught up in the drug scene. Then Pastor Cliff introduced us to Jesus and our lives were changed overnight. Some of you remember the change."

Several in the congregation nodded in agreement.

"Then, last year, my sister called me and said she had found the solution to our wounded hearts in a seminar being taught by a psychologist headquartered here in Denver. I remember telling her, 'I've already found healing for my heart, Carol. I've accepted Jesus as my Savior. He washed me white as snow.'

"Carol's response was, 'You're repressing your memories, Ellen. Hidden underneath that cheerful veneer is a heartbroken little girl crying for comfort. You owe it to her to go back into the past with a psychologist so you can deal with all the unresolved issues of what Dad did to us.'

"I said to her, 'But, Carol, I've forgiven Dad. He didn't know the Lord. I still love him in spite of what he did to us. I want him to know Jesus, too.'

"Carol said, 'You're just not in touch with your true feelings, Ellen. You've got to learn to hate Dad and make him pay for what he did before you can really forgive him.'

"I had never heard Carol sound so bitter. I promised I would read the book on the wounded heart, so I bought it at the Christian bookstore. As I read it, I began to sense an uneasiness growing in my heart. My old anger and hurts returned, only worse than before. It began to affect my feelings toward Walt and I withdrew from him. I went out to attend a seminar on sexual abuse with my sister, and came back convinced that only a psychologist could really understand my problems and how to deal with them.

"My anger and bitterness continued to grow until I couldn't separate my anger at my father from my bitterness toward Walt. Soon I forgot all about the person who actually abused me and I directed all my venom at my husband.

"I began regular therapy with a psychologist at $90 an hour and it was causing us deep financial stress. On top of that, I spent hours on the phone with my sister. If Walt dared to complain about the expenses, I just got even more angry. He couldn't win. I was angry if he tried to talk to me about my attitudes, and angry if he kept quiet.

"I began to realize that I wasn't getting better, but now my pride kicked in. I was too embarrassed to admit that therapy was only making matters worse. Walt kept begging me to go to a biblical counselor with him and I finally agreed. We met with a counselor Pastor Cliff recommended, but I didn't like what he had to say. Still, I had to admit to myself that he seemed to know what he was talking about.

"I still had enough faith in God to believe that the Scriptures are true, so when the counselor began sharing verses with me, I found that my heart responded. I began to remember what it was like when I first accepted Christ— how free, how clean I felt. I remembered the joy Walt and I had shared and I wanted that again.

"I finally agreed to see the biblical counselor again. This time Pastor Cliff was present. They had me read 2 Peter chapter 1 out loud until I understood the deception I had bought into. It was almost like Saul's experience in the Bible. It seemed like scales fell from my spiritual eyes, and I could see the love of God clearly again! Hallelujah!"

Shouts of "Amen!" and "Praise God!" filled the auditorium. The congregation was visibly moved as some dabbed tears from their eyes. Cliff's face beamed with joy. Someone began singing the chorus, "I Cast All My Cares Upon You," and soon everyone was singing praises to the Lord.

After a few minutes, Cliff went to the pulpit and looked out over the crowd. "I want to tell you the rest of the story," Cliff said. "Nearly a year ago, a woman heard me preach that the Scriptures are sufficient to meet every need we face. She believed me and so she called to set up a counseling appointment with me. I met with her, and when she told me of the severe problems she was suffering, I froze.

"You see, folks, in seminary I was taught that we pastors can deal with minor problems, but that for severe dysfunctions we should refer our people to psychologists or psychiatrists. At the very least, pastors should have psychological training themselves if they plan on counseling. It sounded so reasonable, and to tell you the truth I didn't want to spend a lot of time counseling people because I had heard the horror stories of how painful it can be. I didn't want to risk my position as a pastor by making somebody in the church angry. And I just didn't want to take the time that counseling requires. I'm ashamed of it, but that's the truth.

"When I told the woman who came to see me that I felt she needed professional help, she looked at me with a sadness I'll never forget. She told me she had been under psychiatric care for years and had not been helped. 'When I heard you preach,' she said, 'I had hope again. Maybe God can help me.' And then I told her she would need to see a real professional to help solve her problems.

"Can you believe it? I've always preached that our Lord is the God of the universe and that He has given us His infallible, inerrant Word to guide us, but when it came time to back up my claims, I realized I didn't believe it myself. I was in error because I did not know God's Word or His power.

"I began to study counseling. I read books by Christians and nonbelievers who said that the church is selling its spiritual birthright for a mess of psychological pottage. I was convicted deeply when secular experts asked why the church was abandoning its role as healer of souls. So I went to a dear Christian brother, Pastor John Kryer at Faith Evangelical Church, and he began showing me why the Bible is the ultimate counseling manual. He has been working with me for several months now, and I tell you tonight, I have committed myself to the task of counseling God's people from God's Word!"

The congregation broke into applause. "Right on, preacher!" Peter Bryant shouted. Wally Phillips smiled broadly while Thelma Trent looked toward heaven, thanking the Lord for the beginning of revival.

"Furthermore," Cliff continued, "I'm asking for your full support in reclaiming our church's role in counseling. I hope to begin a training course to equip our elders and laypeople to help me as the load increases. I'm asking that you back me up when I have to confront sin from the pulpit and in the counseling office. Some people will get angry at me—I know that. But if I'm afraid of preaching all of God's Word for fear of losing my job, then I don't deserve to be a pastor anyway.

"I'm asking our elder board, on behalf of our church, to write to our denominational offices and seminary to encourage them to rebuild their counseling courses on biblical principles alone. If they refuse, I suggest that our church move our financial support to the schools that truly follow biblical counseling.

"I plan to suggest to other churches in our denomination that they do the same. If enough pastors and churches become aware and return to the Word of God, and encourage our denominational leaders to do the same, we can make a difference in these important days before us.

"My dear people," he said as he looked at their glowing faces with a heart full of love, "I ask your forgiveness for doubting the Word of God. I'm going to do what I can to inform other pastors everywhere I go that Christians are being deceived by psychology. That, as Paul warns in Colossians 2:8, we have been taken 'captive through hollow and deceptive philosophy, which depends on human tradition and the basic principles of this world rather than on Christ.'

"From now on, I pledge to you, as God gives me strength, I will follow Paul's example in Colossians 1:28 and 'proclaim [Jesus Christ], admonishing and teaching everyone with all wisdom, so that we may present everyone perfect in Christ.'"

PART FIVE

Appendices

Appendix A:
A Biblical Theory of Psychology

■ ■ ■

The Meaning of *Psychology*

The term *psychology* is ordinarily defined as the science which examines the mind, mental states and processes, human nature, and behavior. The word comes from a combination of the Greek word *psuché* or *psyché* (which originally meant "the breath" or "the breath of life," and came to represent the concept of the inner man, the immaterial or invisible part, or the soul) and the suffix *ology*, which denotes any branch of science or knowledge. Technically, then, psychology is supposed to be the science or study of the immaterial part of man.

We have already discussed the reasons that psychology cannot be considered a true science, but is more accurately understood as a philosophy or secular religion. We also saw the impossibility for psychologists to define and differentiate between the nonmaterial parts of man. We will see why when we examine what the Bible says about the inner man.

Heart

The Scriptures use at least four terms to describe the immaterial part of man: the heart, soul, spirit, and mind. The descriptions and functions of these aspects of man seem to overlap.

The biblical term *heart* (*lawbab* in Hebrew; *kardia* in Greek) is the clearest summary of the innermost center of the human being. Perhaps the closest psychological term to the heart is the *ego*, the Latin word for "I," borrowed by Freud to denote the "self." Peter describes the inner man as "the hidden man of the heart" (1 Peter 3:4 KJV), or the "inner self" (1 Peter 3:4 NIV). It is the center of one's being

335

(Proverbs 4:23), where he believes and exercises faith (Luke 24:25; Romans 10:9,10). It is the location of the human deliberation, where wisdom is employed. Understanding is said to be the function of the mind (Job 38:36), yet the connection to the heart is undeniable. The heart is where a person discerns the difference between right and wrong (1 Kings 3:9).

The heart is the center of courage, emotions, and will. "Therefore we do not lose heart. Though outwardly we are wasting away, yet inwardly we are being renewed day by day" (2 Corinthians 4:16).

The heart is the center of man's character—who he really is (Matthew 15:18). "The good man brings good things out of the good stored up in his heart, and the evil man brings evil things out of the evil stored up in his heart. For out of the overflow of his heart his mouth speaks" (Luke 6:45).

The Bible describes the heart of man as inclined toward evil. "The hearts of the people are filled with schemes to do wrong" (Ecclesiastes 8:11). "The hearts of men, moreover, are full of evil and there is madness in their hearts while they live" (Ecclesiastes 9:3). "The heart is deceitful above all things and beyond cure. Who can understand it?" (Jeremiah 17:9). "Inside they are full of greed and self-indulgence" (Matthew 23:25). "For from within, out of men's hearts, come evil thoughts, sexual immorality, theft, murder, adultery" (Mark 7:21).

Soul

The term *soul* (*nephesh* in Hebrew; *psuché* in Greek) is also used to denote the eternal and immaterial part of man. "Do not be afraid of those who kill the body but cannot kill the soul. Rather, be afraid of the One who can destroy both soul and body in hell" (Matthew 10:28). Revelation 20:4 clearly relates the soul to the distinct and conscious personality of the human being that continues after death.

In Psalm 42:1,2 the soul is described as that part of man that reaches out to God: "As the deer pants for streams of water, so my soul pants for you, O God. My soul thirsts for

God, for the living God." It seems to be the emotional center of man. It is the soul that is full of anxiety (Psalm 94:19), trouble (Psalm 88:3), joy (Psalm 94:19), and praise (Psalm 103:1). The Scriptures connect the soul with being "downcast" and "disturbed" (Psalm 42:5,6,11; 43:5) and in need of finding rest in God (Psalm 62:1,5). The soul becomes weary (Psalm 119:28) and faints due to sorrow (Psalm 119:81; 126:6), yet it is the soul that gains hope as it waits on the Lord (Psalm 130:5).

The emotions of the soul can be affected by one's choice, according to Psalm 131:2: "I have stilled and quieted my soul; like a weaned child with its mother, like a weaned child is my soul within me." Lest one be tempted to use this verse as a proof text for the "inner child" theory, note that this child is still, quiet, and satisfied, resting safely in the arms of God.

Spirit

The term *spirit* (*neshamah* in Hebrew; *pneuma* in Greek) also refers to the inner man. Proverbs 20:27 equates it with man's "inmost being." It is the breath of life that has come from God, for "the body without the spirit is dead" (James 2:26; cf. Matthew 27:50). But it is more than just animation, for it is connected with understanding: "It is the spirit in a man, the breath of the Almighty, that gives him understanding" (Job 32:8) and thought (1 Corinthians 2:11). It is the immortal aspect of man, according to Ecclesiastes 12:7: "the spirit returns to God who gave it" and Acts 7:59: "While they were stoning him, Stephen prayed, 'Lord Jesus, receive my spirit.'" Like the soul, the spirit longs for God (Isaiah 26:9), and it too is connected with the concept of the heart (Isaiah 57:15; Ezekiel 11:19; 18:31). As the immaterial part of man, it is contrasted with the body when Jesus said, "The spirit is willing, but the body is weak" (Matthew 26:41). The spirit communes with God, but the mind must also be involved (1 Corinthians 14:15,16).

Interchangeable Terms

Comparing numbers of passages on the terms *heart*, *soul*, and *spirit* (Deuteronomy 4:29; 6:5; 10:12; 11:13; 13:3;

26:16; 30:2; 1 Samuel 14:7; 1 Kings 2:4; Job 7:11; Isaiah 26:9; 1 Thessalonians 5:23; and so on) indicates that they are used almost interchangeably. In many cases the term *mind* can also be interchanged for heart, soul, and spirit. Since the descriptions and functions of these entities overlap at so many points, it would seem impossible to make a clear and absolute distinction between heart, soul, mind, and spirit. For that reason, many biblical counselors prefer to define man as consisting of two parts, the material and the immaterial, or body and spirit (*spirit* meaning the totality of soul, heart, and mind).

They support this dichotomy on philosophical grounds as well, to contrast their position with the integrationist argument for the threefold nature of man—body, soul, and spirit. Integrationists emphasize the three-part division and have held that illnesses of the body should be treated by physicians, dysfunctions of the soul (and mind) should be handled by psychologists and psychiatrists, and problems of the spirit should be dealt with by the church. More and more, however, since some integrationists define the soul as the combination of body and spirit, spiritual healing has also been taken over by the psychotherapeutic industry.

A Different Trichotomist Argument

Dichotomists—those who hold that man consists of only two parts, body and spirit/soul/heart/mind—have a good argument. The Scriptures do indeed use the terms interchangeably, from a functional point of view. But I would like to present the possibility of a different trichotomist position—that man consists of three parts: body, life (spirit), and mind (heart, soul)—while disputing the integrationist claim that therapy of the soul (mind and emotions) belongs to a separate priesthood of psychologists.

Proof texts can be found to support both positions. Psalm 63:1 presents a dichotomy: "My soul thirsts for you, my body longs for you," as does Matthew 10:28: "Do not be afraid of those who kill the body but cannot kill the soul." First Thessalonians 5:23, however, can be used to support the trichotomist position: "May God himself, the God of peace, sanctify you through and through. May your whole spirit, soul and body be kept blameless at the coming of our Lord Jesus Christ." The same is true for Mark 12:33: "To love him with all your heart [the inner man], with all your understanding [the mind] and with all your strength [the body]." The problem is that Mark 12:30 presents a *four*-part division: "Love the Lord your God with all your heart and with all your soul and with all your mind and with all your strength." It would seem obvious that the Bible is not trying to convey three distinct parts to be treated by three separate disciplines.

My support for a trichotomy is based on a different foundation entirely—the Trinity. God has given us many illustrations of the Trinity in our natural universe: time (past, present, and future), three dimensions (length, width, and height), the three states of water (liquid, gas, and solid), and so on. Of course, these illustrations are limited, for no created thing can adequately explain the essence of God.

Genesis 1:27 says that "God created man in his own image, in the image of God he created him." Let me explain why it is possible for that image to be triune, consisting of the material (the physical body), life itself (called "the breath of life" or the spirit), and the soul (spoken of as heart, soul, or mind).

There are different kinds of "life." Plants are living organisms which, though carbon-based, are categorically different from lumps of coal. The plants are material and the coal is material, both having physical substance. But plants have a mysterious capacity for life (metabolism, growth, and reproduction) that inanimate objects do not. Scientists can analyze the chemical composition of plants and can mix the precise amounts of elements contained in a plant seed. They can mold those chemicals into the shape of a seed, placing them in the correct sequence and layer. They could even inject actual plant DNA into their formula. Yet if they were to place their artificial seed in the ground, it would eventually dissolve into the soil without producing a plant. A living seed, however, will spring to life when provided with the proper conditions of soil, water, air, and sunlight. The plant has something rocks do not contain—life itself.

Animals move beyond plant life in complexity. The Bible says that they have a spirit of sorts: "Who knows if the spirit of man rises upward and if the spirit of the animal goes down into the earth?" (Ecclesiastes 3:21). They are able to experience and express emotions such as fear, love, and compassion. They have limited mental processes which enable them to learn and respond. The Bible refers to the mind of animals: "Let his mind be changed from that of a man and let him be given the mind of an animal" (Daniel 4:16). It is clear from this passage that the minds of animals and men are different quantitatively (in capacity) if not categorically.

God's image in man would therefore be something in addition to material substance and life itself. I intentionally say "in addition to material substance" even though God is a Spirit (John 4:24) and therefore immaterial (Luke 24:39). His image in man is not the physical, but the material aspects of man do reflect certain characteristics of God. Facial expressions, for example, may communicate compassion, love, anger, judgment, and other of God's attributes. Hands, muscles, and other work-related parts of man reflect the productivity of God. Sexual reproduction reflects the creative aspect of God. Though God is not material, all matter has come from God and is held together by the force of His will (Colossians 1:17). Matter, then, is not antithetical to God, but reveals His creative power and imagination.

What is it that makes man different from animal life and evokes the image of God? The evolutionist would contend that the only difference between animals and humans is that man has developed further than his anthropoid cousins and since, according to their faith, there is no God, man is not reflective of the divine in any sense. Behavioral psychologists treat their patients on the assumption that man is just a more highly developed animal. But there is an emptiness in this philosophy that repels even the irreligious.

What is it that sets man apart? Most integrationists and biblical counselors would agree on this point: The most important difference between human and animal life is man's spiritual immortality—the eternal nature of his soul and his capacity to commune with God. So then man is composed of matter, life, and spiritual immortality. But when it comes to functionality and counseling, there are only two distinguishable parts—the material (body) and the immaterial (heart/soul/spirit/mind).

The Mind

Because of the subject of this book, I have deliberately placed the mind as our final consideration. Counseling deals with every area of human life, material and immaterial. The portal to the immaterial part of man is the mind. It is vital, therefore, to understand major Bible teachings about the mind.

Not surprisingly, we are told that the mind is that part of man which seeks to understand by processing thoughts (Ezekiel 38:10) into a rational order (Job 38:36). The mind guides a person in his understanding and decisions (Ecclesiastes 2:3) by following a logical sequence of inquiry: "So I turned my mind to understand, to investigate and to search out wisdom and the scheme of things and to understand" (Ecclesiastes 7:25). Such learning is a result of conscious effort: "I applied my mind to know wisdom and to observe" (Ecclesiastes 8:16); "Daniel...you set your mind to gain understanding" (Daniel 10:12).

The mind encompasses both deliberate reasoning and involuntary thought, such as dreams. Daniel spoke to the king of the "dream and the visions that passed through your mind as you lay on your bed"(Daniel 2:28). It is recorded that "in the first year of Belshazzar king of Babylon, Daniel had a dream, and visions passed through his mind as he was lying on his bed" (Daniel 7:1). Involuntary thought may be somewhat analogous to the psychological concepts of the unconscious and the subconscious. However, in contrast to psychological theory, there is no hint in Scripture that the individual is powerless over involuntary thought, for the following reasons: 1) The mind, in partnership with the heart, is responsible for one's attitudes and behavior: "I the LORD search the heart and examine the mind, to reward a man according to his conduct, according to what his deeds deserve" (Jeremiah 17:10); and 2) man's involuntary thoughts can be "programmed" or influenced by what one feeds his mind: "Finally, brothers, whatever is true, whatever is noble, whatever is right, whatever is pure, whatever is lovely, whatever is admirable—if anything is excellent or praiseworthy—think about such things" (Philippians 4:8); "the mind controlled by the Spirit is life and peace" (Romans 8:6).

The Bible recognizes the fact that impaired thinking exists. Deuteronomy warns Israel of the consequences of unfaithfulness to God: "The LORD will afflict you with madness, blindness and confusion of mind" (Deuteronomy 28:28). "Your eyes will see strange sights and your mind imagine confusing things" (Proverbs 23:33). Jesus' family mistakenly believed He had gone over the edge with a messianic complex: "When his family heard about this, they went to take charge of him, for they said, 'He is out of his mind'" (Mark 3:21). Paul was accused of insanity because of his belief in Christ's resurrection: "At this point Festus interrupted Paul's defense. 'You are out of your mind, Paul!' he shouted. 'Your great learning is driving you insane'" (Acts 26:24).

Demon possession was, and is, the most severe form of mental problem humans can suffer. It may be associated with violent behavior: "When [Jesus] arrived at the other side in the region of the Gadarenes, two demon-possessed men coming from the tombs met him. They were so violent that no one could pass that way" (Matthew 8:28). Demon possession can also contribute to speech dysfunction: "While they were going out, a man who was demon-possessed and could not talk was brought to Jesus" (Matthew 9:32); other physical ailments: "Then they brought him a demon-possessed man who was blind and mute, and Jesus healed him, so that he could both talk and see" (Matthew 12:22); seizures and self-destructive behavior: "'Lord, have mercy on my son,' he said. 'He has seizures and is suffering greatly. He often falls into the fire or into the water'" (Matthew 17:15); and uncontrolled screaming: "Just then a man in their synagogue who was possessed by an evil spirit cried out" (Mark 1:23).

The power of God working through Christ was more than sufficient to heal those who were suffering from demon possession. "Crowds gathered also from the towns around Jerusalem, bringing their sick and those tormented by evil spirits, and all of them were healed" (Acts 5:16). "When they came to Jesus, they saw the man who had been possessed by the legion of demons, sitting there, dressed and in his right mind" (Mark 5:15).

The Natural Mind

The Bible describes three conditions of the human mind: the natural mind (also described as "depraved"), the carnal mind, and the spiritual mind. The natural mind is the human without God: "The man without the Spirit does not accept the things that come from the Spirit of God, for they are foolishness to him, and he cannot understand them, because they are spiritually discerned" (1 Corinthians 2:14). Though he is aware of the existence of God and His moral laws, he chooses to ignore God, hoping that He will go away.

The Bible explains some of the ways human minds can become impaired. A primary cause is the deliberate turning away from God. Romans 1:28 says, "Furthermore, since they did not think it worthwhile to retain the knowledge of God, he gave them over to a depraved mind, to do what ought not to be done."

Having given man freedom of choice, God allows us to choose our mindset. The contrast between sinful thinking and spiritual thinking is explained in Romans 8:5: "Those who live according to the sinful nature have their minds set on what that nature desires; but those who live in accordance with the Spirit have their minds set on what the Spirit desires." Paul goes on to picture the inevitable results of the two different ways of thinking: "The mind of sinful man is death, but the mind controlled by the Spirit is life and peace" (Romans 8:6).

Paul describes natural thinking as "the sinful mind" that "is hostile to God" (Romans 8:7). Man is not passively ignorant about God; he is actively antagonistic toward Him. The human mind is, by nature, rebellious toward God's precepts. "It does not submit to God's law, nor can it do so" (Romans 8:7).

Biblical pathology reveals that unregenerate man has a mind that is willfully blind and distorted. It is incapable of perceiving and understanding spiritual truths without the direct aid of God (John 6:44). As a result, man is plunged into a cycle of sin and destruction such as described in Romans 1:18-32:

> [18]The wrath of God is being revealed from heaven against all the godlessness and wickedness of men who suppress the truth by their wickedness, [19]since what may be known about God is plain to them, because God has made it plain to them. [20]For since the creation of the world God's invisible qualities—his eternal power and divine nature—have been clearly seen, being understood from what has been made, so that men are without excuse. [21]For although they knew God, they neither glorified him as God nor gave thanks to him, but their thinking became futile and their foolish hearts were darkened. [22]Although they claimed to be wise, they became fools [23]and exchanged the glory of the immortal God for images made to look like mortal man and birds and animals and reptiles. [24]Therefore God gave them over in the sinful desires of their hearts to sexual impurity for the degrading of their bodies with one another. [25]They exchanged the truth of God for a lie, and worshiped and served created things rather than the Creator—who is forever praised. Amen. [26]Because of this, God gave them over to shameful

lusts. Even their women exchanged natural relations for unnatural ones. [27]In the same way the men also abandoned natural relations with women and were inflamed with lust for one another. Men committed indecent acts with other men, and received in themselves the due penalty for their perversion. [28]Furthermore, since they did not think it worthwhile to retain the knowledge of God, he gave them over to a depraved mind, to do what ought not to be done. [29]They have become filled with every kind of wickedness, evil, greed and depravity. They are full of envy, murder, strife, deceit and malice. They are gossips, [30]slanderers, God-haters, insolent, arrogant and boastful; they invent ways of doing evil; they disobey their parents; [31]they are senseless, faithless, heartless, ruthless. [32]Although they know God's righteous decree that those who do such things deserve death, they not only continue to do these very things but also approve of those who practice them.

This is such an important passage in developing a biblical psychology that we need to study it thought by thought. Verse 18 plainly declares that man has willfully suppressed the truth. I believe it can be demonstrated that a large percentage of "mental problems" are self-generated by people who are unwilling to face the truth about themselves, their choices, their actions, and the consequences that inevitably result. Psychology calls this process "denial."

According to verse 19, God has made the truth about Himself obvious to human beings. He explains in verse 20 that the world around us clearly reveals His existence, His power, and even His personal nature, such as His provision for all mankind: "He causes his sun to rise on the evil and the good, and sends rain on the righteous and the unrighteous" (Matthew 5:45). People are even aware of the difference between right and wrong. According to Romans

2:15, "they show that the requirements of the law are written on their hearts, their consciences also bearing witness, and their thoughts now accusing, now even defending them." As a result of this universal information, "men are without excuse" (Romans 1:20).

The result of man's willful rejection of God is that "their thinking became futile and their foolish hearts were darkened" (Romans 1:21). The increasingly dysfunctional mindset of modern man is no mystery. It does not require years of psychological training to understand why people are having so many problems of living. It is the natural consequence of turning one's back on God: "Their foolish hearts were darkened." Confusion, depression, sadness, and suffering are inevitable without the healing work of Christ.

The ultimate example of denial is found in verse 22: "Although they claimed to be wise, they became fools." The incredible arrogance of evolutionary scientists, psychologists, sociologists, and historians is revealed in their confident statements of falsehood. Regardless of what form it takes—"Man is the product of billions of years of evolution" or "Man's problems can be solved through education" or "We need the scientific findings of psychological research to solve man's deepest problems"—the root of their foolishness is rejection of God and His Word. "They exchanged the truth of God for a lie, and worshiped and served created things rather than the Creator" (verse 25).

In God's place, man has set up a variety of idols (verse 23). Man's favorite idol in our day is man himself. Listen to God's response in verse 24: "Therefore God gave them over...." What a terrifying phrase—"God gave them over." Does it appear to you that our world has gone mad? That society is crumbling in front of your very eyes? There is a reason: "God gave them over."

The results are described in ugly detail: sexual impurity (verse 25), degradation (verse 25), shameful lusts (verse 26), lesbianism (verse 26), male homosexuality (verse 27), and the personal suffering that such perversions bring. Venereal diseases, AIDS, loneliness, abuse, suicide, and a host of other self-destructive consequences have flooded our society because man turned from God and He "gave them over to a depraved mind" (verse 28). The media provide ample illustrations of this depravity as pornography oozes its slimy stench by way of movies, television, rock music, magazines, and videotapes. The term "indecency" has become meaningless to the pornographically desensitized modern mind.

The accurate biblical term for nonorganic "mental illness" is mental depravity. It infects every area of human existence. This condition produces "every kind of wickedness, evil, greed and depravity. They are full of envy, murder, strife, deceit and malice. They are gossips, slanderers, God-haters, insolent, arrogant and boastful" (verses 29,30). This is not a picture of basically good people who are just dysfunctional, as psychology insists. Humans are willful rebels, intent on disobeying God at every opportunity. Humans actually *look* for new ways to offend God. "They invent ways of doing evil" (verse 30).

Mental depravity poisons the basic social unit of the family: "They disobey their parents" (verse 30). It impairs the ability to make wise choices: "They are senseless" (verse 31). Mental depravity destroys belief systems and personal integrity: They are "faithless" (verse 31). It produces brutal violence and all kinds of abuses: They are "heartless" (verse 31). It convinces individuals and nations that survival of the fittest is an appropriate sociological tool: They are "ruthless" (verse 31).

To underscore the truth that man consciously rejects God's principles for living, verse 32 says, "Although they know God's righteous decree that those who do such things deserve death, they not only continue to do these very things but also approve of those who practice them." Part of the approval comes because psychology has convinced a willing public that morality is relative and guilt is nonexistent. No one is responsible for anything. Everyone is a victim back through every generation, until ultimately the finger of blame points to God.

By the way, believers have no cause for pride when comparing ourselves to unbelievers. Paul reminds us that "all of us also lived among them at one time, gratifying the cravings of our sinful nature and following its desires and thoughts. Like the rest, we were by nature objects of wrath" (Ephesians 2:3). He repeats, "Once you were alienated from God and were enemies in your minds because of your evil behavior" (Colossians 1:21). As forgiven sinners, we need to reach out our hands in humility, compassion, and love.

The Carnal Mind

The second type of mind described in the Scriptures is the carnal mind. This describes a person who has a knowledge of God but is still living in obedience to his old nature. Paul describes such people as "those who live according to the sinful nature [and] have their minds set on what that nature desires" (Romans 8:5). This is a condition similar to Solomon's: "As Solomon grew old, his wives turned his heart after other gods, and his heart was not fully devoted to the LORD his God" (1 Kings 11:4).

Jesus used a parable to describe carnal-mindedness: "Those on the rock are the ones who receive the word with joy when they hear it, but they have no root. They believe for a while, but in the time of testing they fall away" (Luke 8:13). Their hearts become hard through the deceitfulness of sin (Hebrews 3:13) and the worries of life (Matthew 13:22). They fall back into former patterns of sin, and as a result "both their minds and consciences are corrupted" (Titus 1:15). Paul pleads with the Galatians, "It is for freedom that Christ has set us free. Stand firm, then, and do not let yourselves be burdened again by a yoke of slavery" (Galatians 5:1).

In his letter to Timothy, Paul writes that the carnal mind has been corrupted and "robbed of the truth" (1 Timothy 6:5). Peter says the carnal mind is like a dog returning to its vomit or a sow to the mud (2 Peter 2:22). He writes about the carnal mind, "If they have escaped the corruption of the world by knowing our Lord and Savior Jesus Christ and are again entangled in it and overcome, they are worse off at the end than they were at the beginning" (2 Peter 2:20). It hardly seems possible that one could be worse off than having never known about Christ, but that is what the passage says. "It would have been better for them not to have known the way of righteousness, than to have known it and then to turn their backs on the sacred command that was passed on to them" (verse 21). How can this be? Because "from everyone who has been given much, much will be demanded; and from the one who has been entrusted with much, much more will be asked" (Luke 12:48).

Most severe counseling problems are caused by natural thinking (the depraved mind) or carnal thinking (the hardened, backslidden mind). The natural mind is characterized by a person who openly rejects God, the Lord Jesus Christ, and the written Word of God. The biblical counselor will seek to evangelize the natural mind by presenting the claims of Christ, praying that the Holy Spirit will open the counselee's eyes to see the truth. One who rejects the authority of the Scriptures can only hope for temporary mental relief found in the shifting psychological theories of the world. But his mind will still be depraved, confused, and dark.

The carnal mind is characterized by one who has "a form of godliness but [denies] its power" (2 Timothy 3:5). When a biblical counselor detects a carnal mind, he must appeal from the platform of scriptural authority. Though the counselee may have returned to his muddy wallow, it is possible that he still has a dim reverence for God and a residual bit of faith in the Word. Psychological therapy will only pull the carnal mind further away from God. While the integrationist counselor seeks to understand the carnal mind through the use of psychological tests, the biblical counselor will apply the Scriptures, for "the word of God is living and active. Sharper than any double-edged sword, it penetrates even to dividing soul and spirit, joints and marrow; it judges the thoughts and attitudes of the heart" (Hebrews 4:12).

The Spiritual Mind

The biblical solution for the natural mind as well as the carnal mind is found in 2 Corinthians 10:5: "We demolish arguments and every pretension that sets itself up against the knowledge of God, and we take captive every thought to make it obedient to Christ." In 1 Corinthians Paul also describes yet a third type of mental condition: the spiritual mind. He says that the spiritual man has "the mind of Christ" (2:15,16). It is "the mind controlled by the Spirit" (Romans 8:6).

According to Paul, the spiritual mind will have several characteristics: "The fruit of the Spirit is love, joy, peace, patience, kindness, goodness, faithfulness, gentleness and self-control" (Galatians 5:22,23). These qualities are a result of conscious choices to submit to the Holy Spirit. "Those who belong to Christ Jesus have crucified the sinful nature with its passions and desires. Since we live by the Spirit, let us keep in step with the Spirit" (Galatians 5:24,25).

Peter touches on this process of sanctification when he says that God's grace (His provision for our needs) and peace (a serenity of mind) are available through "the knowledge of God and of Jesus our Lord" (2 Peter 1:2). This is a mental as well as a spiritual process. Peter lists a sequence of qualities the spiritual mind should have: faith, goodness, knowledge, self-control, perseverance, godliness, brotherly kindness, and love (2 Peter 1:5-7). And Paul summarizes the descriptions of a spiritual mind: "The fruit of the light consists in all goodness, righteousness and truth" (Ephesians 5:9).

Appendix B:
A Special Word for Pastors

It isn't enough merely to warn believers about psychological counseling. One reason today's Christian is more likely to seek out a psychologist than a pastor for counsel is that many pastors have not prepared themselves to guide their people through life's trials. Our integrationist brethren have the right to ask, "Then what do you suggest?"

As a pastor, I understand the immense pressures and already-impossible schedules that pastors face. I realize how difficult it is to find time to read, to study, and to prepare oneself for counseling on top of the required preparation for weekly sermons and Bible studies.

I also recognize the seeming futility of investing precious hours with counselees who want instant relief from suffering but do not want to change sinful thinking and behavior patterns. The counselee's personal motivation is the greatest single factor in producing change, and because such motivation is often lacking, it is easy for a pastor to become discouraged and to feel that counseling is a waste of time. Nonetheless, counseling is still part of the shepherd's call, and to perform the task effectively, pastors must prepare themselves.

Who among us would deny that many, if not most, pastors are currently incompetent to counsel their people effectively? But the challenge before us is this: If we will not take the time to become competent, to whom will our people turn? The evidence is that they will turn to psychiatrists, psychologists, and social workers.

It is time that we reclaim our God-given mandate to shepherd our flocks. The Word of God which is so powerful from the pulpit on Sunday is just as powerful in the counseling office throughout the week. The Scriptures which can move congregations to repentance are able to convict individuals as well. If we refuse to counsel from God's Word, how will we answer the Lord when He calls us to account for the condition of our people (Hebrews 13:17)?

Suggestions for Becoming Competent to Counsel

Perhaps you are asking, *How* can I prepare myself to effectively counsel God's people? After being fully convinced of the truth and power of God's Word, the most important step is to have a thorough working knowledge of the Scriptures. Nothing can provide this for the pastor except his own diligent study—formal or informal—under the illumination of the Holy Spirit (1 Corinthians 2:14).

If one has difficulty in locating specific passages dealing with personal problems, there are excellent study tools available. For counseling purposes, I highly recommend the *Thompson Chain Reference Bible*. If I could own just one volume, this would be the one. It is now available for computer[1] so that rapid topical searches can be done.

Assuming the pastor has an adequate grasp of the Bible, there are additional steps he can take to acquire counseling skills. One should become acquainted with Christian counseling literature, both theoretical and practical. Be aware, however, that most "Christian counseling" books are written from the integrationist perspective. Jay Adams has provided foundational biblical counseling material both in theory (*Competent to Counsel* and *A Theology of Christian Counseling*) and in practice (*The Christian Counselor's Manual* and many other helpful volumes). A number of authors have set forth important documentation regarding psychology and integrationist systems. Several other books are listed in the notes which will be of help in settling this important issue in a pastor's mind. And appendix C lists some of the resources that I have found helpful in preparing to counsel.

It will take time to read and absorb the amount of material that is required to gain a comprehension of proper counseling techniques, but any pastor who has spent years in study and in the weekly preparation of sermons is well equipped to do this sort of independent study.

A pastor does not have to avoid counseling his people until he has read a massive amount of literature, however. The basic material that counselors need is readily at hand in the Bible and in biblical counseling manuals. Diagnosing specific problems is time-consuming, but a thorough knowledge of the Word, patience, skillful questioning, and common sense will usually expose the problems which require guidance.

As in every discipline, practical experience becomes an excellent teacher. Trial and error in counseling, however, can produce some damaging effects, and unfortunately that is how many pastors have approached counseling. To supplement one's personal study of counseling techniques, pastors can gain insight by sitting in on counseling sessions with other experienced pastoral counselors. Older pastors can mentor younger ones. A group of pastors can join together to share counseling experiences, insights, and techniques.

Role-playing is useful in thinking through some of the problems a pastor will face. Adams has published a volume of case studies for this very purpose. A pastor can gather several men and women to act out authentic situations in which he will play the role of counselor. The others can help critique his substance, methods, and style of counseling.

A Few Words of Caution

Pray for God's wisdom as you open His Word to guide His children. You are dealing with people's lives and your advice can have a lasting impact on a counselee.

For your own legal protection, I suggest that you limit your counseling to your own congregation, and even then, be sure that your people sign a counseling contract that explains the kind of counsel you offer and the limitations of confidentiality. Your church constitution or bylaws should clearly state something to the effect that the principles of Matthew 18 will be used as a guideline for church discipline and that "discipline may include actions based on information that is revealed in a confidential setting."[2]

If you do occasionally counsel someone from outside your church, be doubly certain that your counseling philosophy is clearly explained beforehand, and require the counselee to sign a contract. You would be wise to have your contract reviewed by a competent Christian lawyer. In today's litigious society you may find it necessary to protect yourself with malpractice insurance, which is available for pastors. Always counsel under the umbrella of the local church, for there is still a measure of protection afforded by the concept of "the separation of church and state."

Be sure that you honor the principle of confidentiality in your counseling ministry. As a counselor, you may not ethically share personal information gathered in counseling sessions without your counselees' permission. Biblically, confidentiality is addressed by the commands against gossip: "A gossip betrays a confidence, but a trustworthy man keeps a secret" (Proverbs 11:13); "He who covers over an offense promotes love, but whoever repeats the matter separates close friends" (Proverbs 17:9). If you love your people, you will not want to relate their sins to others. As Peter reminds us, "Above all, love each other deeply, because love covers over a multitude of sins" (1 Peter 4:8).

On the other hand, a responsible counselor will not promise absolute confidentiality, for there may be cases where a person is suicidal or presents a danger to others and appropriate action may require certain authorities to be informed. In your counseling contract, you should clearly state that counseling confidentiality does not extend to areas that pose a danger to the counselee or others.

I recommend that you purchase a copy of *Christian Counseling and the Law*, by Steve Levicoff[3] for a complete examination of counseling liabilities.

Do not think that you will avoid the danger of a lawsuit by refusing to counsel your people. One pastor I know was sued by a former church member even though the pastor does not personally counsel and the church had not exercised discipline. Another church in Denver is being sued because they refused to counsel an unbeliever. So don't shy away from this important ministry thinking you will be immune from litigation.

Maintain a correct relationship with your counselees at all times. Avoid expressing your compassion and concern with physical touches. There is *never*—and I mean *never!*— any justification for a pastor to become romantically or sexually involved with a counselee. I recommend that you counsel a member of the opposite sex with your mate present. If that is not possible, be sure that there are others nearby who are able to visually monitor you. I have a large window in my office door so that my secretary and staff can look in at any time during a counseling session.

Ultimately, your best protection is to be Christlike in all you do. Love your people. Confront them lovingly, respectfully, and firmly. Guide them gently along the path of obedience to the Lord. Be courageous, and do the work God has called you to do.

Get Started!

The biggest hurdle you will face in counseling your people is your own inertia. I know that by experience! No doubt you are already too busy and over-committed. The temptation will be to refer hurting people to outside counselors, but in so doing you may miss some of the greatest opportunities to edify your flock that you will ever have. Your people *need* your counsel and guidance from God's Word.

So I plead with you, fellow-pastor, consider carefully and prayerfully the evidence I have presented. Make the commitment to prepare yourself, determine to guide your people with the Scriptures, let them know that you are available, and hold on for an exciting new adventure in ministry.

You *can* counsel your people!

Appendix C:
Resources

Listed in the order I would recommend them.

■ ■ ■

Books on Counseling Theory

Competent to Counsel. Jay E. Adams. Grand Rapids: Zondervan Publishing House, 1970.

The Christian Counselor's Manual. Jay E. Adams. Grand Rapids: Baker Book House, 1973.

Introduction to Biblical Counseling. John F. MacArthur, Jr. and Wayne Mack. Word Publishing, 1994.

Self-Confrontation. John C. Broger. Rancho Mirage, CA: Biblical Counseling Foundation, 1990.

Ready to Restore. Jay E. Adams. Phillipsburg, NJ: Presbyterian and Reformed Publishing Company, 1981.

A Theology of Christian Counseling. Jay E. Adams. Grand Rapids: Zondervan Publishing House, 1979.

How to Counsel from Scripture. Martin Bobgan. Chicago: Moody Press, 1985.

A Christian Directory. Richard Baxter (written in 1664-65). Ligonier, PA: Soli Deo Gloria Publications, 1990.

The Psychological Way/The Spiritual Way. Martin and Deidre Bobgan. Minneapolis: Bethany House Publishers, 1979.

Medical and Drug Information Resources

None of These Diseases. S.I. McMillen. Old Tappan, NJ: Fleming H. Revell Company, 1984.

The Family Doctor. A computer program on CD ROM with medical information, charts, and basic information on drugs.

Physicians' Desk Reference. Edward R. Barnhart, ed. Oradell, NJ: Medical Economics Data, 1993.

American Medical Association Encyclopedia of Medicine. New York: Random House, 1989.

Heavy Drinking. Herbert Fingarette. Berkeley: University of California Press, 1989.

Complete Guide to Prescription & Non-Prescription Drugs. H. Winter Griffith. Los Angeles: The Body Press, 1989.

Complete Guide to Symptoms, Illness & Surgery. H. Winter Griffith. Los Angeles: The Body Press, 1989.

Books on Psychology

The Psychological Society. Martin L. Gross. New York: Random House, 1978.

Psychological Seduction. William Kirk Kilpatrick. Nashville: Thomas Nelson Publishers, 1983.

Psychology As Religion. Grand Rapids: William B. Eerdmans Publishing Company, 1977.

Christ Esteem. Don Matzat. Eugene, OR: Harvest House Publishers, 1990.

The Death of Psychiatry. E. Fuller Torrey. Radnor, PA: Chilton Book Company, 1974.

The Shrinking of America. Bernie Zilbergeld. Boston: Little, Brown and Company, 1983.

Psychoheresy. Martin and Deidre Bobgan. Santa Barbara: EastGate Publishers, 1987.

The Seduction of Christianity. David Hunt and T.A. McMahon. Eugene, OR: Harvest House Publishers, 1985.

Books on Psychological Terminology and Theory

Baker Encyclopedia of Psychology. Grand Rapids: Baker Book House, 1987 (integrationist perspective).

Resource Groups

National Association of Nouthetic Counselors
5526 State Road 26 East
Lafayette, IN 47905

Christian Counseling and Education Foundation West
(offer conferences for medical doctors and biblical counseling)
3495 College Avenue
San Diego, CA 92115

Biblical Counseling Foundation
P.O. Box 925
Rancho Mirage, CA 92270
(619) 773-2667

Christian Counseling and Education Foundation
1803 E. Willow Grove Avenue
Laverock, PA 19118
(215) 884-7676

L.I.F.E. Fellowship
11500 Sheridan Blvd.
Westminster, CO 80020
(303) 451-LIFE

Trinity Theological Seminary
(Bible counseling courses by extension)
4233 Medwel Drive/P.O. Box 717
Newburgh, IN 47629-0717
(812) 853-0611

The Master's College
21726 Placerita Canyon Road
P.O. Box 221450
Santa Clarita, CA 91322
(805) 259-3540

The Master's Seminary
13248 Roscoe Blvd.
Sun Valley, CA 91352
(818) 909-5627

Biblical Theological Seminary
200 North Main Street
Hatfield, PA 19440
(215) 368-5000

Westminster Theological Seminary
(Philadelphia campus)
Chestnut Hill
P.O. Box 27009
Philadelphia, PA 19118
(215) 887-5511

(Escondido campus)
1725 Bear Valley Parkway
Escondido, CA 92027
(619) 480-8474

Notes

Chapter 1—Christian Counseling Today

1. Joseph M. Stowell, "A Multitude of Counselors," in *Moody*, May 1991, p. 4.
2. Ibid.
3. Ibid.
4. Lynn Garrett, "Is Christian Psychology Possible?" in *Wellspring*, Fall 1991, p. 7.
5. Ibid.
6. Gary R. Collins, *Can You Trust Psychology?* (Downers Grove, IL: InterVarsity Press, 1988), p. 94.
7. Ibid.
8. Ibid.
9. Ibid., p. 95.
10. Ibid.
11. Ibid., p. 96.
12. Ibid.
13. Ibid., pp. 96-97.
14. Ibid., p. 17.
15. Lawrence J. Crabb, Jr., *Basic Principles of Biblical Counseling* (Grand Rapids: Zondervan Publishing House, 1975), pp. 11-12.
16. *Ibid.*, p. 17.
17. Lawrence J. Crabb, Jr., *Effective Biblical Counseling* (Grand Rapids: Zondervan Publishing House, 1977), p. 47.
18. *Ibid.*, p. 48.
19. William Glasser, *Reality Therapy* (New York: Harper & Row Publishers, 1965), pp. 42-43.
20. Crabb states that the opinion is "largely justified. Churches have a woefully simplistic understanding of the problems people experience. A fair number seem to glory in their ignorance by insisting there is no need for an inside look" (Dr. Larry Crabb, *Inside Out* [Colorado Springs: NavPress, 1988], p. 51). I do not know of any biblical counselor who believes there is no need to look inside one's heart. True biblical counselors simply believe that one should look at the heart through the lens of Scripture without the distorting filter of psychology.
21. Crabb, *Inside Out*, p. 107.
22. Ibid., p. 108.
23. Ibid., p. 96.
24. Ibid.
25. Ibid., p. 103.
26. Ibid., p. 186.

Chapter 2—The Myth That Psychology Is Scientific

1. Michael J. Martin, "Bumps & Brains, the Curious Science of Phrenology; the Wrong Idea at the Right Time," *American History Illustrated*, September 1984, p. 43.
2. Gary R. Collins, *Can You Trust Psychology?* (Downers Grove, IL: InterVarsity Press, 1988), pp. 129-30.
3. Robert M. Hazen and James Trefil, *Science Matters* (New York: Doubleday, 1990), p. 149.
4. Ibid., p. 1.
5. Ibid., p. 247.
6. Ibid., p. 250.
7. Martin L. Gross, *The Psychological Society* (New York: Random House, 1978), p. 195.
8. Ibid., p. 196.
9. Ibid., p. 202.
10. Collins, *Can You Trust?*, p. 109.
11. Crabb, *Basic Principles of Biblical Counseling*, p. 22.
12. Frank B. Minirth and Paul D. Meier, *Happiness Is a Choice* (Grand Rapids: Baker Book House, 1978), p. 15.
13. Ibid., p. 25.
14. Ibid., p. 172.
15. Ibid., p. 225.
16. Frank B. Minirth, *Christian Psychiatry* (Old Tappan, NJ: Fleming H. Revell Company, 1990), p. 144.
17. Ibid., pp. 144-45.
18. J.W.N. Sullivan, *The Limitations of Science* (New York: Mentor Books, 1933), p. 127.
19. Hazen and Trefil, *Science Matters*, p. 245.
20. Ray M. Jurjevich, *A Psychologist's Ventures in Faith* (Glenwood Springs, CO: Ichthys Books, 1987), p. 259.
21. Hazen and Trefil, *Science Matters*, p. 87.
22. E. Fuller Torrey, *The Death of Psychiatry* (Radnor, PA: Chilton Book Company, 1974), p. 158.
23. Gross, p. 16.
24. Bernie Zilbergeld, *The Shrinking of America* (Boston: Little, Brown and Company, 1983), p. 87.
25. Gross, *Psychological Society*, p. 207.
26. Zilbergeld, *Death of Psychiatry*, p. 87.
27. Jeffrey Moussaieff Masson, *Against Therapy* (New York: Atheneum, 1988), p. ix.
28. Ibid., p. 248.
29. Gross, *Psychological Society*, p. 6.
30. Tim Stafford, "Franchising Hope," *Christianity Today*, May 18, 1992, pp. 22-26.

Chapter 3—The Myth That Psychology Is Effective
1. Gary R. Collins, *Can You Trust Psychology?* (Downers Grove, IL: InterVarsity Press, 1988), pp. 26-27.
2. *Rocky Mountain News,* January 30, 1992, p. 51.
3. Martin L. Gross, *The Psychological Society* (New York: Random House, 1978), p. 23.
4. Ibid.
5. Martin and Deidre Bobgan, *The Psychological Way/The Spiritual Way* (Minneapolis: Bethany House Publishers, 1979), pp. 19-20.
6. Gross, *Psychological Society,* p. 40.
7. Martin and Deidre Bobgan, *Psychoheresy* (Santa Barbara, CA: EastGate Publishers, 1987), pp. 46-47.
8. Collins, *Can You Trust?,* p. 45.
9. Ibid., p. 46.
10. Judi Striano, *How to Find a Good Psychotherapist, A Consumer Guide* (Santa Barbara, CA: Professional Press, 1987), p. 79.
11. E. Fuller Torrey, *The Death of Psychiatry* (Radnor, PA: Chilton Book Company, 1974), p. 47.
12. Collins, *Can You Trust?,* p. 28.
13. Otto and Miriam Ehrenberg, *The Psychological Maze* (New York: Holt, Rinehart and Winston, 1977), pp. ix-xii.
14. Torrey, *Death of Psychiatry,* p. 27.
15. Archibald D. Hart, *Me, Myself & I* (Ann Arbor, MI: Servant Publications, 1992), p. 100.
16. Thomas Szasz, *The Myth of Psychotherapy* (Syracuse: Syracuse University Press, 1987), pp. 193-205.
17. Ibid., pp. 194-95.
18. Collins, *Can You Trust?,* p. 28.

Chapter 4—The Myth That Psychology Is Motivated by Compassion
1. Susan Miller and Kenneth L. Woodward, "These Souls Were Made for Shrinking," *Newsweek,* September 14, 1992, p. 60.
2. Gary R. Collins, *Can You Trust Psychology?* (Downers Grove, IL: InterVarsity Press, 1988), p. 40.
3. Bernie Zilbergeld, *The Shrinking of America* (Boston: Little, Brown and Company, 1983), p. 142.
4. Otto and Miriam Ehrenberg, *The Psychological Maze* (New York: Holt, Rinehart and Winston, 1977), p. 69.
5. Judi Striano, *How to Find a Good Psychotherapist, A Consumer Guide* (Santa Barbara, CA: Professional Press, 1987), pp. 14-15.
6. Collins, *Can You Trust?,* p. 41.
7. Ibid., p. 41.
8. Denis Donovan, ed., "Marketing: Developing the Right Attitude," *Psychotherapy Today,* February 1991, pp. 1-2.
9. Ibid.
10. Ibid.
11. Thomas Sowell, "There's no problem so big that we can't make it worse," *Rocky Mountain News,* February 20, 1992, p. 49.
12. Charles Krauthammer, "Crazy crimes can lead to courtroom insanity," *Rocky Mountain News,* February 10, 1992, p. 35.
13. Ibid.
14. *The American Medical Association Encyclopedia of Medicine* (New York: Random House, 1989), p. 678.
15. "Violent Crime and Hard Time," *Rocky Mountain News,* October 23, 1992, p. 72.

Chapter 5—The Myth of Psychological Labels
1. Erica E. Goode, "Sick, or just quirky?" *U.S. News & World Report,* February 10, 1992, pp. 49-50.
2. Ibid.
3. Ibid.
4. Gary R. Collins, *Can You Trust Psychology?* (Downers Grove, IL: InterVarsity Press, 1988), p. 134.
5. Ibid.
6. Ibid., p. 135.
7. William Glasser, *Reality Therapy* (New York: Harper & Row Publishers, 1965), pp. 45-46.
8. E. Fuller Torrey, *The Death of Psychiatry* (Radnor, PA: Chilton Book Company, 1974), p. 36.
9. Ibid.
10. Ibid., p. 37.
11. Ibid., p. 40.
12. Herbert Fingarette, *Heavy Drinking* (Berkeley: University of California Press, 1989), pp. 2-3.
13. Ibid., pp. 2-4.
14. Ibid., p. 22.
15. Ibid., pp. 23-24.
16. Ibid.
17. Torrey, *Death of Psychiatry,* p. 54.
18. Glasser, *Reality Therapy,* pp. 42-43.
19. Garth Wood, *The Myth of Neurosis* (New York: Harper & Row, 1986), p. 60.
20. Thomas Szasz, *The Myth of Psychotherapy* (Syracuse: Syracuse University Press, 1987), p. 195.
21. Ibid., p. 196.
22. Ibid., p. 194.
23. Collins, *Can You Trust?,* p. 135.
24. Lawrence J. Crabb, Jr., *Effective Biblical Counseling* (Grand Rapids: Zondervan Publishing House, 1977), p. 31.
25. Glasser, *Reality Therapy,* p. 44.
26. Wood, *Myth of Neurosis,* p. 62.
27. Goode, "Sick, or just quirky?" pp. 49-50.
28. Ibid.
29. I originally wrote about the DSM's (Diagnostic and Statistical Manual) designation of PMS (premenstrual syndrome) in partial jest, but I discovered that it does indeed list it under the category "mental disorders—not otherwise specified." The task force reviewing PMS for the DSM of the APA (American

Psychiatric Association) now calls PMS "premenstrual dysphoric disorder" or PMDD. Perhaps too many people understand what PMS stands for and the experts need a new code. See *Newsweek*, March 15, 1993, "Is It Sadness or Madness? Psychiatrists Clash Over How to Classify PMS," p. 66.

Chapter 6—The Myth That Psychology Is Trustworthy

1. William T. Kirwan, *Biblical Concepts for Christian Counseling* (Grand Rapids: Baker Book House, 1984), p. 24.
2. Gary R. Collins, *Can You Trust Psychology?* (Downers Grove, IL: InterVarsity Press, 1988), p. 65.
3. *The Columbia Encyclopedia*, 3d ed. (New York: Columbia University Press, 1963), s.v. "Psychoanalysis."
4. Thomas Szasz, *The Myth of Psychotherapy* (Syracuse: Syracuse University Press, 1987), pp. 195-96.
5. Lee Coleman, *The Reign of Error* (Boston: Beacon Books, 1984), p. 130.
6. Bernie Zilbergeld, *The Shrinking of America* (Boston: Little, Brown and Company, 1983), p. 146.
7. Ibid., p. 149.
8. Coleman, *Reign of Error*, p. 148.
9. Harold M. Silverman, *The Pill Book, Guide to Safe Drug Use* (New York: Bantam Books, 1989), p. 3.
10. James W. Long, *The Essential Guide to Prescription Drugs* (New York: Harper & Row, Publishers, 3d Edition, 1982), p. 345.
11. Ibid., p. 346.
12. Ibid., p. 348.
13. Ibid., p. 209.
14. Collins, *Can You Trust?*, pp. 37-38.
15. Ibid., p. 38.
16. Ibid., pp. 38-39.
17. There are several volumes available to help a lay person evaluate medications that have been prescribed. H. Winter Griffith has published the *Complete Guide to Prescription & Non-Prescription Drugs*, which contains important information: the brand names under which the drug is sold, whether the drug is supposed to be habit-forming, what its primary purpose is, dosage information, possible adverse or side effects, warnings and precautions, and possible interactions with other drugs or substances. The book retails for $15, but can be purchased for less at discount outlets.

    The *Physicians' Desk Reference*, commonly referred to as PDR, is a more expensive source book, but contains a great deal more information. With this volume, a counselor can research a drug by manufacturer, product name, category, generic name, and chemical name. It provides a full description of the "indications and usage, dosage, administration, description, clinical pharmacology, supply, warnings, contraindications, adverse reactions, overdosage and precautions" for each drug. By looking up a specific drug, the counselor can learn how the drug is metabolized, what organs are affected, the duration of drug effect (especially important if additional drugs are prescribed), how a person's age affects drug metabolism, and other significant information. This reference work will require a larger investment, somewhere between $40 and $60.

    Another helpful reference is the *American Medical Association Encyclopedia of Medicine*. This volume explains many of the medical terms that commonly confuse the layperson. It is available for about $25. *U.S. News & World Report*, May 20, 1991 edition provides a helpful list of the "10 Top Drug Books" and the "10 Top Medical Books" available to the general public. University libraries provide other valuable sources of medical information for the layperson. The purpose of such information is to provide a counselee sufficient data so he knows what he is taking and why the drug was prescribed.
18. Silverman, *Pill Book*, pp. 2-3.
19. Collins, *Can You Trust?*, p. 89.
20. Ibid., pp. 89-90.
21. Ibid., p. 90.
22. Ibid., p. 91.
23. Lyle E. Bourne, Jr. and Bruce R. Ekstrand, *Psychology, Its Principles and Meanings*, 3d ed. (New York: Holt, Rinehart and Winston, 1976), p. 20.
24. Ibid., pp. 21-22.
25. Ibid., p. 1202.
26. B.F. Skinner, *Beyond Freedom and Dignity* (New York: Bantam/Vintage, 1971), frontis page.
27. Richard Wollheim, *Freud* (Glasgow: William Collins Sons and Co. Ltd., 1971), pp. 16-17.
28. Collins, *Can You Trust?*, p. 91.
29. Ibid.
30. Ibid.
31. Ibid., p. 92.
32. Szasz, *Myth of Psychotherapy*, pp. 30-31.
33. Collins, *Can You Trust?*, p. 83.
34. O. Quentin Hyder, *The Christian's Handbook of Psychiatry* (Old Tappan, NJ: Fleming H. Revell Company, 1976), p. 49.
35. Ibid., pp. 52-53.
36. Lawrence J. Crabb, Jr., *Inside Out* (Colorado Springs: NavPress, 1991), p. 184.
37. Robert H. Schuller, *Self-Esteem, the New Reformation* (Waco, TX: Word Books, 1982), esp. chapter three.
38. Dan B. Allender, *The Wounded Heart* (Colorado Springs: NavPress, 1990), p. 188.
39. Frank B. Minirth, *Christian Psychiatry* (Old Tappan, NJ: Fleming H. Revell Company, 1990), p. 75.
40. Clyde M. Narramore, *The Psychology of Counseling* (Grand Rapids: Zondervan Publishing House, 1960), p. 174.
41. Ibid., p. 178.
42. John D. Carter, "Maturity," in *Psychology and Religion* (Grand Rapids: Baker Book House, 1988), pp. 173-74.
43. Ibid.
44. Gary R. Collins, *Effective Counseling* (Carol Stream: Creation House, 1972), pp. 160-61.
45. *Baker Encyclopedia of Psychology*, David G. Benner, ed. (Grand Rapids: Baker Book House, 1985), p. 618.
46. Ibid.
47. Collins, *Can You Trust?*, p. 84.
48. Szasz, *Myth of Psychotherapy*, p. 183.

49. E. Fuller Torrey, *The Death of Psychiatry* (Radnor, PA: Chilton Book Co., 1974), p. 107.
50. Ibid., p. 108.
51. Collins, *Can You Trust?*, p. 86.

Chapter 7—The Myth That Psychology Can Heal the Past
1. Dan B. Allender, *The Wounded Heart* (Colorado Springs: NavPress, 1991), p. 186.
2. Ibid.
3. H. Norman Wright, *Making Peace with Your Past* (Old Tappan, NJ: Fleming H. Revell Company, 1985), p. 30.
4. Ibid., chapter 4.
5. Collins, *Can You Trust?*, p. 104.
6. Ibid., p. 105.
7. Ibid.
8. Dave Hunt and T.A. McMahon, *The Seduction of Christianity* (Eugene, OR: Harvest House Publishers, 1985), p. 174.
9. H. Norman Wright, *Self-Talk, Imagery, and Prayer in Counseling* (Waco, TX: Word Books, 1986), p. 59.
10. Ibid., pp. 118-19.
11. Bill Scanlon, series in *Rocky Mountain News*, September 13,14,15, 1992.
12. Ibid.
13. Ibid.
14. Ibid.
15. Ibid.
16. Ibid.
17. Ibid.
18. Ibid.
19. Ibid.
20. Ibid.
21. "Borne on His Wings," *Willow Creek Magazine*, 1990; reprinted in *The Beacon*, February 1992, pp. 3-5.
22. Nat Hentoff, "Don't Always Believe the Children," *Rocky Mountain News*, December 31, 1992, p. 53.
23. "Presumed Guilty," *The Daily Herald* (Chicago), October 7, 1992.
24. Ibid.
25. Ibid.
26. William Glasser, *Reality Therapy* (New York: Harper & Row Publishers, 1965), pp. 42-43.
27. Wright, *Making Peace*, pp. 40-41.
28. Paul Yonggi Cho, *Solving Life's Problems* (Plainfield, NJ: Logos International, 1980), p. 45.

Chapter 8—Psychology and Christianity
1. Martin L. Gross, *The Psychological Society* (New York: Random House, 1978), pp. 34-35.
2. Ibid., p. 45.
3. William Kirk Kilpatrick, *Psychological Seduction* (Nashville: Thomas Nelson Publishers, 1983), p. 14.
4. Ibid., p. 15.
5. Ibid., p. 16.
6. Ibid., pp. 17-18.
7. Ibid., p. 20.
8. Ibid., p. 23.
9. Paul C. Vitz, *Psychology As Religion* (Grand Rapids: William B. Eerdmans Publishing Company, 1977), p. 9.
10. Ibid., p. 7.
11. Ibid., pp. 9-10.
12. Gary R. Collins, *Can You Trust Psychology?* (Downers Grove, IL: InterVarsity Press, 1988), p. 101.

Chapter 9—Psychology and the Church
1. Gary R. Collins, *Can You Trust Psychology?* (Downers Grove, IL: InterVarsity Press, 1988), p. 127.
2. Ibid.
3. Ibid., p. 128.
4. Richard H. Cox, ed., *Religious Systems and Psychotherapy* (Springfield, IL: Charles C. Nelson, Publisher, 1973), p. 420.
5. Ibid., p. 421.
6. Jeffrey Moussaieff Masson, *Against Therapy* (New York: Atheneum, 1988), p. 235.
7. Collins, *Can You Trust?*, p. 97.
8. Lawrence J. Crabb, Jr., *Effective Biblical Counseling* (Grand Rapids: Zondervan Publishing House, 1975), p. 37.
9. Collins, *Can You Trust?*, p. 163.
10. Ibid., pp. 128-29.
11. Wendy Kaminer, *I'm Dysfunctional, You're Dysfunctional* (Reading, MA: Addison-Wesley Publishing Company, Inc., 1992), p. 121.
12. Ibid., p. 125.
13. William Kirk Kilpatrick, *Psychological Seduction* (Nashville: Thomas Nelson Publishers, 1983), p. 14.
14. Ray M. Jurjevich, *A Psychologist's Ventures in Faith* (Glenwood Springs, CO: Ichthys Books, 1987), pp. 267-68.
15. Robert H. Schuller, *Self-Esteem, The New Reformation* (Waco, TX: Word Publishers, 1982), p. 14.
16. Ibid.
17. Ibid., p. 64.
18. Kaminer, *I'm Dysfunctional*, p. 18.
19. Schuller, *Self-Esteem*, p. 68.
20. Ibid., p. 38.
21. Kilpatrick, *Psychological Seduction*, p. 23.
22. Cox, *Religious Systems*, p. 424.
23. Collins, *Can You Trust?*, p. 83.

24. Lawrence J. Crabb, Jr., *Inside Out* (Colorado Springs: NavPress, 1991), p. 49.
25. Collins, *Can You Trust?*, p. 128.
26. Collins, *Search for Reality* (Wheaton, IL: Key Publishers, 1969), p. 21.
27. Jay Adams, *A Theology of Christian Counseling* (Grand Rapids: Zondervan Publishing Co., 1979), p. 43.
28. Collins, *Can You Trust?*, p. 71.
29. Ibid.
30. Ibid., p. 72.
31. Ibid., p. 59.
32. Ibid., p. 71.
33. Lawrence J. Crabb, Jr., *Effective Biblical Counseling* (Grand Rapids: Zondervan Publishing House, 1977), p. 40.
34. Ibid., pp. 42-43.
35. Ibid., p. 43.
36. Adams, *Theology*, pp. 39-40.
37. Ibid., p. 135.

Chapter 10—Psychology and the Christian Counselor

1. Gary R. Collins, *Can You Trust Psychology?* (Downers Grove, IL: InterVarsity Press, 1988), p. 79.
2. Ray M. Jurjevich, *A Psychologist's Ventures in Faith* (Glenwood Springs, CO: Ichthys Books, 1987), p. 213.
3. Ibid., p. 214.
4. Ibid.
5. Thomas Szasz, *The Myth of Psychotherapy* (Syracuse: Syracuse University Press, 1987), p. vii.
6. Jeffrey Moussaieff Masson, *Against Therapy* (New York: Atheneum, 1988), pp. xi-xii.
7. Jurjevich, *Psychologist's Ventures*, p. 214.
8. Collins, *Can You Trust?*, p. 81.
9. Ibid., p. 82.
10. Gary Collins interviewed by James Dobson, "Christians and Psychology" (Focus on the Family, cassette CS 502).
11. Ibid.
12. Collins, *Can You Trust?*, p. 121.
13. Ibid., p. 124.
14. John Neuhaus, "Religion and Psychology," *National Review* (February 19, 1988), p. 46.
15. Lee Coleman, *The Reign of Error* (Boston: Beacon Books, 1984), p. 4.
16. Ibid.
17. Ibid.
18. Archibald D. Hart, *Me, Myself & I* (Ann Arbor, MI: Servant Publications, 1992), pp. 17-18.
19. Ibid., p. 20.
20. Jay Adams, *The Christian Counselor's Manual* (Phillipsburg, NJ: Presbyterian and Reformed Publishing Company, 1981), pp. 9-10.
21. Harold J. Leavitt, *Managerial Psychology* (Chicago: University of Chicago Press, 1978), p. 11.
22. Martin and Deidre Bobgan, *The Psychological Way/The Spiritual Way* (Minneapolis: Bethany House Publishers, 1974), pp. 25-26.
23. Martin L. Gross, *The Psychological Society* (New York: Random House, 1978), p. 4.
24. Neuhaus, "Religion and Psychology," p. 46.

Chapter 11—Psychology and the Bible

1. Robert H. Schuller, *Self-Esteem, The New Reformation* (Waco, TX: Word Publishers, 1982), p. 48.
2. Jan Karel Van Baalen, *The Chaos of Cults* (Grand Rapids: William B. Eerdmans Publishing Company, 1960), p. 99.
3. Gary R. Collins, *Search for Reality* (Wheaton, IL: Key Publishers, 1969), p. 21.
4. Walter R. Martin, *The Kingdom of the Cults* (Minneapolis: Bethany Fellowship, 1977), p. 18.
5. Quoted by David Noebel in *Understanding the Times* (Manitou Springs, CO: Summit Press, 1991), p. 51.
6. Paul Kurtz, "Is Everyone a Humanist?" in *The Humanist Alternative*, Paul Kurtz, ed. (Buffalo: Prometheus Books, 1973), p. 177. Quoted by Noebel, *Understanding the Times*, p. 57.
7. Harold R. Rafton, "Released Time or Democracy," *The Humanist*, Spring 1947, p. 161. Quoted by Noebel, *Understanding the Times*, p. 61.
8. Noebel, *Understanding the Times*, p. 63.
9. Erich Fromm, *You Shall Be as Gods* (New York: Holt, Rinehart and Winston, 1966), p. 7, quoted by Noebel, *Understanding the Times*, p. 357.
10. Ibid.
11. Collins, *Can You Trust?*, p. 103.
12. Ibid., p. 104.
13. Ibid.
14. Ibid.
15. Bill Zika, "Meditation and Altered States of Consciousness," in *Christian Counseling and Psychotherapy* (Grand Rapids: Baker Book House, 1987), p. 132.
16. *Baker Encyclopedia of Psychology* (Grand Rapids: Baker Book House, 1987), p. 224.
17. Ibid.
18. Ibid.
19. Collins, *Can You Trust?*, p. 143.
20. Ibid.
21. Archibald D. Hart, *Me, Myself & I* (Ann Arbor, MI: Servant Publications, 1992), p. 7.
22. Ibid., p. 9.
23. Ibid., pp. 17-18.
24. Ibid., p. 43.
25. Ibid., p. 69.
26. Ibid., p. 74.
27. Ibid., p. 76.
28. Ibid.

29. Ibid.
30. Don Matzat, *Christ Esteem* (Eugene, OR: Harvest House Publishers, 1990), pp. 28-29.
31. Ibid., p. 29.
32. Ibid., p. 30.

Chapter 12—A Biblical Foundation for Counseling
  1. John MacArthur, Jr., *Our Sufficiency in Christ* (Waco, TX: Word, Inc., 1991), p. 57.

Chapter 13—A Biblical Place for Counseling
  1. Martin Bobgan, *How to Counsel from Scripture* (Chicago: Moody Press, 1985).
  2. Jay Adams, *Ready to Restore* (Phillipsburg, NJ: Presbyterian and Reformed Publishing Company, 1981).

Chapter 14—A Biblical Method for Lasting Change
  1. Lawrence J. Crabb, Jr., *Inside Out* (Colorado Springs: NavPress, 1991), p. 49.

Appendix B—A Special Word for Pastors
  1. HyperBible is available for Macintosh and IBM formats and can be purchased through computer catalogs, or direct from Beacon Technology, Inc., 631 Elkton Drive, P.O. Box 49788, Colorado Springs, CO 80949-9788, (719) 594-4884. Tell them I sent you!
  2. Steve Levicoff, *Christian Counseling and the Law* (Chicago: Moody Press, 1991), p. 81.
  3. Ibid.

Subject Index

DATE DUE
